ORAL
PLEASURE

Books by Jerzy Kosinski

Novels

The Painted Bird
Steps
Being There
The Devil Tree
Cockpit
Blind Date
Passion Play
Pinball
The Hermit of 69th Street

Essays

Passing By
Notes of the Author
The Art of the Self

Nonfiction
(*Under the pen name Joseph Novak*)

The Future Is Ours, Comrade
No Third Path

ORAL PLEASURE

Kosinski as Storyteller

Compiled, transcribed, and selected by
Kiki Kosinski

Edited by
Barbara Tepa Lupack and Kiki Kosinski

Grove Press
New York

Published simultaneously in Canada
Printed in the United States of America
FIRST EDITION

ISBN-13: 978-0-8021-2033-5

Grove Press
an imprint of Grove/Atlantic, Inc.
841 Broadway
New York, NY 10003

Distributed by Publishers Group West

www.groveatlantic.com

12 13 14   10 9 8 7 6 5 4 3 2 1

For Dita von Fraunhofer-Brodin
and Tony von Fraunhofer

In memory of
Jerzy and Kiki Kosinski

"If you are already lovers," advises a recent article on how to please a man, "don't be afraid to give him oral pleasure." Now I distinctly remember when I arrived in the United States, to me, oral pleasure meant Haggadah. What else is there? I mean the rest is a pleasure, no doubt about it. But true oral pleasure comes from storytelling. You are now experiencing—at least I pray that you are experiencing—such oral pleasure. I don't want to be too intellectual about it, but to play on words, as the Hasidic Jew has always done, I am giving you my head. This is the supreme act of oral pleasure, and therefore you laugh and have a good time.

Jerzy Kosinski

CONTENTS

On Storytelling

On Censorship

On Autofiction

On Poland

On the Holocaust

FOREWORD

Kiki Kosinski

This book is of Jerzy's voice, and of his voice alone. But it is a virtually unknown voice, a softer voice that is seldom visible in his novels. The pieces clearly indicate his intelligence, psychological insights, marvelous humor, and his incredible interpretations and awareness of life in America and Europe. Some are hilarious and all are profound.

INTRODUCTION

Barbara Tepa Lupack

The title that Kiki Kosinski chose for this volume was *Oral Pleasure*. She liked that title because it evoked images of sex and sexuality—images that were certainly a vital and often controversial part of Jerzy Kosinski's fiction. She also knew that "oral pleasure" suggested something equally stimulating and provocative: a narrative tradition of storytelling. As Kosinski himself explained, true oral pleasure derives from the creation and telling of stories and, for him, the best storytelling derived from the Eastern European cultural tradition in which he was raised.

That tradition, based as it was in more than a thousand years of Polish-Jewish history, involved looking at the world indirectly, through a mediated form—the form of language—which allowed a pause, a reflection, an opportunity for vision and revision. The storyteller, therefore, had a unique perspective: not simply a "recorder of events" or "a communicator of any particular set of historic references," he was instead—in Kosinski's words—"a voice of fantasy, imagination, humor, and sexuality" who could mix and fuse and propose information in any fashion he wished. He could tell his story as he originally conceived it or—a day or a week or a year later—he could choose to turn it into a different event entirely. That was the storyteller's prerogative; that was his freedom.

A good storyteller ultimately felt liberated enough to tell any kind of story he wanted to. Not subjected to competition, he became instead a pivotal point of entertainment. His narrative gift, which marked him as a man of both wisdom and imagination, made him a valued member of the community, "the closest thing to being a shaman." Yet, Kosinski observed, the storyteller did not interfere. He did not seduce. He did not promise. He did not preach. Instead, he drew on the fundamental truths of personal and human experience to tell his story and then allowed his listeners to take from it only what they wished.

Best known for his fiction, Jerzy Kosinski—the consummate storyteller—was born in Łódź, Poland, on June 14, 1933, and immigrated to the United States in December 1957. Within two years of his arrival he wrote his first book, *The Future Is Ours, Comrade* (1960), under the pseudonym Joseph Novak. Subtitled "Conversations with the Russians," the sociopsychological analysis of collective behavior in the Soviet Union became a Cold War best-seller that was serialized in the *Saturday Evening Post* and condensed in *Reader's Digest*. A second study of totalitarianism, *No Third Path*, followed in 1962. Yet despite his success as a writer of nonfiction, over the next few years Kosinski turned exclusively to fiction so that he could tell the kinds of meaningful stories he really wanted to tell. His first novel *The Painted Bird* (1965), based on the experience of war in his native Poland, was hailed as a masterpiece of both Holocaust literature and modern fiction. Translated widely, it won France's Prix du Meilleur Livre Étranger. *Steps* (1968), his innovative second novel, received the prestigious National Book Award. The short but wickedly satiric *Being There* (1971) not only reached the best-seller list but also inspired a successful movie adaptation, for which Kosinski wrote the prize-winning screenplay. Subsequent works such as *The Devil Tree* (1973), *Cockpit* (1975), *Blind Date* (1977), and *Passion Play* (1979) became significant links in his cycle of novels, in which the picaresque protagonists sought to survive the assaults on their selfhood by various social and political forces and by other adversaries. *Pinball* (1982)—whose dual protagonists (an aging classical composer whose work is out of favor with the public and a young electronic rock genius whose popularity is so extreme as to become threatening) discover that they share secrets as well as values—examined issues of identity and privacy that are even more relevant today than they were when the novel first appeared. And his final novel, *The Hermit of 69th Street* (1988), an "autofiction" written in part to rebut the allegations made by the *Village Voice* questioning the authorship of his fiction, signaled a new and exciting direction in contemporary fiction, the promise of which Kosinski, who committed suicide on May 3, 1991, had only begun to fulfill.

Kosinski was more than just a gifted novelist. He was an avid sportsman, for whom skiing and polo playing served not only as pleasant diversions from his writing routine but also as physical and metaphysical challenges. (In his fiction, several of the protagonists—including Fabian in *Passion Play*, a polo player who shuns team play in favor of one-on-one encounters, away from the fickleness of the public—test themselves accordingly.) A tireless promoter of human rights causes, Kosinski supported the efforts of the American Civil Liberties Union (founded by his old friend Roger Baldwin) and the International League for Human Rights, abhorred all forms of censorship and attempts to suppress the First Amendment, and was dedicated to the Jewish Presence Foundation that he founded and the American Foundation for Polish-Jewish Studies, which he chaired. Nor did he shy away from controversial causes that he found compelling: he corresponded, for a time, with convicted killer turned author Jack Henry Abbott, who was granted parole and later stabbed to death a young aspiring writer, and he raised a stir among Jews and non-Jews alike by suggesting that the erection of so many Holocaust memorials and museums created "a second Holocaust" that celebrated Jewish extermination instead of Jewish achievement. As two-term president of the American Center of the PEN (Poets, Essayists, Novelists) Club, the international organization of writers, he worked to free imprisoned artists overseas. An accomplished photographer, he exhibited his work in galleries in Warsaw, New York, and Chicago; as an actor, he made a stunning film debut as the Bolshevik bureaucrat Grigory Zinoviev in the film *Reds* (1981), produced and directed by his friend Warren Beatty.

For a few years in the late 1960s and early 1970s Kosinski was also a Guggenheim Fellow at the Center for Advanced Studies at Wesleyan and a professor of prose and literature at Princeton and Yale, where he instructed undergraduates on the importance of words as tools and weapons. Immensely popular in the classroom, he often shocked his students into new ways of thinking. Reportedly, on the opening day of his seminar on "Death and the American Imagination" at Yale, twenty students were expected but far more actually turned up. Kosinski winnowed the number by announcing that the class would confront the experience of death as directly as possible, through visits to hospitals, morgues, and mortuaries. "Regrettably," he added, "in order for the experience of death to be complete, it will be necessary for one member of the seminar to die." His announcement resulted in a mass rush to the exits. Another time, when he was lecturing on creativity and reality, he declared that he had invited teachers from a professional dance studio to offer instruction in tap dancing, and that, at the end of the class, he would make an important point. The professional dancers proved laughingly inept, but the students kept practicing the steps the dancers showed them. Afterward, Kosinski shared a lesson in reality: the dance instructors were fakes yet the students—because they had been *told* the instructors were professionals—never questioned their authority. The event had been carefully staged.

Above all, Kosinski was a brilliant raconteur. A favorite of the talk show hosts Merv Griffin, Dick Cavett, and Larry King and of late-night comedians such as Johnny Carson and David Letterman, he fascinated television audiences with his dark exotic looks and attire, his accented but staccato-paced delivery, and his sharp wit. At the Academy Awards ceremony, where he was a presenter, he brought the house down with his brief but clever remarks. In print, radio, and television interviews, he created an unforgettable persona. Describing his strange penchant for secrecy and concealment, he spoke of the weapons he kept hidden and the disguises he wore when he ventured out late at night, and he told of eavesdropping on people's conversations as a way of learning about himself and about how others perceived him. He also repeated tales about Plato's Retreat and the various sex clubs he frequented, places in which he felt safe because the patrons were more concerned about self-recognition than the recognition of others. And at the celebrity-studded soirees and the exclusive beaches of the rich and famous where he often held court, he regaled his hosts with tales of his legendary pranks. Some of those pranks were amusing but benign, such as the time he posed as a spastic just to get to the head of the queue at a French post office or hid under a desk and tickled the ankle of a visiting diplomat so terrified by stories he had heard of the tarantulas in the area that he leapt into the air. Others were more shocking, such as the blind dates he claimed to have arranged for macho polo players with beautiful women who turned out to be transsexuals. In more formal appearances before such distinguished groups as the Century Association and the Philadelphia Stock Exchange, Kosinski spoke eloquently but usually extemporaneously, with few, if any, notes to guide him. He was, in short, a great storyteller, just as his native tradition had prepared him to be.

Storytelling, in fact, was both Kosinski's vocation and his avocation. He told stories in his fiction—evocative and often brutal tales of men and women in conflict with forces that try to repress them and suppress their individuality; and he told stories in his own life—anecdotes he relished and usually embellished for dramatic effect, as purveyors of the narrative tradition are wont do. And often, as oral tradition allows and even demands, he deliberately blurred the line between the two. "Once you are a novelist," he noted, "you make a story of everything."

To be sure, Kosinski's life was the stuff of great stories. He spoke often of that extraordinary life in his interviews and his lectures, and he wrote about it in his novels. Traumatized by his precarious situation as a Jewish child in wartime Eastern Europe, he learned—as a young adult—to defy Marxist doctrine and eventually plotted a successful escape from Stalinist Poland. Arriving virtually penniless in New York at the age of twenty-four, he was fluent in several languages but not English. Within a few months, while working a succession of odd jobs that included parking cars and scraping paint from the hulls of ships, he taught himself his new language, won a grant from the Ford Foundation, and secured a place in the graduate program in sociology at Columbia University, where he turned his class notes on collective behavior into his first book. He soon met and married Mary Hayward Weir, the widow of the National Steel Corporation tycoon Ernest T. Weir, and, through her money and influence, he embarked on the jetsetting lifestyle of the superrich. Yet, even while living the American Dream, he never forgot his nightmarish wartime experiences, which he used as the basis of his acclaimed first novel. Mary's trust, however, made no provision for him, and after her death he found himself once again on his own—by now, though, as a successful writer of fiction. Over the next twenty years he published eight more novels and achieved an enviable personal and literary celebrity. His constant companion and devoted assistant was Katherina ("Kiki") von Fraunhofer, a prominent former advertising executive and Bavarian aristocrat who later became his wife.

In 1982 Kosinski found himself threatened again, this time by the scandal that followed accusations reported in the *Village Voice* that he was a liar, a CIA stooge, and a literary fraud who employed others to write large portions of his fiction. Although most of the charges were unproven, Kosinski knew that irreparable damage had been done to his reputation, and he spent much of the next few years battling the rumors. His final work, a nontraditional novel without a conventional plot, offered a fictional rebuttal of the allegations and gave Kosinski the new narrative form he had been seeking. Essentially a story about storytelling, the novel featured a fifty-five-year-old half–East European, half–American Holocaust survivor named Norbert Kosky ("Kosinski without the 'sin'") who is wrongly accused of artistic fraud.

It is no wonder, therefore, that Kosinski believed "the random succession of pain and joy, wealth and poverty, persecution and approbation" in his own life was "even more eventful than that of his fictional characters," or that he often imagined his own life as a fiction and perceived of himself as a fictional character. He recalled, for instance, that in the chaos of postwar Eastern Europe, when he felt buffeted by competing ideologies, he turned to Stendhal's novel *The Red and the Black* and imagined himself as the protagonist Julien Sorel, who realizes that things were neither red nor black but somewhere in between. Later, alienated and alone in New York, Kosinski conceived of himself as a character from the works of Dos Passos, Hemingway, Faulkner, or Balzac; in such a way, he "wandered through the first few months, accepting various identities and surviving in a city which was rather hostile."

As Kosinski wove even the most traumatic incidents from his life into his fiction, his biography became an increasingly vital part of his storytelling. Because "what we remember lacks the hard edge of fact," he explained, "to help us along we create little fictions, highly subtle and individual scenarios which clarify and shape our experience. The remembered event becomes a fiction, a structure to accommodate certain feelings." Yet memories, he suggested, are neither literal nor exact; if they have a truth, "it is more an emotional than an actual one."

Indeed, if the essential truth of personal experience is conveyed through the "remembered event" and not through the "hard edge of fact"—that is, through memory that is more emotional than exact—then, for the writer of fiction, the emotional impact of an event is of greater consequence than the actual details of that experience. Whether Kosinski's boyhood muteness was literal (as he initially contended) or symbolic (as he later conceded), the event itself was authentic. Whether or not he was physically separated from his parents and forced to flee peasant villages alone during the war, his fear of being discovered and betrayed was just as real. Whether he lost sixty or sixty-two members of his family in the Holocaust, whether or not he actually dropped a Bible while serving Mass, whether or not he carried a cyanide capsule in case his escape from Poland failed—the feelings evoked by memory were in effect the same and became a metaphor for his reality. Consequently, those biographers and literary critics who delight in finding or chronicling inconsistencies in Kosinski's remembrances of his experiences often miss the larger point—and the underlying truth—of his novels and stories.

In his oral narratives as in his writing, Kosinski repeated certain themes and anecdotes. Yet even when the details of the different versions varied, the essence of the story remained the same. And that story usually harked back to his Eastern European past, particularly to the narrative aspect of the Polish-Jewish tradition from which he learned his very first stories. The more Kosinski searched for new forms, in fact, the more he tapped into the old, original ones.

The interviews, lectures, presentations, and media appearances represented in this volume reveal Jerzy Kosinski at his storytelling best. At times witty and humorous, at times clever and punning, at times serious and provocative, Kosinski shared his personal and cultural experiences through his stories; in turn, he experienced—and shared—"the supreme act of oral pleasure."

All of the material in this volume is previously uncollected; most is previously unpublished. Yet unlike his novels, which Kosinski meticulously and notoriously revised, even into final galleys, the various talks and interviews in *Oral Pleasure* expose another side of Kosinski by demonstrating his spontaneous command of language and ideas and his remarkable ability to galvanize his audiences. His way with words, as one interviewer confirmed, was "inspiring," "majestic," and "pure magic." At the same time, the various pieces enhance our appreciation of his fiction, to which they serve as an essential complement.

The material has been grouped loosely into sixteen sections, according to certain recurring themes. But there is a necessary overlap among the categories, just as there are necessary repetitions within the pieces themselves. Insofar as possible, however, the integrity (especially of the longer interviews and lectures, in which Kosinski typically addressed a broad range of topics) is preserved by printing the pieces in full.

A final note. Although transcripts of some of Kosinski's media appearances were available (albeit often in incomplete form), the talks printed herein were preserved entirely thanks to Kiki Kosinski, who usually accompanied her husband to his engagements and taped his remarks on a small tape recorder that she held on her lap. Given the vagaries of such electronic recording, occasionally portions of the material were inaudible or missing. Consequently, the material has been edited for gaps, length, and major redundancies between pieces, but every effort has been made to retain the original voice. Mrs. Kosinski also supplied details about dates, places, and other particulars and offered numerous invaluable insights in the preparation of this volume, which would not have been possible without her vision, support, and generous assistance.

Unfortunately, Kiki Kosinski did not live long enough to see the volume in print. She died on May 25, 2007, shortly after the manuscript was completed. It was her original intention that *Oral Pleasure* serve as a testament to the spontaneous wit and verbal dexterity of her beloved "Jurek" by revealing facets of his personality unfamiliar to some of his readers. Ultimately, though, it is as much a tribute to Kiki's own talent and tenacity, and a confirmation of her singular role in promoting and preserving Jerzy Kosinski's literary legacy.

On Autobiography as Fiction /
Fiction as Autobiography

My novels are always confrontational. And my characters are often survivors who pose as conquerors. . . . In all of my novels, the viewpoint is that only by being imaginative toward your own life, perhaps by perceiving yourself as a character in a drama, can you make it meaningful. By being exposed to a confrontational novel, readers have their own notions of life challenged.

How can any novelist write anything that is purely fictional without openly involving himself? My novel is fiction, true. But it stems from my life—autobiography combined with fiction. Why pretend it isn't?

THE PRACTICE OF FICTION

In his radio interview with Barry Gray in April 1982, Kosinski discussed a wide variety of topics, from his wartime experiences (which he described in terms that were symbolic as well as literal—and which he fictionalized in *The Painted Bird* and other of his works) to his early years in the United States, from his fascination with language and its absence to his love of sports, from his practice of fiction to his philosophy of life.

BARRY GRAY: I am fortunate indeed to have with me Jerzy Kosinski, the great writer, novelist, and actor. How many radio programs have you now done?

JERZY KOSINSKI: Actually, very few. Three or four, I think. No more than that.

BG: How do you decide whether or not to do a program? I'm just curious.

JK: I like radio. Radio is the closest medium I can think of to writing fiction. If you are listening to us right now, you don't see us. You have to put your mind to work. You have to envisage us and what we are talking about. In this way, the mental process of listening to radio is the same as reading fiction. You read *Pinball* and you have to imagine the characters.

My private mission is to sponsor radio, at least in the neighborhood, and I happen to live in this neighborhood. It is my spiritual neighborhood as well as my physical neighborhood.

BG: I have now read *Pinball,* and I am puzzled as to how you translate this novel to the screen—and it will be transferred to the screen, will it not?

JK: Only if I choose to do so, and I have not made up my mind yet.

BG: You've been offered the opportunity.

JK: You always get offers. I think that in this country you get offers for everything. The trick is not to agree too quickly to anything.

BG: The thing that puzzled me in our first meeting and that still puzzles me is how Jerzy Kosinski has managed to retain his sanity into the beginning of his middle years, considering his background. You were an instant away from being put to death by the Nazis. An instant.

JK: Yes, but at the same time, so were hundreds of thousands of other Jewish children.

BG: But that doesn't change anything. It's like saying there are four million poor, but you are the one who feels raw hunger. You are the one who is hungry, not the other four million.

JK: I guess. I somehow refuse to see myself as being in any way singled out. I like to think that I was part of a large terrible historical process, a historical process which nevertheless involved hundreds of thousands of people exactly like me.

BG: But have you never wondered what it was that saved you? Was there a strange power? Was it a spiritual thing? Was it a lucky number? Was it the stars that took you out of that line and saved your life? What was it that happened? Have you never thought of that?

JK: I do once in a while. But I was six when the war began and when I was separated from my parents. Then I moved alone from one peasant village to another.

BG: You don't mind my bringing this up?

JK: No, not at all. It was very much a part of my life. My parents sent me to what they thought would be the safety of a remote village, in a pattern followed by many middle-class Jewish families. Jews were required to go to the concentration camps, and eventually everyone knew that meant the gas chambers. The middle-class Jewish families would pay for the upkeep of their children by non-Jews. There were people who specialized in that process, in taking a child and depositing him in a foster-parent home of sorts, where the child would be required to hide, not to speak too easily, and never to betray the Jewish identity.

In my case, what happened was that instead of being entrusted to some-one professionally reliable, my parents for some reason had chosen a man who was an acquaintance of my father and who was on his way to the Soviet Union. Now, keep in mind that in 1939 the Soviet Union was not at war with Germany. In fact, they had just signed a peace treaty, so there was a chance that this man who was a Polish Communist before the war—a very reliable man, or so my parents thought—would take me with him to the Soviet Union. And so they gave him some money and jewels and appar-ently a family Persian carpet. He took the valuables, and then he took me with him. Again, I was only six. But somewhere on the way to the Soviet border he changed his mind. Or maybe his mind was changed by what he saw: the terrible war that was taking place, hundreds of people fighting for every place on the train, children everywhere. And I was a nuisance, a very talkative six-year-old Jewish child.

Two or three days into the trip on that train, which seemed to stop and go, stop and go, he just left me with some peasants at one of the small railroad stations. He gave them some money and probably said, "Do whatever you can with this kid." And then my war began. I might add that I was a very spoiled only child. My father was substantially older than my mother, so I had sort of double attention—which, in fact, to answer your question, might have been responsible for my surviving. I was so spoiled as a child that whenever something awful happened to me, even something as awful as being left at a station with two peasants who were

5

obviously not very friendly and who saw me as a nuisance right away and who got rid of me promptly . . .

BG: And a Jewish child . . .

JK: Yes, a Jewish child who was a menace to everyone there. They already knew the penalty for harboring a Jew or a Gypsy. I think that being so spoiled, I saw myself as rather sweet and pleasant and others ignorant of what they were doing. Now, this was a good feeling to have, because whenever someone would hit me or push me around or refuse to keep me, I just told myself that he or she didn't know what a nice child I am. I hate to say it, but I think this feeling accompanied me throughout the war.

BG: And saved your life.

JK: Yes, and maybe saved my life, in the sense that at no time did I see myself as being altogether victimized. There were, however, two brief moments during the war when I considered committing suicide. I remember at one point that I threw myself off a tree. But I selected a tree that was not tall enough, so clearly I didn't mean to die. Another time it was a fence, and again nothing happened. So I guess that I survived by being positive in some way about my own value. And that's how the war passed.

BG: The world according to Jerzy Kosinski. When the man who was supposed to be your guardian absconded and left you with the two peasants, what did they say?

JK: This was already in a territory where the peasants spoke a dialect. He didn't talk to them in front of me. He merely told me that they were going to take me to a place where my parents would come to pick me up.

BG: And you believed it, of course.

JK: I believed him. I went with the peasants, and they found an old woman on the outskirts of a village. She was very old, and she died shortly afterwards.

BG: This was Poland?

JK: Poland, in November 1939, two months after the war began. The country had been invaded by the German army, and Jews were beginning to be rounded up for the concentration camps. The old woman kept me for a while and then she died. And, of course, I had to go to another village. By then I knew my parents were not coming back, and by then I started a sort of game: each time a peasant family would take me, they expected to be paid for my upkeep. You see, between 1939 and 1942, there were sufficient numbers of Jewish children still living in the countryside with non-Jewish foster parents, since the myth of the rich Jews who would come to ransom their kid was still very much alive. So whenever I would come alone, the peasants were quite eager to keep me for a few weeks. And I maintained the myth that someone, either my parents or a messenger sent by them, would soon come to claim me. After two or three weeks, nobody was showing up. And then by 1941 . . .

BG: How did you get that smart?

JK: I could see what was happening. The peasants were very nice to me in the beginning. They would show me the photographs of other Jewish children whom they had kept before or who somehow passed through the village, or they would tell me about neighbors who had Jewish children. Occasionally, they brought a photograph to reassure me that there were other Jewish children around and that I should be positive and not run away, for heaven's sake, otherwise, the messenger with the money would come and I wouldn't be there. So then I would feed into these expectations. I would say, "Oh, definitely, so and so will be coming. A man will be coming with jewelry and Persian carpets and with all kinds of other things." But, of course, the man never came.

BG: And then they quickly discovered . . .

JK: Yes, this worked until 1942, more or less. I lived in about twenty different villages over two years. Then the situation changed and I had to move very quickly. After 1942, there was a major penalty for anyone who harbored a Jew. This was part of the Final Solution of the Jewish problem.

BG: When peasant couple B transferred you to peasant couple C, they kept you for three weeks or so. How did they explain that they were giving you away?

JK: They would not give me away.

BG: You would run away.

JK: I realized that they were going to get rid of me. There were examples around.

BG: And so then you would go. How did you attach yourself to a new couple?

JK: I would not. I would just run away from the village as quickly as I could. I could sense the change of climate and knew that I would not be welcome anymore. And I was afraid, frankly, that something bad might happen to me. As a matter of fact, from time to time, when the money was not forthcoming, the peasants would tell me what could happen to a Jewish child alone, a child whose presence endangered the whole village.

BG: What kinds of things did they tell you?

JK: I knew that I could be delivered to the Germans. I knew I was not supposed to talk about my background. I was not supposed to drop my pants because I was circumcised. I was not supposed to walk in the daylight. I was not supposed to be out when there was a holiday. I was not supposed to talk to strangers. I was supposed to sit on the farm or in the basement or wherever and wait for the money that would pay for my upkeep. I was also made aware that some of the Jewish children who used to live in the village were no longer there. Or maybe they were, but underground. And so, knowing all of this, I would run away and start the whole thing again in the next village. Positive face, positive attitude—here I am. They would ask me, "Why are you here?" and I would say, "The peasants who kept me in the other village—unfortunately something happened to them. They had

8

other Jewish children, and I wasn't welcome anymore." And, of course, I would add that the man with money would be coming very soon and that I hoped he would know where I am, and so forth.

BG: It's like Charles Dickens. How did you know which Polish couple to attach yourself to?

JK: You just know.

BG: Weren't the other children cruel?

JK: Yes, of course they were. Children are cruel, even to their friends. And here I was at the mercy of everybody. Occasionally, part of my war was fighting off children and dogs. The disadvantage I had was that I could not hurt any other kid. He or she had parents and relatives. Everyone could hurt me, so I was an easy target. I was also an easy target in the sense that once I was selected as a target, I had to accept being a target and do nothing about it. Not enter into any open fight. Not attract attention. Eventually I developed what you might call an instinct. I could sense in someone's look that he was getting hostile and that maybe he would try to drown me, or maybe that he was drinking too much vodka and was preparing himself to commit some unpleasant physical act that might end my life. Then I would run away. I still run away when I feel I am not welcome.

BG: Weren't you once thrown into human waste up to your armpits?

JK: A bit deeper than that. There was a reason for it. But these are not necessarily pleasant subjects.

BG: I don't really want to be pleasant, Jerzy. Please, I want to hear this story, if I may. Do you mind?

JK: No, I don't mind. In 1942, after the Germans had announced the Final Solution of the Jewish problem in Eastern Europe, anyone—any family, any individual, any community—harboring a Jew was to be punished by death. That included those who were immediately responsible as well as those indirectly responsible. The Germans exhibited posters everywhere, and the posters portrayed Jewish families. As you can see, I do look rather

9

Jewish, and it just so happened that the male child on one of those posters looked exactly like me. The hooked nose, the olive skin, the slightly tubercular frame—there I was on every poster in every village. Clearly this made my upkeep much more difficult. Except for the Catholic church, which was responsible for my surviving, no one dared to keep me. The minute I would show up in a village, someone either threatened to deliver me to the Germans, at which point I would run away again, or tried to find a place for me by contacting the church.

In one particular village not too far from the railroad, where the German trains were carrying Jews to the concentration camp at Treblinka, the peasants realized that I was a terrible, terrible menace. So the church was contacted, and the local priest found a place for me. I could serve as an altar boy at the early Mass, at six o'clock in the morning, along with the young priest, an anti-Nazi who was also hiding in the church to avoid recognition. There was literally no one in the little village church at this hour. But, in the beginning of June, there was a large religious holiday, and the main priest needed six altar boys, three on each side of the church. One boy did not show up. I was hanging around the church, and since, with my face turned away from the parish, my looks were similar to those of the absent boy, the priest said, "Why don't you serve at the Mass?" He was the major figure in the parish, so of course I agreed in order to assure myself food and shelter for another few days.

During the Mass, it was my turn to transfer the Bible from one side of the altar to the other. I wrote about the experience in a remote way in one of my novels, *The Painted Bird*. It was a dramatic moment, almost a turning point in my life. Corpus Christi Day, one of the most important Christian holidays. The Bible was heavy, and it stood on a huge stand. There was just not enough strength in me to move it, and I knew this ahead of time. But I was not brave enough to whisper to another altar boy to change places with me, because I was afraid that in the act of leaning toward him I would reveal my profile to the people in the church.

Now, my profile looked exactly like the profile on that poster which was hanging outside of the church. Since I preferred to face Christ rather than my fellow man, I got up and took it upon myself to transfer the Bible. It did not work. I lifted the Bible and managed to move back with it, to kneel with it, but it overturned. There was a terrible outcry from the congregation, who took it as a bad omen. Some supposed I might be drunk; others realized I was an obvious outsider. Quickly, some of the men nearest to me picked me up, probably to prevent others in the church from taking a better look at me. Imagine this episode in its historical context. What if there was a Catholic German soldier in the back or on the balcony next to the organist? The whole village would suffer as a result.

My rationalization is that the men knew that if they just pushed me around, I would return to the village and endanger everyone there. So what they did was probably the wisest thing to do under the circumstances. They threw me into the pit of human excrement, not too far from the church, which was used as a toilet.

BG: What did you do?

JK: I guess I almost drowned. The pit was very deep, probably five or six feet down. They covered it once a year and built another one. I was then nine years old.

BG: Four feet tall.

JK: Right. The pit had a very dense substance with all sorts of viscosity to it. It literally sucked me in and filled my lungs and stomach, so I almost drowned. Yet at the same time it was heavy enough to bounce me up in a way, so even though I did not know how to swim—not that you could swim in it—I managed to crawl out. From that point, it took me a while to come to terms with what actually happened. I stopped talking. I became mute possibly as a result of the trauma. I haven't resolved it—maybe because of the fall in the church and the sheer tension that I had developed before the fall, maybe as a result of the trauma which preceded being thrown in the excrement pit. I knew where they were dragging me. I knew the place very well. I used the toilet very often myself. Maybe it was the sheer horror of the substance itself. In any case, this was a turning point: Corpus Christi Day of June 1942.

BG: The scene which you have just described is in fact from an earlier book, *The Painted Bird*. How many books have you written?

11

JK: I have written eight novels, in some twenty years.

BG: Eight novels in a language which was obviously not yours to begin with.

JK: But which became mine when I came to this country.

BG: I told you on the phone when we spoke earlier this week, the thing that is amazing to me—and I would add shameful to me, as one who is native-born—is your ability to handle the language. It is pure magic. You have a majesty with words which is inspiring. It's awesome. How did this come about?

JK: Well, I am very pleased. It probably came about, in a way, by being pleased that finally there was something I could do that would not make me dependent on other people. I would not have to depend on society outside. I could use the very democratic institution of language.

BG: How did you know you could write?

JK: I always wanted to write, even when I was in high school. In Eastern Europe, however, we all knew that there was no point in writing. The political system prevented free expression. So when I was in school I used photography to express myself.

BG: Let's go back to those terrible moments, when you crawled out of that well of excrement. You were filthy . . .

JK: That is probably when I turned into a writer of sorts, because I lost the power of speech. I became mute for the next five years.

BG: How did you know you were mute?

JK: Because when I reached the next village, I could not speak . . .

BG: So you arrived at the next village. You must have looked like an apparition.

JK: Yes, I was an apparition. That's why no one wanted to talk to me. And when I wanted to talk to some of them, I could not.

BG: What did you do about a change of clothing?

JK: I quickly washed my pants and shirt in a nearby pond of sorts, a marsh, really. It was very warm, the beginning of June. I dried off, vomited, got very sick, and knew very well there was no point in going back. I was afraid that this time they could drown me. I spent about a day or a day and a half hanging around in the woods, to recover from the experience.

BG: No food?

JK: I still don't eat as much or as often as you think. And then I went to the next village to look for a place to stay, hoping that someone would pick me up again, hoping that someone would assume that someone would show up to pay for me. By then I had washed the shirt—it was actually a sack. I was wearing a sort of a brown sack and sandals, which we made ourselves, from pieces of wood with little straps. A couple on a cart stopped me. They wanted to talk to me, asked me who I was, but I could not tell them. That is when I realized that I was mute. I thought that it was a result of having swallowed excrement. Frankly, in the beginning, I thought it would pass. I really did not know that the muteness was going to last. I assumed it was a temporary disease, something that was in my throat. I kept thinking that my voice was stopped in my neck rather than in my spirit.

BG: So you arrived at the next village, and you found more problems. At which point did your life begin to be mobile upward?

JK: I think that was the moment. Ironically, the loss of speech became very peaceful spiritually. I discovered spiritual peace once I realized that I simply could not speak. I did not worry anymore about being asked questions because I knew I could not answer them. And so I turned inward. I became far more preoccupied with what I thought and with things that I saw, and human contact became manipulative for me only in terms of getting food. So I became much more self-reliant. I changed villages very quickly, one after another. I would often use the railroad. I would hang on to a train. I started to steal. I became much more enterprising. I got myself a comet, a little device which I described in *The Painted Bird,* a little preserve can with holes in it. You can cook in it, you make a fire in it, and it keeps you warm as you walk.

You asked before how I became a writer. When I came to New York in 1957, twenty-five years ago, I did not know English very well. I had a rudimentary knowledge of English, some knowledge of French, Russian, Polish. And Latin—not a great help in New York. I looked at myself once again as being mute. Although I had actually regained my speech at the age of fifteen, in New York I saw myself as being mute once again. I said to myself, "So what, Kosinski? This is no worse than when you were a kid. From now on, imagine what you as a mute person would like to do in the United States."

BG: What happened to you during the years of your muteness?

JK: The war, the rest of the war, which went on for another four years. And the orphanage after the war. My parents found me in the orphanage. My parents survived the war.

BG: How did they find you?

JK: Again, in the relatively messy circumstances of postwar life, when the country tried to organize itself, Poland itself was like one big orphanage. I listed the city in which we lived before the war as the one to which I wanted to be sent back by the Soviet army. So after a short period with a Soviet outfit, I—together with a great number of other children—was delivered to the orphanage in Łódź, the city in which my family had lived. Months later, someone obviously noticed the name or maybe the great resemblance between me and my mother. My parents were around. They too had come back to Łódź. And so they showed up to claim me. I might add I did not really want to go with them. I didn't remember them too well. I saw myself as being quite different than I was before the war. I didn't want parents any-more, I wanted to be on my own. But I was mute so I had to go with them.

I was sent to a special school for the handicapped. And the YMCA, an American institution which was very active in Poland at that time, helped me a great deal. They took care of me; they rehabilitated me in a way. They used the fact that I knew how to ride horses—because I was employed with animals from time to time in some of the villages—to turn me into a horseman. They also taught me how to ski. Those two sports—skiing and horseback riding—required no communication with other children. Then, by 1947, I regained my speech in a skiing accident. I fell. Again, there was a moment of tension that preceded the fall: I knew I was approaching a huge drop and I wasn't able to stop. Then I fell and was hospitalized. Again, just as suddenly as I had stopped talking, I picked up a telephone and began to speak.

BG: The words just fell right out of you.

JK: Yes, the phone rang and I picked it up.

BG: When you met your parents after all those years, how did you feel?

JK: That really they were a nuisance, that they were two older people broken by the war. They looked quite pathetic to me. I saw myself as a free creature. Here they wanted to claim me. What for? Meanwhile, they had adopted another child during the war, a Jewish child who was then five years old. I confronted this other kid, and there was a competition. The kid was normal. I wasn't. I was in the orphanage for retarded children, most of whom were crippled, physically crippled, with no legs or no hands, with broken jaws, blind, deaf, or mute. Although everyone thought I was a deaf-mute, I was not. I was merely mute. But I had a way of reassessing my identity. There were things I knew how to do better than anybody else. I could throw a stone with great precision. I could steal better than most. I could disguise myself very well. I could pretend to be someone else. And here my parents wanted to turn me into a child and sort of match me against another kid. So this was not easy, and I became almost a criminal child. I would run away at night. Not really run away—I would just go out at night. Very often I was picked up by police and delivered back to my parents. So I think it was a difficult time for them.

    The irony is that, once I got my speech back, the inner peace ended and the real trouble started with the Communist State. I became openly hostile to any attempt at spiritual collectivization. I felt the purpose of human life was to live it individually, that the meaning we would discover was the meaning in our own selves. That philosophy is still very much a part of me, and I have used it in all my novels since. Well, the Communist State in Poland was not about to put up with this. They would try to enroll me in the Party; they tried to force me to wear a green shirt and red tie. I was not going to do it. I was not going to march in any marching column, because a marching column for me evoked the image of the Nazis. Anything marching in a column was my mortal enemy. The trouble really began and soon led to my conviction that I should get out of Eastern Europe. So even though I became relatively successful as a student and as a social scientist—I specialized in the nineteenth century to avoid any contact with their Communist twentieth century—I planned my escape. And I escaped to the United States in 1957 at the age of twenty-four. Once I arrived here, I was mute again. Happy again, and free to pursue what I saw as my own private destiny.

BG: You mentioned Latin and all those languages. Where did you learn Latin?

JK: At the university in Poland. It was an obligatory language in school. Also, since my father was a classical scholar, there was encouragement at home.

BG: When you met your parents again, did you hate them for having abandoned you?

JK: No, because most of the children in the orphanage were abandoned. War meant children being abandoned. That is what war was all about. The relationship with my parents was hardly important. What was important to me was how to take care of myself. They appeared to be a threat, a threat to my identity. What if they were going to imprison me? What if they were going to give me to someone again? What if they were going to do this or that? I wanted to be on my own.

BG: How did you finally get out of Poland?

JK: It was a complex process which required two years. I did not want to leave behind me anyone responsible for my departure, since anyone responsible for my escape would then be liable for it. Briefly, what I did was this: I invented four nonexistent bureaucrats. I described the process in *Cockpit,* one of my novels. At the time, I was a scientist at a prestigious state scientific institution. I invented four bureaucrats who were very important—so important, in fact, that the only way to get in touch with them was to write to them. There was no way to telephone them; they were unlisted, like most of the important men in the Communist State. And these four nonexistent men, all of whom were affiliated with the academic institution of which I was a part, ultimately supported my petition for a passport to the United States. All the state organizations, state agencies, and police had to correspond with them. I pretended that each of the bureaucrats had authorized me to pick up his mail. It worked very well. I would go downstairs to the main mail office, and after claiming the mail I would answer the letters in their name.

BG: And you made this all up yourself?

JK: Yes, since I couldn't possibly bring anyone else into it. Anyone who became part of my plan would then be punished and get sent to prison.

BG: You made up four scientists?

JK: Four sets of stationery, four rubber stamps, and so forth. Three of them were in favor of my departure; one was against. The other three, of course, countered the negative influence. In the course of almost two years, after hundreds and hundreds of letters from various state agencies, I managed to secure a passport for Jerzy Kosinski to leave for the United States, and no one knew anything about it.

BG: How did you dream up this plan, this scheme?

JK: I knew the bureaucracy quite well. I was very much part of it. At one point, my father said to me, "You know, this place is a jungle." And I took this as a motive. Bureaucracy is a jungle, and the Communist bureaucracy is a triple jungle. The building in which I was employed had twenty-five hundred distinguished men and women working in it, and some seventeen hundred additional workers. Among them were some seven hundred and

17

fifty people whose names were listed somewhere but whom no one had ever seen. Four more, I reasoned, would not make a great difference. And they didn't.

BG: Jerzy, how did you get this job in Poland?

JK: The initial job was the result of a state competitive examination. I was a very good student. I was probably one of the best and certainly one of the youngest students at the university in Łódź. I had two master's degrees—one in political science, one in history. I had great support from professors who opposed the Communist system and to whom, in fact, I was an example that some students still would not enroll just in anything. And so even though the majority of the institution could be counted as my enemy and saw me as an enemy—that is, a student who refused to join the student union, a student who refused even to consider joining any political association or organization—there were some professors, among them a rector and a dean of the old guard, who encouraged my opposition. They kept saying, "This is the only chance we have." But I wasn't the only one. There were others. Not that many, though, maybe some six or seven out of two or three thousand who had simply given up. So in a way I was privileged—ironically, privileged that there were others who helped me to survive the hostile atmosphere of the Communist university. Once I passed the competitive examination, I received a state scholarship and automatically became a grantee at the Polish Academy of Science, the highest scientific body in the country. You do not have anything like this in the United States; here the country is not a pyramid. In a Communist state, the whole country is one particular pyramid, and the Academy of Science sits on the very top. I was only twenty years old. I had energy. I had mental resources and I wanted to get out, so I embarked on this major plan of invention. And it worked.

BG: So, at twenty-four, how did you get the money to come to the United States?

JK: The money came with the passport. I was paid by the State to get out. Once I received the passport—I still have all these things with me, I brought them in my suitcase, the only inheritance I have, proof of the best plan of my life—they paid for my trip, because it was assumed I was going for research, state-sponsored research in the United States. So I paid for my ticket on SAS Airlines in Polish currency provided by the Polish government.

BG: And when you got here?

JK: When I got here I knew nothing. I was lost. So I went to the YMCA, an organization with whom I had a history. I knew the YMCA would have a way of verifying who I was. Even though I could not pay, they gave me a room, and I started to function in New York like thousands and thousands of other refugees.

BG: What did you do on your first day?

JK: I went to the cafeteria and then I walked around the neighborhood. It was another village to me, this time a bigger village than the villages I was accustomed to. But it was another village, and I was a mute person in a very big village. And I loved the village.

BG: And you did not speak a word?

JK: There was no need.

BG: Did you have any money?

JK: I had three dollars and eighty cents left from the initial five dollars I was allowed to bring with me. This was the foreign currency the Polish government allowed you to take: five dollars, of which I spent a dollar twenty on Coca-Cola in Copenhagen when I was changing planes, because I wanted to taste the forbidden fruit of the West.

BG: How was it?

JK: Terrible. I learned to like it since but not at the time.

BG: So with a few dollars and change . . .

JK: I had some black-and-white film which I was willing to trade but the YMCA said, "No, you do not have to." They told me about a man who came three or four times a week and who would try to get me a job. I registered downstairs, and someone came. And I was employed rather quickly. I think on the following day I was already working.

BG: So you got a job as a photographer?

JK: No. I was scraping paint from the Day Line cruise ships. The unions would paint the ships, but someone would first have to scrape off the old paint. The unions did not want to do it at the time, so they used all kinds of Mexicans, Greeks, assorted Latinos—and I among them. They paid thirty-five cents an hour to scrape off the paint, to chip it off. And that's not easy work. It was December.

BG: Cold. Cold and on the water. So you worked eight hours a day, and you got approximately three dollars.

JK: Through the night. It was done at night.

BG: That's even worse.

JK: Somehow it was not quite legal. There was a minimum wage already. At the time, it was a dollar an hour. We were paid thirty-five cents an hour. While I was a legal alien, there were probably many who were not legal, so we were all employed illegally. But that was fine. I didn't mind it. It was a new country. I had to pay a price. I didn't speak the language. I made no provision for coming to the United States. I spent so much time and energy getting out of Eastern Europe that it was my fault, in a way, that when I arrived here my English was really rudimentary.

BG: How then did you learn your English?

JK: I started to learn right away. Keep in mind, I was a scientist. Language is not a mystery. You listen to a radio program. You have a dictionary next to you. You read the newspapers. You translate things for yourself. You buy paperbacks, grammars, synonym finders, word finders, phrase finders. In six weeks I managed quite well.

BG: What kind of words were you using in those first six weeks?

JK: Verbs, primarily. The verb is very important. But again, I don't necessarily think that verbal communication is so essential in human contact. I am sure that in your life in New York you come across people who speak rather haltingly, and yet you communicate with them and you like them and you help them.

BG: I also meet a lot of people who speak very fine English whom I don't like at all, and I have nothing to say to them.

JK: Language can be a barrier. In my case, the absence of language was a kind of bridge: most of those who worked with me didn't speak English at all. So, in a way, it was encouraging. There I was in a country that did not require proficiency in English as a major aspect of one's existence.

BG: You were still living at the YMCA? And you were coming in what, at four, five, six o'clock in the morning? And you would sleep until one or two in the afternoon?

JK: Yes. Then I would start looking for the sources of other employment—and of language.

BG: Did you ever steal?

JK: Let's say that, from time to time, I experimented with it. The irony is that I used to steal little tins of caviar. At the time, caviar was sold in supermarkets. The tins were small and could very easily be concealed. I would go inside and drop them into the sleeve of my coat. Then I would retrieve them from the inside of the sleeve and deposit them in the pocket of my shirt. The reason I would pick up caviar was that it is highly nutritious and it is filling.

BG: It's also very good.

JK: I wasn't really fond of it. As a student in Eastern Europe, occasionally I visited the Soviet Union to do some work in the archives there. And, of course, we would get caviar in Russia. I wasn't very fond of it but I knew that it was nutritious, easy to steal, easy to conceal, so from time to time in New York I would feed myself.

BG: And where did you get a job to get away from the ship?

JK: There were several. Once I started to speak, there were many jobs I held in rapid succession. I would clean bars because somebody discovered I did not drink and that made me a perfect employee. The bars had to be cleaned, bottles dusted off, particularly after four o'clock in the morning. Eventually I began to drive and managed to become a member of the Teamsters. I had to get some money to pay for my membership, but then I started to drive a truck with another driver. It was a great opportunity to listen to the radio and to learn the language. I was quite well paid. When the other man was driving, I could read the newspaper, pick out the words I did not know. I embarked on a massive program of self-improvement, as simple as that. I had to know everything about the American environment, including the American spiritual environment. I literally wasted no time. This is the answer to your initial question, "How is it that one comes from abroad and begins to speak in a foreign language?" You do it because it is your future, because you have no way back, because your whole body, your soul, muscle, energy, waking state, sleeping condition directs itself toward the goal, which is the future. And in my case the future was something I wanted to do on my own, and that was to write. And that's all.

BG: How did we look to you as a people? What did you think of our society? You had come from the worst, having had experiences which are almost indescribable, and here we were a fat and happy country.

JK: I didn't see it as a "fat and happy country" because probably it isn't a fat and happy country. Maybe it was at a certain time—and is to us now, from time to time—but when you arrive in New York when I arrived, when you work with those I worked with, it's a country of very hardworking, committed people. People committed to their existence. In many, many ways, it's different than Europe. There is no fear, at least there wasn't then. Less tradition, perhaps. But it's a country whose environment encouraged me, and I guess many others, to do what it was I wanted to do. So I saw the environment as very supportive.

BG: You have written eighteen novels . . .

JK: Eight. I wish there could have been eighteen.

BG: Oh, there will be. What are you working on now?

JK: Another novel. What happened was that the first seven novels I wrote composed a cycle. They are connected. In a way, they follow certain aspects of my life. They are to a degree autobiographical. My latest novel *Pinball* stands outside of that cycle.

BG: So there is a change coming.

JK: Yes. And now the next one I think will be almost entirely independent. *The Painted Bird* opened the cycle of the novels. It was followed by *Steps,* then *Being There,* from which I made a film with Peter Sellers. Then *The Devil Tree, Cockpit, Blind Date, Passion Play*—this is the cycle of seven novels that started with *The Painted Bird* and ended with *Passion Play. Pinball* stands outside of that cycle. It's much more intimate in a way, and it looks at, hypothetically, an artist who has created a cycle of novels.

BG: And a phenomenal book, which I recommend unconditionally. I hesitate to talk about a novel on the air because it is very difficult to discuss it without giving away the story, and I don't want to do that. I merely say that if this audience believes me, you will rush to buy *Pinball,* which kept me awake. I simply could not put it down, and I called you the next day to tell you that I had never been so enthralled with a book. At which point did you begin to feel that you had come and seen and conquered?

JK: I have always felt this. I learned then that my life is what I feel within me and that I cannot, cannot in any way, rank myself against others. I cannot rely on the reaction of others because my life is my gift. When I got out from that excrement pit, I suddenly realized that my whole reliance on the community, my whole joy of being an altar boy, my whole joy of being embraced by people even though my presence threatened them, was no victory. I realized that I had to look inward. Now, here I am, a forty-nine-year-old man, and I think exactly the same way. I was formed in that excrement pit, although I did not know it right away. You asked me before, "How does one get out of a pit of human excrement? What does one do with oneself?"

In such a moment, one has to like oneself. Otherwise, what do you have? That is the lesson I learned then. So when I came to New York, it was no different for me. I came to another village, a village which was going to try to define me on its terms, and I was not going to let it.

As I mentioned to you before, when I was seventeen, my father felt that I was sufficiently balanced, sufficiently out of my muteness, sufficiently grown-up, sufficiently rebellious, so we began to talk. My father was a very wise scholar, almost a Talmudic man, who translated Abraham Joshua Heschel simply for the joy. The lesson of Heschel was that you have to look within yourself to find that which is good. It is not a condition that you can arrive at through artificial means, said Heschel. You cannot arrive at it by societal dynamics; you do not arrive at it statistically; you do not arrive at it by competing with others. You arrive at it spiritually by rejoicing that you are here because you don't have to be here. So I rejoiced when I came to New York, and I still rejoice. I have the same feeling right now with you because this is my moment, a moment for which I am responsible. I am not going to compare this moment to other moments, because that is artificial. The other moments do not exist to be rated. And I am not going to worry about tomorrow's moment, because tomorrow may not come. So what I have right now is myself and you. This is our moment. This is our life. Driving a truck—great experience. Learning a new language—great experience.

Eventually I became a chauffeur for a black businessman. Well, not quite a businessman. Let's say a businessman from Harlem.

BG: Can I say a black pimp?

JK: No, no, no, he owned some restaurants. Actually, he did not own them, he managed them.

BG: You made it sound as though there was something illicit going on.

JK: There was something. There is always something going on. You know, he was a free spirit, a lovely man. He followed my truck because he liked the way I drove it. He decided I drove with great precision. I probably did; I like driving. He waved me to a stop. I was convinced he was an agent of the

FBI. Who else would drive a green Cadillac? He offered me a job. He said, "Do you want to drive for me? I need somebody who drives like that." And I thought, "Why not?" I think I broke the color barrier: I became one of the very first white chauffeurs in Harlem. I still have photographs of myself in hat and gloves and this beautiful Cadillac surrounded by my black friends. I was called "Mr. Foreigner." They wouldn't bother with Jerzy Kosinski. "Mr. Foreigner" was a much better phrase. I had great fun. During this time, I discovered the American nightclub and music, and an entirely different psyche. Harlem in 1958 was a place of a different type of entertainment. I used some of this experience in *Pinball,* and I used some of it in *Steps.* My employer would use me to break the color barrier in some of the American nightclubs that did not welcome blacks. He would give me money, and I would go as a foreigner from the United Nations. I would reserve three or four tables in some very fancy New York nightclubs. Those clubs did not prevent blacks from entering, but they would say all the tables were reserved, and if a black would actually manage to sit at a table he would not be served. So I would go. I would reserve the tables. And I would ask the captain to open a few bottles of wine, claiming that in my country it was a custom for guests to arrive at the table after the bottles of wine were already open. The real reason was that once the bottles of wine were open, we would have to be served.

BG: Of course.

JK: Then I would tip the captain very generously, and I would wait for my United Nations friends. And indeed they would arrive—all blacks from Harlem, speaking their own brand of English. We would have great fun, to the horror of everyone else in the restaurant. But it was too late. Ten bottles of the most expensive white wine or red wine were already open. Those were very joyous days.

I was also racing for one of my employers. One race that generated a great deal of excitement, a great deal of trouble, and a great deal of money was a very complicated game which used regular cars, on regular city blocks. I described it in one of my novels, *Steps.* But the game was very dangerous and was played late at night.

25

BG: You are not talking about "chicken," are you?

JK: No. I am talking, ironically, of knocking books off of parked cars. Rather thick volumes were attached at random to several cars parked on the side of the street. Then, in the course of a single green light, the driver would drive through two city blocks at great speed and try to knock off as many of these books as possible. But it had to be done almost by instinct. You really could not see much, so you had to drive as closely and tightly as possible to the cars parked on your right side—in other words, on the far side from the driver. Then the books that had been knocked off were counted. If you knocked off twelve books and the guy after you knocked off only eight, you won. People would bet on you. This was the game that I played. So, before I began to write books, I knocked them off. Just as well.

BG: So as a race car driver in Harlem, you were obviously making money.

JK: Oh, yes, a great deal of money, which I would spend just traveling around. I wanted to know as much about New York as possible, and about other places. I would fly to Las Vegas, and to California, and then come back. My employer was good to me. He was actually a very generous man.

BG: When did that period of your life end?

JK: It ended quickly since I tried to start a legitimate career. By then I had learned the language sufficiently well to apply for a Ford Foundation fellowship, and I got it. So I enrolled at Columbia University for my postgraduate studies. From then on, I became a student at Columbia and I normalized my life. That was only six or seven months after I arrived. When I met with the Ford Foundation officials, they probably wondered not only about my Harlem-accented English but also about my dress, my manner, the kind of car I arrived in. It was a marvelous period. Here I was alone in the United States, my new country. I loved it because it left me alone. I could do anything I wanted to do. I wasn't harming anyone. I was not asked to do anything. I found everyone quite generous with their feelings and emotions. No meanness. Here I am speaking twenty-five years later and still feel the same.

BG: What did you think of American girls?

JK: I did not think about them that much. I liked them. I liked the variety of physical types, which, of course, is unparalleled in Europe. But frankly I think what fascinated me about the United States more than anything else was the sheer variety of human experience possible here. You can redefine yourself from moment to moment. You can change professions. You can be as free as you want. Society places no restrictions on you. I was aware of the poverty, but at the same time I saw possibilities for transcending it. Coming from Eastern Europe, I knew what it was like to live in a society that was frozen, that did not allow transcending of the condition, that the condition was defined and frozen by the State. So given the fluidity of the American experience, I saw freedom as a potential here which I found absent in Eastern Europe.

BG: If I had been in your position, I would have felt anger at those who accepted the conditions in this country that were imposed on them and seemed to do nothing about it. Didn't you feel a little anger at those who were poor and remained poor, those who were uneducated and remained uneducated?

JK: No, actually I did not. I felt that maybe there was a reason, maybe a historical reason, maybe some inability to come to terms with their own existence, maybe some fault in the system itself. I did not know the country well enough. Obviously, it isn't a perfect system. The issue for me at the time was how it compared in its potential to the system I left behind, the Communist system. So then I became a student. I started to write, right away at the university. I began my "writing career," quote unquote, with nonfiction, which I wrote under a different name because I did not want to discuss it. I wanted my books to be published and to let them do their own work.

BG: What name were you writing under?

JK: Joseph Novak. As Joseph Novak, I published two books on social science, on collective society, on collective behavior—subjects that I knew

27

quite well and subjects that troubled me. Doubleday published my first book. The *Saturday Evening Post* condensed it and the *Reader's Digest* serialized it. Now, that was not bad for a beginner.

The advantage of writing under a different name is that you can recommend the book to everyone because they do not know that you have written it. So I ran around Columbia University recommending Joseph Novak as the best writer of the century. Too bad so many people disagreed after they read Novak. But at least I had my fun.

Then an important moment occurred in my life. I met my wife [Mary Hayward Weir] who was the widow of a very distinguished American businessman from West Virginia. I met her two years after I arrived in the United States, and I married her in 1962, four years after I arrived. Then my life changed drastically. She represented a long tradition of cumulative wealth, of Protestant outlook, in Pittsburgh and West Virginia. She was a very accomplished woman in her own right. Ironically, like my father, she was interested in classical subjects, particularly in ancient Greece. My life changed very dramatically. Suddenly the Western world became a private enterprise. We could go everywhere. We would travel a great deal and in great luxury. I saw things I couldn't even think about and couldn't imagine. I took upon myself the only expense that I could afford: the tips. And I might add that the tipping ruined me. When Mary died, in 1968, I was absolutely penniless. All the money Novak made—by then I had also published my first novel, *The Painted Bird*—was spent on tips. I was left literally penniless, and once again I had to start to think what to do.

BG: When you say "penniless," what do you mean?

JK: I had no money. When Mary died, I had something like seven hundred dollars left. My wife was enormously wealthy. During the marriage, her estate funds paid for our living expenses. In fact, she was on a trust from her late husband. There was no cash involved, and when she died, whatever she owned reverted to the trust. But during her lifetime, whatever we needed was paid by the trust, except the tips, and I took care of the tips. When she died, therefore, I found myself without tipping money—which, in my case, by then, was my living money.

After *The Painted Bird* was published, it was not well received. Like all of my novels, it got very mixed reviews. I think the violence of the novel—one of the subjects we talked about on this program—is not necessarily pleasant. There is a great deal of violence and sexuality in my books. So *The Painted Bird* was not an encouraging experience. The Joseph Novak nonfiction had been a success. But I did not want to write nonfiction anymore. I wanted to be Jerzy Kosinski. I wanted to write with my own voice, and I wanted to be responsible for what I wrote, to answer for what I wrote, not to hide behind a pseudonym anymore. So then I applied for a Guggenheim fellowship, which the foundation generously gave me, and I wrote my second novel, *Steps*. Again, it was not well received: a few good reviews, too much violence, a certain sexuality that was bothersome to Americans, I think. Nevertheless, it set me on a writing career.

I started to teach English. By then I was connected to the language; by then the English language was part of my life. Keep in mind that when I write I have no foreign accent. There is a redeeming quality to writing in another language. You can express yourself as freely as you want in terms of those for whom you write. You are also part of a long tradition. I somehow incorporated myself into the tradition of the English language, which is a tradition that I inherited very late in life. There was no other tradition I could possibly usurp. So this was my kingdom. I decided therefore to work in my kingdom. Then I started to teach English at Wesleyan in Connecticut, then at Princeton, and then at Yale. So several years passed during which I would, in my foreign-accented English, teach my native American students the principles of composition, of correct usage, and so forth. A very rewarding experience.

BG: How did the students react when they walked in and heard this Polish-Harlem accent?

JK: Obviously, they were not there to learn my accent, though I do not think it would have harmed them. It is better to have an accent than to have none. At least you have something.

BG: You must have been the darling of the campus.

JK: I was not. In fact, I think many of the students found me manipulative, and justly so. I told them from the beginning that we were not there to like each other. We were there to learn from each other.

BG: What do you mean by manipulative?

JK: Manipulative in the sense that I would very often set traps for them. I would, for instance, analyze a text I told them was written by Faulkner in his typical style. I would say, "Let's analyze the syntax and the usage." Everyone in class would strain to analyze the page, only to be told at the end of the class that it had no meaning whatsoever. I bashed the page out before the seminar. Not a single sentence made any sense at all. In other words, I would set them up. That is what learning is for. You have to be on guard. Learning means being able to discriminate.

BG: I don't think that's manipulative at all.

JK: But many of them did think that. I had other tests of this sort. Eventually they came to regard whatever it was I had done with great suspicion, which is precisely what I think education is for.

BG: And they became much, much better in life for it.

JK: Let's hope. I enjoyed it a great deal—except that, after a while, I decided that it was too comfortable an existence for a novelist who, after all, writes from experience. I like experience.

BG: You couldn't stand the check every week?

JK: Too safe, too safe. Yale is a paradise. It's an intellectual clinic. You do not want to leave there. You just want to sit there, breathe, read, go to the beach, ride the horses, and be surrounded by young students who you somehow feel are your children. Hypothetically, they are; they will live longer. They will outlive us. I had no family, and I saw the community, the academic community, as an extension of sorts—and an easy extension, easy family, good relatives. Finally I said to myself, "You have to get out."

So ten years ago I left Yale. I became for a while the president of PEN, an association of writers and editors that does a great deal of things for writers, poets, and playwrights who have no means, who need help. PEN is an international association, but I was the president of its American Center. I served two terms, which was a valuable experience. And in a way it gave me a sense of contributing to the life that was very generous to me. By working with PEN, I tried to help those who were not as privileged and lucky as I was.

BG: This paid you enough to live in the style to which you had become—

JK: No. PEN was not a paying job. In fact, I paid all my own presidential expenses. I was writing novels. I had, by then, four novels: *The Painted Bird*, *Steps*, *Being There*, and *The Devil Tree*.

BG: *Being There*, of course, was the one that broke through financially, no?

JK: No. None of my books actually did. *Being There* I turned into a film, but only three years ago. At the time, my novels . . . Let's set the record straight: I am a very marginal novelist. I don't want our listeners to be misled. Just because I played in *Reds* and just because you are very kind to me and to my fiction, we should not overexaggerate its impact.

BG: You are also a brilliant actor.

JK: Ah, that's something else!

BG: I left that out because I have a feeling that somehow you want to keep that in the wings, that it is just a peripheral part of your activity. But your performance in *Reds* is Academy Award–worthy. Professional actors would be proud of that performance.

JK: I am glad. But at the time I lived off my novels, and I am a very marginal novelist. I am not widely read.

BG: I hate interviewers who interrupt but I must ask. Why do I have the impression that you like to live high on the hog? That is an idiom for living well.

JK: I don't.

BG: Why do I have the impression that yours is a . . .

31

JK: Because I play polo?

BG: . . . an acquired taste of Rolls-Royce, good leather, wine, cigars, good food, et cetera?

JK: I am so pleased I make this impression. Actually, in fact, it's the opposite.

BG: Austere?

JK: Not by design. I like it that way. I live in a two-room apartment. When I was married, we lived in many, many homes at the same time. There were Rolls-Royces, private places. There were hired limousines and chauffeurs. Still, I kept all my personal belongings in my bedroom. It troubled my wife, and it troubled our servants. I wanted to have everything in my bedroom, because I live in one room. I learned how to play polo. I loved playing polo. I play a great deal of polo. Obviously, it is an expensive sport, depending on who you are and how you play. I am an experienced player, and I am in great demand by those who need their horses played. So I play on other people's horses.

BG: As the expression goes, they have to be worked.

JK: That's right. In other words, I pay for it. I play on them and I have to exercise them. I have to clean them. I have to tack them. When I come in to visit, the chief groom goes on vacation. That's how I am able to play polo all over the world.

BG: The last time you were here, you told me that all of your belongings could hang in half a closet.

JK: Not can. They do.

BG: Essentially you said the same thing here again. Why do you believe your needs are so minute, so meager, if you will?

JK: They are not minute spiritually. I think they are enormous spiritually. I am always hungry spiritually. I want to know things. I am curious about people. I am curious about places. Maybe because of this, I am not competitive. Even in polo, I refuse to be rated. I don't like to play for points. I like to ski and play polo for fun.

BG: You've never wanted to own a polo pony?

JK: I don't want to own anything. Ideally I want to use an object that belongs to other people and have fun with it. They like to own it; I gladly rejoice at their owning it. I don't mind renting things.

BG: Your friends are among the most beautiful people in the world. They have a great deal of money. They own everything. What do you think of that?

JK: And I own everything . . .

BG: The power of that ownership . . .

JK: I own my perception, and my memory can retain so much stuff. My perception is the greatest possession that I have. It's no worse or smaller than anything else. I am not saying that I am poorer or that I am richer. I am saying that mine is a different form of wealth. I see myself as a very wealthy human being. I have retained a great number of things, and a great number of people, and a great number of moments in my head. It's the largest bank I know. There is no larger bank than that.

I am not here to please anyone. I am here to coexist—to exist peacefully. This has been my credo, and I think it paid off, to use a financial phrase. I see myself as unique. I am not here to rate myself against others, and therefore I am not here to collect objects. I am not here to project myself onto the outside. In fact, if anything, I have to increase the effort of concretizing the quiet eminence of my being—that is, to look within. My writing fiction is, in a way, one way of doing this. My writing fiction is a very democratic process: you don't impose; you don't say to anyone that it is needed, that it is necessary, that it is science or fact.

BG: You're saying fiction, but I have a feeling that there is a great deal of verity in your fiction.

JK: But I present it as fiction.

BG: It may be presented as fiction, but you are writing about life as seen through the eyes of Jerzy Kosinski. And included, I am sure, are many of the experiences of Jerzy Kosinski. No?

JK: Yes, but again, I don't try to say that it is important to see it as that.

BG: Your work—*Being There,* for example—will probably be looked upon, thirty-five, forty, fifty years hence, as one of the most important books ever done about our political system, which is changing even as we sit here. And *Being There* is part of that change.

JK: That's the advantage of fiction to me, that in a way it offers possibility. It doesn't say that it's statistics. It doesn't say that you have to believe it. It merely says that it is plausible. And usually it is more than plausible; it's probable.

BG: We have seen half a dozen changes in the Kosinski life beginning with the lad of six, through the time at the YMCA, the cafeteria, Harlem, the fellowship, and the novels, et cetera. Where do you see Jerzy Kosinski in 1990?

JK: I want to know where I will see myself tonight. That's all I worry about: about myself right now.

BG: I am not speaking of worry.

JK: I worry about it in the sense that I love life. It would be untrue if I said that I wouldn't want to be around. I do want to be around. But I want to be around tonight—no more than that.

BG: I want to be around tonight, but I would also like to be around for another forty or fifty years. In fact, I'd like to be around forever.

JK: I don't have that same feeling. If I were to depart ultimately tonight, I would depart a very happy man. I would be grateful that it lasted as long as it did, that it took me to so many places, very often against my will. I don't mind the Second World War. If I could relive my life and be asked, "Would you like to omit the Second World War?" I would say leave it exactly as it was, because it made me a wiser man and, I like to think, a better man. And maybe it purified me from some of the longings and some of the notions that I would have had, had I been a plain middle-class Jewish child bent on simple accomplishment and simple accumulations of wealth.

BG: You bring to mind a thought. What did you think of American Jews when you arrived here?

JK: It is only recently that I joined the American Jewish community. For a long time I felt that it would be very difficult for me to confront them. I tried once or twice. It's a different experience; we are indeed an Atlantic apart. I felt somehow that it would be improper for me to expect that they should know what I'm talking about. On the other hand, I wouldn't want not to say what I felt that I ought to say. Only two weeks ago, I spoke to survivors of the Holocaust and was much more outspoken.

BG: What did you say to them?

JK: I said that, for the first time, I was saying exactly what I thought, that our experiences of the Holocaust are different. Even though we try to share the experience, it is actually very difficult to do. The dimensions are so different for an American Jew who lived here during the Second World War, and, let's say, for me. I also said that frankly I am perplexed why I have no family, that here I am, a forty-nine-year-old man without a single relative left in the world, while so many American Jews have all their relatives. So part of this is, possibly, jealousy, and I don't like to be jealous. Part of it is bitterness, and as a Jew I cannot be bitter. Part of this is regret, that all my relatives perished and there are not even graves. Yet every American Jew that I have met has relatives and graves. Again, as a Jew, I don't want the joy of my current life to be spoiled by regret. So for a long time I avoided facing American Jews precisely because I did not want to be anguished or jealous or regretful. Now, perhaps I am wiser, maybe older, and maybe strong enough not to be anguished and not to be regretful and not to be jealous.

35

BG: You told me how the polo started. It started because you were working with and riding horses. Any other loves?

JK: Skiing and polo. Actually both sports are quite remarkable. Let me say that sports for me are reminders of how frail one is, and how temporary one is. When you ski the Alps or the Rockies and you are alone on an enormous slope, you feel so insignificant. That's the moment that I think one should rejoice that one is still around. Horses, it's a different matter. Polo is a sport of enormous energy, energy that is mobilized instantly. You change horses every two to three minutes. They are specially trained. It's a mixture of abandonment and control. You can be true to the sport and safe to yourself only if you are both ultimately abandoned and ultimately in control. That is what downhill skiing is, and that's what polo is. The mixture of abandonment and control to me typifies my whole life. They are, in fact, the predicament of our existence.

BG: What will you do tonight?

JK: I don't know yet. I have to define my mood. I have an invitation to a birthday party for a very close friend of mine. I think I will probably go to it, although I never commit myself definitely. I always say I might come, because I can come only when I really feel like coming. Otherwise, it would be dishonest. I don't want to go to someone's birthday party when I don't feel like going.

BG: You live every day in that same way?

JK: I try to. I really try.

LITERATURE AS IDENTITY

In a radio interview for the British Broadcasting Corporation in December 1985, Kosinski spoke of the effects of his personal trauma and sense of estrangement on his writing, the ways that literature helps to define identity, and the importance of personal and political freedom.

INTERVIEWER: Could you go back and describe your family and the experience of your formative years?

JERZY KOSINSKI: It is rather typical. I was born in Poland in 1933. At the age of six, because of the Second World War, I was separated from my parents, as were hundreds of thousands of other children. My parents were middle-class Jews. I survived the war, was reunited with my parents, and stayed in Poland, where I completed high school and went on to study at the university and later at the Academy of Science. Then, at the age of twenty-four, I left for the United States. That is basically the first half of my spiritual life. And the second half of my spiritual life began when I left for the United States in 1957; the second half still continues, with this interview that we are doing.

INT: What sorts of things happened to you during the war?

JK: Nothing of any importance, really. I do not like to talk about it because I have already written a book about a nameless child in a nameless country.

So I always hesitate when I have to speak about my own past, since in some way this might indicate that the book is autobiographical. But it was written to be a novel, and it was published as a novel, like all my novels. I would be just as reluctant to talk about any other experience of mine if I had portrayed it in one of my novels. There is a very good reason for that: I want the reader to imagine the experience on his or her own.

INT: You are obviously speaking about your first novel, *The Painted Bird*, which is a harrowing and violent account of a young boy wandering through the countryside in Eastern Europe.

JK: In a nameless country.

INT: Presumably, one imagines, Poland.

JK: Well, maybe one imagines another country—depending upon where one imagines it.

INT: The boy is subjected to a series of horrifying, traumatic experiences. You have said that the book uses the stones of your childhood to build a new wall. What did you mean by that?

JK: I mean that, like any other novelist, I picked up the fragmentary impressions and memories which very often are fused with each other to create a universal childhood. A childhood is always traumatic, regardless of whether it takes place in France, Germany, or Austria, or in the United States, or in Latin America. A child grows into a grown-up world. Since *The Painted Bird* was the first of my novels, all of which are about conflict, I properly began my own story of man with the story of ultimate conflict, the story of a child in conflict with the world. The child happened to be Jewish; the world happened to be the world of the Second World War in an unnamed country. War is equally tragic everywhere, and that was the point the novel tries to make. As a story of trauma, it is just as applicable to one country as it might be to another. We are all affected by one wall or another.

INT: This wall that you talk about—is it a wall that separates you from something, or separates you from people?

JK: Not at all. We all exist within the wall. It is a mutual spiritual enclosure in which we find ourselves. We all face that wall. And we all may be imprisoned by it.

INT: And at the same time it encloses us, doesn't it also—for you, at least—shut out what we may see as conformity? Isn't *The Painted Bird*, the title of your book, a metaphor for nonconformity?

JK: Not necessarily. It may be a metaphor for one who is estranged, one who tries to conform but is disliked by others. As I see it, the boy in *The Painted Bird* is as normal as any other bird in the flock, but for some reason he is singled out as being different, even though he is not. He is like any other man.

INT: Do you see yourself as being singled out?

JK: I see myself as being singled out by my individual life, but no differently than any other man is. At the same time, I see myself as being brought together with others because of this condition. It is a condition in which one is unique—no doubt about it, every man and every woman is—but at the same time one discovers oneself in the uniqueness of others. We have a great deal of seemingly unique things in common. We survive wars, we travel from one country to another, we listen to one another, we marry one another. And so I see the world as being oppressive and liberating at the same time, depending upon how one approaches it and how one is approached by it.

INT: You say "oppressive and liberating." Are you talking about any particular part of the world? Are you using these words because you come from a part of the world which is totalitarian?

JK: I do not. I speak because I come from the human condition, which is at once oppressive because it threatens us on many, many levels and in many forms, some of which are political, but which at the same time is profoundly liberating because it renders us spiritually free to define ourselves on our own, preferably in political conditions which allow it. That is why I am in the United States. Which means once again, I like to think, that I speak from a very personal point of view but also from a point of view which really knows no borders, which if anything is bordered by the conditions of life: by disease, by death, by happiness, by an attempt to define one's life as closely to oneself as one can, regardless of which country it takes place in.

INT: Is it necessary for you to define your life through writing?

JK: I think it is, because writing is probably the only thing I can do totally on my own, spiritually on my own, philosophically on my own, physically on my own, and for which, therefore, I am totally responsible. It is something that gives me a sense of identity. It is something that—I do not want to use the word "justifies," because I do not have to justify anything in a spiritually free world—something that gives me a sense of purpose. In other words, I can experience something today, even during this interview, or I can see something today that perhaps I can use spiritually. I repeat: this is a spiritual operation in which the human experience suddenly becomes an individual event that otherwise might be restricting, becomes a universal event open to scrutiny by others and as such liberates me from the notion that it was created only for me.

INT: Was it essential for your survival to leave Poland? In 1957, you had Khrushchev in power in the Soviet Union. You had Gomulka back in power in Poland after a period of exile. And things tightened up again, did they not, after a period of freedom? In that tightening up, of course, it was intellectual freedom that suffered most.

JK: I left Poland because I wanted to get out from the conditions which were mainly defined for me politically. I found those conditions to be unbearable, simply because I was not a political being, because I resented with every fiber of my body the very political system which took over Poland after the war. I found it offensive religiously; I found it indefensible from any moral point of view; I found it based on pure power in the worst sense of the word—not even a national or regional power but a foreign power. And so I felt that if my life were to be defined by forces other than my own, I might as well take it upon chance and try to get out from what for me was, without doubt, a totalitarian state.

INT: Of course, you would not have been able to write.

JK: I would have not been able to live as a human being. Writing, in fact, was not of prime concern for me at the time. I was twenty-four; I was a student at the academy, an assistant professor in sociology. I had no reason to think I would be a novelist. I simply wanted to express myself as a human being, as one human being expressing himself to another. But even such communication was often impossible. The system rendered it punishable by law, depending upon what you were confessing to another human being. So basically, in coming to the United States, I was running away from the most restrictive universe that I could imagine.

INT: How important do you think political freedom is for a writer?

JK: It depends upon how the writer defines his or her life. If he defines it in terms of being published, then achieving political freedom could be very difficult, since his books might not be published. Therefore his definition of himself would suffer greatly, I think. But if he defines himself in terms of expression that is aimed not at others but rather at himself, then it is an entirely different matter. Yet there is no doubt that for most writers the totalitarian system creates a filter of censorship which is impossible to avoid and which operates on many, many levels.

INT: So writing in English was a way for you to take on a new identity?

JK: Since I could not express myself as a writer in Poland, clearly, obviously, I could express myself only in English and only in the United States. Hence the United States became, through language, the country of my expression. Keep in mind that I published two works in Poland in Polish, but they were both on scientific topics. I published them at the age of twenty and twenty-two. They were nineteenth-century monographs. I could not express myself freely on the subjects of the twentieth century, and certainly I could not express myself clearly on the subjects that interest me most: daily life and my communion with other people. Communion, meaning all sorts of relationships, most of which I write about in my novels. This is what interests me; this is what my life is all about.

41

My life centers around my writing. I have no other "me" than that. I have no business to speak of, no family, as you know. Whatever I do leads to writing, and everything stems from it. My whole life is created around my typewriter, and my typewriter goes with me everywhere I go. In fact, my typewriter is in my head. I could not use such a typewriter, such an inner typewriter, in any country of the Eastern Bloc, where it would be owned by the State. Here I can sit in this very room, and I can write anything I want, even about this very interview.

INT: You talk about your life being your writing, and writing being your life. Isn't this a very lonely process?

JK: No, not at all. The very fact that you are here means that obviously there are some who read and whose curiosity is carried on all the way to the BBC. Hence I can safely assume that my physically solitary act, the physical act of sitting behind my desk at my typewriter and scheming stories to tell others, is not a solitary act at all. In fact, it brings me much closer to all kinds of people whom I could not possibly meet without it.

INT: You have written quite a lot of novels.

JK: In under twenty years I wrote eight novels. By comparison, in twenty-five years, Balzac wrote seventy-five.

INT: One of your novels, *Steps*, is made up of tales which, I suppose, could best be described as perverse. You yourself have said—

JK: I do not "suppose" it at all.

INT: So *Steps* is not perverse?

JK: That is the view of one particular reader.

INT: But you yourself have said that it is cruel. What I want to ask you about is how human beings can manipulate each other, and how this manipulation is preconditioned by . . .

JK: By the State, by all the cruel devices of life around them. *Steps* is about the cruelty of the staircase of life. That staircase is very often created for

42

us by others, including the totalitarian state. If indeed *Steps* is cruel, the cruelest part is not the cruelties inflicted on individuals by individuals, but the ones inflicted on them by the State, by nameless bureaucracy. That is where the true cruelty of *Steps* can be found.

INT: Do you think there is as much to criticize here in America as there is in a totalitarian state in Eastern Europe?

JK: I am sure there is as much, but it is an entirely different thing. No society is an ideal society. The American society is hardly ideal: it is riddled by conflict, both potential and actual. In many ways, it is unjust. In many ways, it is a society which I would imagine would need a great deal of insight to become better. Nevertheless, it is a society which is free to improve itself, a society in which I, as one of its citizens, can do my very best to change it, to fight the things which I find intolerable, oppressive, difficult, and so on. This is the very freedom that obviously I would not have in a totalitarian state.

INT: Do you see yourself as a participant in life or as an observer?

JK: I see myself definitely as a participant in life because I love life, and I will be profoundly sorry when it ends. I think life is an extraordinary gift, a gift like no other, and one that should be worshipped moment to moment. Every novel I have written is written in that very manner: incidents, episodes, little steps, one step at a time because unless you take one step at a time you will miss the whole. We know our life only at one particular moment: that is how it comes to us. Which means I see myself not only as a participant; I see myself as an overly eager participant. I see myself trying to squeeze as much life as I can into every unit of time, including this interview, because at this moment, this is the only spiritual reality I have. I must be aware of it, and this awareness should make me a better man.

AUTOBIOGRAPHICAL ASPECTS

OF *THE DEVIL TREE*

Kosinski was keenly aware of the fact that many critics and reviewers tried to find exact parallels between his fiction and his life. Prior to the publication of his fourth novel, *The Devil Tree* (1973), he corresponded with William Jovanovich, of Harcourt Brace Jovanovich (publisher of *Being There* and *The Devil Tree*), about the matter of autobiographical aspects of his fiction, especially in his most recent work.

As you might know, all my novels have been considered more or less autobiographical, and continual critical efforts have been made to find in my fiction a revelation of my own personal life or the lives of individuals close to me. This happens despite my intentions to illustrate events familiar to us all, to illustrate the common denominators of everyday experience. Thus, for instance, at the time of the publication of *Being There*, some attempts were made to parallel the story of the Rands and Chauncey Gardiner to my own life, and even to the family of my late wife, Mary Hayward Weir.

Now, with the imminent publication of *The Devil Tree*, I am certain such extraliterary pursuits will continue, especially since, like *Being There*, *The Devil Tree* is grounded in a specifically American environment. It would be impossible, of course, for any writer's life to have no impact on his fiction.

I assume, however, that certain readers and critics will look for ways to prove my fiction merely an extension of my private history. And the more determined and inventive of them will no doubt insinuate the corollaries they are looking for.

Nevertheless, it is important to remember that the primary concern in writing fiction is imaginative, that the imagination creates molds into which experience can fit. For example, I feel reasonably sure that new attempts will be made at finding counterparts to the Whalens of *The Devil Tree* among my former wife's family. But even the most superficial comparison of the two will reveal that my fictional characters bear an equal resemblance to many Americans of similar social and economic standing. Furthermore, specific details reveal important differences: for instance, unlike Ernest T. Weir, who died of old age, Horace Sumner Whalen drowns while relatively young. Unlike Mrs. Whalen, with her various mansions, her yacht, her famous diamonds, and her "quarter of a billion dollars in municipal bonds alone," Mary Hayward Weir was never "a heavy industry duchess." She was poles apart (indeed, a Pole apart) from Mrs. Whalen. Furthermore, Ernest T. Weir had several children, none of whom, as far as I know, lived in Burma or Africa, only to become, as Whalen's only child Jonathan did, sole heir and majority shareholder.

These are just random examples of significant differences between fact and fiction. *The Devil Tree* magnifies many times these differences and proves how tangentially my imaginative projections are connected to my actual past. This fact was upheld by two lawyers, representing two major law firms, who read the manuscript and the galleys of *The Devil Tree*. Both of them are familiar with the circumstances of my life and with the lives of the remaining members of my former wife's family.

Like *The Painted Bird*, *Steps*, and *Being There*, *The Devil Tree* establishes archetypal characters and situations in an attempt to condense or crystallize situations common to all of us. After reading the galleys of *The Devil Tree*, a friend of mine called it a meditation on contemporary American life, in which every incident is a composite of many everyday circumstances. If *The Devil Tree* is indeed such an open-ended "meditation," it is more concerned than any of the previous novels with the process, rather than the effect, of these circumstances. It is also the most societal, in the degree to which it reflects contemporary events. The media tell the story of Whalen and his generation almost daily; the essence of this story is the inability of many young Americans to fulfill the moral trust imposed upon them by their parents while living off the financial trust their parents established for them.

Thus, as literary characters, Jonathan and Karen are partially inspired by young Americans reflected in the mass media as well as by those I have encountered during the past few years, both here in America and abroad. In the same way, Horace and Katherine Whalen's life story is a distillation of the lives of an entire generation which developed America's industry while building their own personal empires.

The characters' important personal traits—whatever it is, for instance, that makes Jonathan "his own event" or allows him to interact with his girl "while he was the audience, and she was on stage"—are also imaginative expansions. In that sense, the characters of *The Devil Tree* cannot be called collective or synthetic aggregations of facts.

In 1965, in my *Notes of the Author on The Painted Bird*, I wrote my German-language publisher that "the transfer of fragments of objective reality to this new dimension in which the literary work arises has a logic of its own and requires the selection and condensation of a large number of phenomena which the writer believes to best document his imagination, best suit his adopted creative outlook." Only now, with *The Devil Tree* ready to go to press, I realize how much it depends on this "selection and condensation" within an even more complex imaginative framework.

In terms of *The Devil Tree*'s philosophy, I believe that none of the characters' actions or states of mind are extraordinary or improbable. The fact that Jonathan and Karen fail to resolve their problems is not necessarily proof of derangement or emotional impotence: they are the products of a schizoid economic and social reality, and their refusal to accept the usual compromises and false solutions can only be seen as a positive factor in Jonathan's and Karen's personalities. And even if their behavior is considered genuinely aberrant, they still must be seen as the products of many conflicting influences, specifically their unhappy childhoods and their economic and emotional inheritances. In fact, by rebelling against the cushioned existence provided for them at birth, Jonathan and Karen in a curious way fulfill the dream of their fathers: the vision of a pluralistic society in which the individual is free to choose his future and to reject his past.

So much for the reason why I have proposed that the note "This book is wholly fiction" should appear in the front of the novel.

"BEING THERE" IN TORONTO

On May 3, 1987, at the invitation of the *Toronto Star*, Kosinski spoke to a Canadian audience on numerous topics, including his Polish background and the challenges he faced as a writer of popular fiction.

Let me first thank the *Toronto Star* for extending an invitation to a novelist whose next book won't be published until next January, a novelist who has basically been in retreat and not visible at all for several years now. That is indeed an act of mercy, and I am very grateful for that. It is not very often that a novelist who is, from a certain perspective, truly self-employed has a chance to confront a living audience in a city that he happens to like a great deal—and a city, I am absolutely convinced, with the best bookshops. My last trip to Toronto practically ruined me, I bought so many books here.

The title of my remarks is "Being There," a phrase that indicates something about the split that I am feeling this evening. "Being There," however, is about far more than a simple split—it suggests a multilayered soul, divided not only in state of being but also in psyche. The novelist Carson McCullers once asked, "Who is a writer?" I would suggest that a writer is both lonely and amorphous. A writer soon discovers he has no single identity but instead lives the lives of all the people he creates, and his weathers are independent of the actual day around him.

Since "being there" also alludes to an actual work that some of you might know, I would like—in a tribute both to the Canadian spirit and to myself—to read a little fragment from a very beautiful poem written by Canadian poet Irving Layton. In that poem, which touches on some motifs familiar to the book and to the movie *Being There*, Layton writes of a man who, "once headlong out of Eden, yet remembers a nameless garden" with "plants vivid and infused with light." While surrounded by images of death—like that of the "drooping" city tree—"just before he trudges on the water, he will firm up and [be] free." And, in another part of his poem, Layton writes: "he is the dream child and poet whose solipsistic fantasies [create] a small world outside. And yet mark this, he makes himself a garden," even though he knows that nature is "bound to growth and ordered decay." But "loathing death, he will cry when an old man dies and will not stay to see his corpse interred."

What I tried to do in *Being There* is what I would love to do in front of you tonight. That is, to be absolutely and entirely pure. But to be entirely pure, one would have to do without an audience; therefore, all of you would have to be out of the picture. A novelist who speaks in front of an audience is no longer pure. He embraces the public persona, which comes decked out and dusted in all kinds of ingredients. Vanity is one of them; need, an authentic need to be confronted by other beings, is part as well.

Chance, Chauncey Gardiner, the protagonist in *Being There*, had none of that. Thus he would be just as pure here as in any other place. But a character with so buoyant a personality, a character so accepting of the world outside, a character able to dismiss reality without denial or hostile thought—I don't think such a character actually exists outside of certain Buddhist communities in Thailand. Nevertheless, I will try to bring some sense of that character here, to have him face you in front of this microphone, in front of the TV camera.

Creativity, as most of you know, whether it be in life or art or any other form, requires a state of abandonment. Chance is utterly abandoned. Even in deep water, he does not drown. He is so pure that perhaps even gravity does not threaten him. I transferred the notion of his being free and abandoned and buoyant from the novel, where it appears in the beginning—page six,

I think, of the paperback edition—to the very end of the film, where it had to be portrayed visually, as Chance walks across water. His umbrella sinks but he does not.

Speaking of freedom: today—the third of May—is no ordinary day for me. The third of May combines two critical events in my life. One is the thirty-ninth anniversary of the state of Israel, and part of my Jewish soul celebrates solidarity with Israel. The second—1791—is especially significant to me as a Pole. It is the date of the first true constitution created in Europe; worldwide, it was second only to the American constitution. The Polish constitution managed, very briefly, to limit the power of the king and to make him the guardian of rights—indeed, one could say, the guardian of human rights. That responsibility also extended protection to the Jews, who, as you know, had lived in Poland for many, many centuries. All of these things were properly noted in today's Toronto newspapers and will no doubt be mentioned again by Elie Wiesel, a friend and a very distinguished Jewish soul, when he speaks here in two days about learning the way to peace.

When I played the character of Grigory Zinoviev in *Reds*—allow me to plug my twenty-minute-long movie career!—I learned, as I said in the movie, that time means everything. So tonight I brought with me an alarm clock. Don't be alarmed: things will be kept within reason, within time.

"Lone ranger of sex and violence," read one review of my seventh novel, *Pinball*. It was an essentially violent review, with a substantially large headline. The author of the review wrote: "I feel like a voyeur reading a Jerzy Kosinski novel. It always seems to lean too heavily towards sadomasochism and pornography. Always has a hero with intimate knowledge of electronics, or cameras, or motorized equipment, or horses, that enables him to achieve his many conquests." Since I am trying to be pure, I must say that is not quite true. I can operate a horse. I cannot operate a gadget; I am totally nonmechanical. "Always with the image of the solitary warrior hiding his vulnerability behind the armor of technical proficiency. His heroes, however, are not simple mechanical devices; they are obsessed humans bringing ordinary disaster. Only their ability to rigidly control their own environment gives them a sense of space."

An author should not argue with a review. But he can argue with an old review, and this one was from 1982. The fact is that the characters whom the author imagines don't really control their environment. They just try to control themselves. They do that for a very simple reason. Unless they control their lives, they may end up losing them. Life happens to be sacred. It has to be—must be—taken moment by moment. Otherwise, the very nature of life, the essence of life, might in fact be lost. Jewish law has always placed a high price on each person's uniqueness. "Your life," the Talmud says, "is more important than anybody else's."

So where does this business of "lone ranger of sex and violence" come from? In truth, I do like sex, but I hate and abhor violence, even though it is a part of my history. Had I been different, had I come from another background, would I write differently? We will ponder this question, too, not because it is my issue but because, to a degree, it is yours as well. Is one violent because one has to respond to a violent environment? Is one preoccupied with sex because it is a force of life? Without sex, after all, there is no procreation. Without procreation, no creation.

My background is the Second World War. Pretty soon, there won't be any people left who lived through that war. It's just as well: time will take care of us. As for me, I survived the war in Poland entirely with Poles, with Catholic Poles. And I did so, I might add, as a Jew. I would not mind being blond and blue-eyed, yet from my profile, even from my full face, you can see that I do not look like a Viking. The fact that, looking the way that I do, I survived in Poland tells you a great deal about the goodness and kindness of those who managed to let me survive under the most horrific conditions.

Poland was the first country invaded by the Nazis and, in four and a half years, it suffered more losses, comparatively speaking, than any of the other countries affected by the war. Poland had a large Jewish community, which had thrived there for a thousand years. Until 1939, in fact, they lived with freedom and, to a degree, with a spiritual expression that could be matched only by life in ancient Israel. But ninety percent of the Jews in Poland, some three million and two hundred thousand of them, died during the war, along with almost three million non-Jews in Poland. It was a disaster in human history like no other.

We all know about the Jewish Holocaust. One third of all Jews in Europe perished during the war. What is less known are the conditions in which Jews and Poles perished in Poland. We know that Jews were number one on the priority list for extermination, but we know much less and speak much less about what actually happened to the Poles. Heinrich Himmler told the SS generals that Poles would have to be disposed of in delayed genocide. And, in fact, the generals almost did so. The mission of the German people, Himmler said, was to destroy the Polish people, and he predicted the disappearance of Poles from the world. To a significant degree, Himmler's prediction came true. About five million non-Jewish Poles were forced into slave labor by the Nazis; more than two million non-Jewish Poles were systematically burned. In terms of the adult population in Poland, practically one out of every two was either enslaved or killed during the war.

I was a child during the war. In 1946, when I was already in my early teens, a well-known Polish weekly announced a competition for drawings by children who had survived the Occupation. The weekly was interested in how the children would portray themselves and the world around them. What came out was an astonishing variety of cruel and distorted images which reflected the children's view of mankind. I wanted to participate in the drawing competition but could not draw well enough to provide an entry.

Soon afterward, the prominent Polish educator Stefan Shulman conducted his own private opinion poll, so to speak. He asked children questions such as "What do you remember from the time of war?" "What happened to your family and relatives?" Almost half of those who were surveyed recalled murders, executions, often face-to-face executions. Later, Professor Shulman wrote an essay, based on his own study, in which he advocated that people who were not trained as writers should nevertheless write about their experiences. He noted that writers are basically dilettantes. You start as a dilettante—and from personal experience, I know that even at age fifty-three you continue as a dilettante. But I trusted Shulman, who felt that someone could be a writer, even without preparation or special study, as long as he simply sat down and wrote. I consulted my father, who said,

"Well, yes. But remember that you write not with your head but, frankly, with your behind. You have to sit for a long time to write. You can't run around. You can't ride your bicycle. If you want to write, you have to sit." So I learned to sit. By 1957 I had already served as editor of my high school paper and had become a writer. I mention this simply because these are my origins. As a novelist, as a storyteller, I would not be here in front of you without Stefan Shulman.

Ironically, a novelist is not necessarily defined by what he writes but rather by what is written about him. At least that is true in this country, the United States. I am sorry—I mean in North America, since I really feel that the United States and Canada are virtually one country. I think of it as a territory, a spiritual territory, since I don't actually divide the world into countries. A writer sees a country as the place where his books are published, a place where he can speak the language in which he writes. So naturally I mean North America.

Once a novelist is portrayed half naked, as I was, on the cover of a magazine [the *Sunday New York Times Magazine*], his profile clearly changes. Once a novelist steps outside of his novel, he becomes a public figure. And once he becomes a public figure—you know this as well as I do—he is no different than any other public figure. To illustrate the predicament of the novelist: a man came to New Haven to interview me for an American newspaper. After the interview, we went to a nearby restaurant, where it just so happened that a birthday party was taking place at another table. The man who was being celebrated must have been the largest human being I have ever seen. As you can tell, I don't have much flesh to hide the soul, so I was astonished at the sheer mass of that man's flesh. I would love to be his size, since I find it an astonishing accomplishment to love life so much. Fat is life. Fat is flesh. Flesh is something I have always envied. Too bad I can demonstrate it only in my novels and not in person.

In any case, in front of the man were three or four chocolate cakes. Personally, I don't eat chocolate cakes; they don't agree with me. And I probably don't have the space for them, even if they did. But I noticed that even after three cakes, this man could easily have eaten more. So I asked the waiter to send him another cake and to charge it to my MasterCharge card. The waiter sent the cake. The man looked at me with gratitude. He probably thought to himself that I could have stuffed myself to no end, that I could have eaten fifteen such cakes, and the fact that I was sending him a cake was a very honest act of admiration. "Hey, thanks, buddy," he said and ate the cake, indicating to his friends that he was moved that a stranger would send him such a thing.

The reporter turned to me and asked, "Mr. Kosinski, why did you do that?" I said that I sent the chocolate cake because I felt that the man would enjoy it—that he could have his cake and eat it, too, or something like that, I don't know—and besides, in the novel that I was writing at that time [*The Devil Tree*], I was going to have a character do a similar thing, though with an entirely different motive in mind. In Eastern Europe, we don't have chocolate cakes. But in my novel, my character would send a chocolate cake to find out whether the man who received it would be silly enough to eat it, knowing that the cake might actually kill him. My character would say when you are that big and have only one heart, an average American heart, there are only so many cakes you can eat.

Well, what came out in print was that Kosinski was basically a chocolate cake killer, and having survived World War Two there was no telling what else I might do. Since the reporter was a veteran of the Vietnam War, readers assumed that he spoke with a ring of truth. Who knows? Maybe he was right. Perhaps you can kill somebody with chocolate cake.

Later, I made the mistake of going on a television show in Washington, D.C.—I think it was called *Panorama*, with Maury Povich—where I was asked to be a cohost. Telegrams from fat people started pouring in. "Mr. Kosinski, you are a fat hater," they said. "You of all people should be ashamed of yourself. You, as a survivor of the war. Why do you want to kill fat people?"

Then, in *Passion Play*, I depicted a fat girl. She was in her twenties, short and plump with an open face. I actually liked her a lot as a character. Her waist was as wide as her hips. Her breasts were large and shapeless. They seemed too heavy for her torso and shifted with every movement she made, pouring from side to side, slapping against her ribs, sloping when she leaned forward. Actually, I found it very exciting: female breasts are a source of life, and the larger they are, the more life they contain. In the novel, she takes the protagonist, who is drunk, back to her house and lets him rest until he feels well enough to move on. And there is a love scene. But that doesn't matter, at least not to my critics. After *Passion Play* was published, the letters began to arrive—letters reinforced, remember, by my literary history in *The Devil Tree*. This is one of the letters that I received.

Dear Jerzy, I have read just about all your fiction and everything the media has to say about you. And I have come to this conclusion. You've got to be one of the meanest little creeps on earth. My God, with all the suffering that you have said you have been through, you treat people like trash. This is, of course, if the things you write are true. I am reading *Passion Play* now. I think the well has gone dry, my man. OK, but what truly sets me off was how you treat this fat girl on page 158. You practically describe this girl as a no-good sow. You shouldn't have messed with her in the first place if you feel her so repulsive. Have you taken a look at yourself lately, kiddo? You could go sucking up ants with that hooter of yours.

Then, as far as your body goes, there was a picture of you on the cover of a magazine. It looked like you had just had the hair waxed off your chest. Also, let me tell you this. It seems like most of the female characters in your books are body-beautiful, acrobatic, pseudo-intellectual whores. You know, there are some women in this world who are not 5' 7", 110 pounds of boobs and legs, who do not summer on Montego Bay or screw around like cats. There are some average people who are actually more than they seem, but why tell you this? You are so-o-o heartless, you probably don't care what real affection is all about. It seems to me the fat girl was just reaching out to you for affection. I hope that when you are old, man, you will know what misery and loneliness is all about.

P.S. Sorry for my grammar. My God, I don't pretend to be a writer. My friends call me "Fat Pat."

Now, obviously, this hurts. It hurts because it simply is not true. But what can a novelist do? Call the letter writer and enter into a personal dispute with her? The fat girl is a character in a fiction of mine. The character exists independently of me. I have no relationship with her; it is the male protagonist Fabian who has the relationship. So how do I resolve Fat Pat's concern? Were we to meet, she would probably take one look at me and say, "Sure, you hate fat people. Look at you."

When I told Harold Pinter about this, he sent me a piece of correspondence he had exchanged with one of his readers. The exchange, he said, had raised the important question of whether a writer should respond to such a letter—in other words, whether a writer should be in contact with his audience. This is the letter that Pinter received.

Dear Mr. Pinter, I would be obliged if you would kindly explain to me the meaning of your play *The Birthday Party.* These are the points which I do not understand. 1. Who are the two men? 2. Where did Stanley come from? 3. Were they all supposed to be normal? You will appreciate that without the answers to my questions I cannot fully understand your play. Yours faithfully, So and So.

Pinter's answer:

Dear So and So, I would be obliged if you would kindly explain to me the meaning of your letter. These are the points which I do not understand. 1. Who are you? 2. Where do you come from? 3. Are you supposed to be normal? You will appreciate that without the answers to my questions I cannot fully understand your letter. Yours faithfully, Harold Pinter.

In his book *Who Is Man?* my spiritual guru Abraham Joshua Heschel wrote "Every generation has a definition of man it deserves." He observed that in the *Encyclopedia Britannica,* the definition of man is "a seeker after the greatest degree of comfort for the least necessary expenditure of energy." In pre-Nazi Germany, however, man—as Heschel noted—was reduced to his simplest parts. Quoting a familiar statement from that time, Heschel observed that "the human body contains a sufficient amount of fat to make seven cakes of soap, enough iron to make a medium-size pail, a sufficient amount of phosphorus to make two thousand match heads, enough sulfur to rid oneself of one's fleas." Heschel concluded that perhaps there was a connection between this statement and what the Nazis actually did in the extermination camps: made soap of human flesh.

If I were to define an American human being, I would say that an average American—in my case, the average American novelist—is an anxious being. Reinhold Niebuhr called anxiety "the inevitable concomitant of the paradox of freedom and finiteness in which man is involved." Rollo May called it "the apprehension cued off by a threat to some value which the individual holds essential to his existence as a self." For me, anxiety manifests itself not only philosophically but also physically. In this age of anxiety, half of all hospital beds in the United States are devoted to psychiatric patients. In five years, one out of ten people in the United States will develop psychiatric complaints serious enough to warrant hospitalization. Magazines portray images of perfectly normal-looking people who reportedly find it difficult to wake early or to start work each morning, or who complain of a "nervous" stomach—and then recommend drugs to reduce their anxiety or to render them passive. That is what made Chauncey Gardiner such an interesting character. He felt no such anxiety. Nor did Peter Sellers when he portrayed him. Sellers, by the way, was part of an outstanding cast of actors that included Shirley MacLaine, Melvyn Douglas, and Jack Warden.

As a writer, I also have a cast. In my case, however, it is a cast of ghostwriters. In fact, I use as many as six hundred ghostwriters—writers like Balzac, Stendhal, and Voltaire, whose body of language, knowledge, and plots influences my own writing. But I retain the ownership of my text. As a writer, I use my voice, which you, as the reader, hear. Do you honestly believe that I would readily surrender my voice? It is the only thing I've got. Do you honestly think that the most powerful editor, even one who might be willing to exchange bodily fluids with me, could possibly sway my mind? No way. An editor inserts a question mark if it is necessary. But an idiosyncratic writer keeps his text the way he or she wants it. Yet, I repeat, no text is ever completely original, because it is shaped by the ghostwriters who came before.

I like to think that my latest book, *The Hermit of 69th Street*, makes a good point. What I do in that novel is what I have done for you here at the microphone: put a footnote at the end of my thought. And in the end I stand more comfortably because I can back up what I say with a footnote, which, in this case, happens to be literary tradition. But even within the literary tradition a writer must be independent and find his own voice. And that is why I stand before you tonight alone, speaking in my own voice.

SYNTHESIZING HISTORY

The Hermit of 69th Street, Kosinski told an interviewer on Lifetime television in 1989, not only reflected his personal history; it also "synthesized" it.

INTERVIEWER: Is it less of an emotional experience to write in English as opposed to conversing in Polish or English?

JERZY KOSINSKI: Less emotional. No doubt about it. Therefore it is more literary, since from the outset I am already detached from the very medium through which I want to express myself.

INT: The Irish writer Samuel Beckett once said that he chose to write in French because it was easier to write without style. Is that true?

JK: Very true. You adopt your own. You create it literally as you go along. And, since you invent it, you don't imitate anyone.

INT: Your life is so fascinating that it does not need the embroidery of an elaborate style. When I say that you wandered as a child it sounds trivial. But it is true, isn't it?

JK: It is true, but it was true of hundreds of thousands of other people. I hesitate when I hear things like this, because it is comparable to praising someone from New York for riding the subway. It was a fact of life.

INT: It was. I read, for example, your friend Roman Polanski's autobiography . . .

JK: Again, not unlike the life of a whole generation.

INT: The children of Jewish parents were often taken into the countryside and looked after by people who did not take great care of them . . .

JK: Now, be careful here. The penalty for harboring a Jew was death. The penalty for not denouncing someone who harbored a Jew was the concentration camp. These are historical dimensions unlike any other.

INT: Indeed, and they are historical facts, and they are abhorrent to us.

JK: This last novel of mine [*The Hermit of 69th Street*] reflects some of this history. Basically, what I tried to do was to confront myself as a historical figure—but for once not as an individual historical figure but as a collectively historical one. I wanted to examine what my head—this head right here—represents. What is inside it? What is the fusion between the American aspects of it and the Eastern European aspects?

INT: In other words, the parts that never leave you. So here you are, a man writing under a dim bulb in a two-room flat . . .

JK: That's me! I spent six years writing *The Hermit*—two years in Switzerland, under Swiss circumstances, but that didn't work. Then I came back to New York and spent four years nonstop behind my desk in a two-room apartment. All right, it wasn't Sixty-ninth Street. It was a different number. But it was close.

INT: You don't deny that it's autobiographical.

JK: No. A great deal of the novel is actually nonfiction. I think it's time to start writing novels that reflect us, novels that are intimate enough to allow us to be free to say whatever we want to say. Why should I pretend that I am not a public figure? Am I supposed to write novels today that are no different from the novels that were being written in the year I was born? Novels like *God's Little Acre*?

INT: Of course, you have the freedom to choose what you write. But you don't have the freedom to choose where you come from or the part of memory that will always be with you.

JK: That's true of every writer. Depending on how you look at it, I think every writer's life is both dramatic and comic, no matter where you live it.

INT: This mélange of past and present, Polish and American—is it continually erupting from your memory and imagination?

JK: I like to see myself as a synthesizer. In fact, the book *The Hermit of 69th Street* is written in that fashion. Depending on which button you push, you get a different melody.

INT: This is a very challenging book.

JK: Actually, I think that it is great, great fun to read, providing that you make an effort—an effort not unlike the effort you have to make to move from black-and-white photographs to video. Is it easier to look at photographs? The black and white is right there. Black and white. Simple. Right? Video means that you have to pay attention. It is a lateral medium. But is it easier to listen to a stupid tune than to complex synthesizer-created music? No.

INT: Obviously not. Yet you are also on record as saying that "Television is my great enemy, and it is pushing the reading public over to the margin."

JK: I think that by now television is my friend. This is the time to say it! And I am saying it because I feel that anyone who has watched as much television as we do is absolutely ready to start watching the pages of *The Hermit*.

INT: Do you think our expectations, our imaginations, have changed because of television, because of video, because of films?

JK: Surrounded by television and other media, the contemporary reader is no longer the reader who used to read Balzac or Dickens or even Caldwell. In *The Hermit*, I am trying to show that it is possible to create adventure through reading, to create escape—and escape, especially from routine, is difficult. Escape means that you find in the text things which other writers have already said, and sometimes better. So why not use their words, the way that clips are used in a documentary?

INT: Are you less free, more inhibited, as an artist because of your celebrity? Over the years, you have been built up; you have been torn down; you have costarred in the movies; your screenplay of *Being There* has been praised. Because of all these things, are you carrying baggage that you don't want to carry?

JK: No. I love it.

INT: You love being . . .

JK: Being there! Without being on television, I would never have written *Being There*. Without acting in *Reds*, I would never have written *Pinball*.

INT: Compared to *The Hermit*, *Being There* is a slim volume with a gentle premise.

JK: Still, it took three years to write. And I was accused of using ghostwriters. If I truly employed ghostwriters, I would have twenty-five books to my credit by now.

INT: Contrast the current novel. It seems so complex and busy, by comparison.

JK: Two different pysches are at stake. Norbert Kosky, the protagonist of *The Hermit*, is Kosinski—without the "sin"! I also imagine Kosky as Chauncey Gardiner endowed with the wisdom stemming from experience. Chauncey Gardiner is absolutely pure. He is open to the world.

INT: You have a fascinating physical life. You sleep four hours, rise, sleep another four hours, drink, eat raw onions. How do you maintain such physical fitness?

JK: It is no longer a conscious attempt. But I do breathe quite differently now. I make an effort to bring more oxygen to the body.

INT: This is an outcome of yoga?

JK: Yes. It becomes a natural process and no longer an exercise. You bring in more oxygen, therefore you burn more calories. You can eat a huge meal and burn it off simply by sitting differently. The ultimate test comes in water—if you can float without movement, if you can get into a swimming pool with no salt added and remain as buoyant as a lotus. If you have enough oxygen in your body and in your brain, where it really counts, you can keep your head above water.

INT: And the result is serenity and increased power and ability to do things that ordinary men cannot.

JK: No, the result is vanity. The result is that I used to hate swimming pools and now I cannot wait to show off. I can even sleep on the water, remain there as long as I want. It is very peaceful and pleasant and euphoric.

INT: You are among the most quotable writers currently writing. Is vanity a big part of your mentality?

JK: Frankly, I think it is a big part of any creative person. Starve vanity and terrible things happen. What else do we have? After spending four years behind a desk, I need the encouragement, the kind things you say here about me. A businessman, a politician, almost anyone else goes out into the world and establishes a bridge between himself and his society. A writer does not have that. As a writer, you have to believe that what you do makes sense. People have told me that *The Hermit* does not make sense. I know they are wrong, but I cannot tell them that.

INT: So you have to go out as the modern world's salesman.

JK: Yes, I have to seek out situations.

INT: If you had stayed in Poland, would your art have developed totally differently?

JK: I would have been a photographer, perhaps, as I used to be. I would have remained a social scientist, but I would not have been free to write the kinds of books I like to write, to be a storyteller, to be self-employed, to remain true to myself, to be without anxiety or fear—just to be buoyant, with or without oxygen or water.

INT: Would you ever return to Poland?

JK: I recently did. It is by far the most buoyant country on earth. Poor economically, but spiritually—I dare to say—one of the richest countries in the world.

INT: It has been a rare treat to have you on this program today. Readers who pick up *The Hermit of 69th Street* will know immediately if they are up to the challenge.

JK: And they will enjoy the book enormously.

On Writing

Writing is the essence of my life—whatever else I do revolves around a constant thought: could I—can I—would I—should I—use it in my next novel? . . . My books are my only spiritual accomplishment, my life's most private frame of reference, and I would gladly pay all I earn to make it my best.

What I need more than anything else when I write is the conviction that others could have written the same thing, because they see the world in fundamentally the same way as I do. And, conversely, that I could change places with them. When I go back to my apartment to write my next novel, I see myself as representing a condition larger than my own.

When you create a fictional character, he becomes a bridge between your experience—extremely idiosyncratic—and that collective experience which you feel you have reached [with readers].

CONVERSATION

WITH GEOFFREY MOVIUS

In his 1975 conversation with Geoffrey Movius, Kosinski analyzed his picaresque protagonists, described the difficulties of writing in a totalitarian system, and expounded on the role of the writer as artist.

GEOFFREY MOVIUS: What subjects or books do you wish more Americans read?

JERZY KOSINSKI: I would like to see all of us more involved—for our own sakes—with imaginative fiction that can bring us closer to our daily existence, with works that would do for us today what the works of Melville, Upton Sinclair, Sinclair Lewis, Dos Passos, Stephen Crane, Flannery O'Connor, Steinbeck, and Fitzgerald have done. I feel that literature is a necessity because it dramatizes the very conditions of life—what Henry James called a "tangle," a predicament, internal as well as external—which the contemporary man or woman experiences as oppressive rather than dramatic. Most of the Americans I know are at the mercy of an underlying personal, economic, or political reality, which they either pay only fractional attention or dismiss as routine with a "what else is there?" attitude. When these realities break through, they have shattering effects.

GM: Can you give some examples?

JK: Watergate, for instance. The FBI, CIA, inflation, fuel crisis, et cetera. We should not expect things at the top to be ideal. Yet the amount of corruption and illegality that has come to light is surprising. Think about the garage mechanic. You assume he'll change the engine oil when you leave your car with him. Why do you expect that? Why should the mechanic be more trustworthy than the American president?

Behind this reluctance to examine what goes on lies the fear of confronting one's role in life and one's immediate reality—a fear of where such confrontations might lead. Judging from the fiction at the beginning of this century, Americans of that period perceived themselves as protagonists in a *drama of life*. They were not yet frozen into a specific social milieu or a single social role. They were on the move, aware of the main chance, and emotionally prepared to face any change. Today, this is not true anymore. Today, even the so-called blue collar worker has become frozen into middle-class values.

Let me give you another example. We are in a recession which may last for years, yet most people refuse to confront this situation at the level of family life. They cling to their houses, to their cars, and to their established way of life rather than start "reducing" and, if necessary, selling some of their "status," even if it is at a loss. They cling to the belief that the future will be better, while in fact it may be very considerably worse. On the immediate personal level, few people show any desire to "concentrate" themselves by reduction, to find out exactly what it is that they want from life, and to build their lives around that very basic need. Instead, almost everybody indulges in a pervasive procrastination, desperately evading the need to focus—either on their cars, on their daily environment, or, for that matter, on the very essence of their existence.

GM: Is that procrastination a function of the pace and pressure under which people live in this country?

JK: Possibly. After all, American popular culture does not encourage concentration on any single aspect of life. Like TV, it promotes a short attention span coupled with channel switching—by remote control, if convenient.

GM: Is it not a self-willed failure of will?

JK: That is a very good question. The failure occurs precisely in that imaginative moment in which we might be able to separate the basic external pressures from our inner concerns and our essential life force and focus. This is what we must recognize. We must develop the life force needed to block external pressures that dilute this personal core.

GM: It was once held that art should aim to instruct by pleasing. Is it still the writer's task to offer the reader a moral model or design?

JK: Well, the "task" of my novels is to give the reader a jolt which could lead to a recognition, to a judgment, a new attitude. Hence I try to make my prose as unobtrusive as possible, the language direct and easy, to facilitate the reader's entry into the arena where the shock is to take place—to move the reader from the waiting room into the examination room, so to speak. Once you are there, a shock: you are mortal, you're vulnerable, you're not protected. Yet you survive. It should be a joyful feeling, the awareness of being alive. At least you now have the knowledge, which is better than the assumption of strength, and the peace and promise of the "happy ending"— all, quite likely, not true.

GM: But doesn't this recognition substitute one type of anxiety for another?

JK: It substitutes "real" for "unreal." But at least the substitute generates new awareness: life may run out. I suppose that is pleasing only if the reader is emotionally and philosophically—or religiously—geared to such a recognition. If he is not, the task, as I have said, is to jolt the reader, to make his familiar and therefore unexamined reality suddenly unfamiliar and demanding explanation. Our lives are often "unseen"; habit dulls them, and the imagination doesn't perceive them as unusual, as dramatic, or as modifiable. Instead, it perceives them merely as "being there." I see the purpose of any imaginative enterprise, from poetry to photography, from fiction to drama and film, to hint at the various possibilities of change: emotional, physical, political, spiritual, any—

GM: A change of will?

JK: An awareness of the power of the individual, personal will to change one's life. And I think the instructive power of the destructive protagonist in fiction might be greater than that of a romantic "Fiddler on the Roof" type of character. Let me explain. Even a destructive character shows us one optimistic aspect of nature: the power of the individual. In a curious way, Iago is a more powerful character than Othello. Iago demonstrates that there is a great deal of energy and an enormous potential—even if wrongly used—for change in each one of us. I am astonished that so few of those who have written about *Cockpit*, my latest novel, realized that Tarden, its main character, might generate a feeling of optimism, a sudden inner statement in a reader. Look how much Tarden does with his life. Yet how many of us are equipped to make a topography of our life and determine what we want?

GM: Let me go back to *Being There*. When discussing your character Chauncey Gardiner, you once referred to Hitler, Mussolini, and Stalin as the "nobodies of the twentieth century" who became powerful because they realized how to use their external characteristics to become charismatic.

JK: I think they were the early apostles of the twentieth century. Admittedly, the historians seldom noticed that they were ordinary men who rose to power solely through the media. I think that reflects upon the historians.

GM: That's a peculiar Horatio Alger angle, and an odd subject for a didactic fiction.

JK: Not so odd upon examination. It's shortsighted to portray these men as Iago-like monsters blessed with special inner powers. Rather, it should be emphasized how ordinary they were. Stalin and Hitler and Mao were not outstanding to their young contemporaries. But they harnessed the political process and its propaganda apparatus with superb skill. Our historiography has failed to analyze this. And our art has failed to present the other end of the spectrum. I have been waiting for years for a novel, or a play, or a film based on the life of Ralph Nader. A truly heroic man, the best example of that enormous positive dynamic energy and power still so common in this country. There's drama there; corporations have plotted against him, tried to neutralize him. And there are dramatic moments—congressional hearings, corporate backdowns.

GM: But there's also Richard Nixon, a pretty ordinary third-string end on his college football team. Then an undistinguished junior congressman. Not to mention the men around him at the fall—all of them very ordinary, limited men.

JK: True. And yet there is already a tendency to look for hidden signs and childhood events that would predict unusual or criminal lives. We won't find significant clues; from the beginning, these were unexceptional men. Don't forget that Himmler, the Gestapo chief, had been a chicken farmer. Events shaped him; he merely carried out assigned tasks.

GM: There must be something in the environment, in the development around such men, that affects them and causes them to seek power. You mentioned Iago. Why, we want to know, did he behave as he did? What made Richard III act as he acted? He was a hunchback. Maybe he was angry at the world because of his deformity. Is there any point in pursuing that sort of search for motivation?

JK: Awareness of the self must eventually lead to an awareness of one's deformities—physical and psychological. Each of us is deformed; nobody is "perfectly average." Sickness deforms us, age deforms us. Social conditions, employment, accidents—all work specific distortions.

GM: William Sloane Coffin said in a television interview that true intellectuals are those whose lives are changed by the ideas they encounter. He also quoted Nietzsche, "I like my truths bloody." What you are saying in some respects sounds very similar.

JK: I mistrust the notion of "ideas" proposed by the twentieth century. For me, a true intellectual defines and redefines himself in very private moments, not at party meetings, not during group therapy. Collective gatherings often provide a forum for an avoidance of self-confrontation.

71

GM: Do you think of yourself as a political writer?

JK: Not directly. I don't propose any political solutions. Indirectly, I think my fiction views social environment in terms of its impact on the psyche, in terms of its drama, its role in one man's life. The fascist, the authoritarian communist, and the capitalist are equally important to me. My attitude toward, let's say, the so-called free-market society is based on its dramatic opportunities: the potential for self-deception, the potential for greed, passion, disguise, escape.

GM: What does Tarden in *Cockpit*, or the spectacle of the America he inhabits, say to the rest of the world?

JK: There is a special quality in Tarden, and I think we all should cultivate special qualities in ourselves. However Tarden uses that quality is his business—and the reader's. William Blake warned us that we must all create our own systems or risk living at the mercy of those of other men. Tarden tries to do this. Perhaps he is an "optimistic" figure because he attempts something which for the rest of us is so difficult to do. In countries with totalitarian regimes, it is impossible. For the readers in these countries, Tarden is a character from a faraway galaxy.

GM: Or the villain hero?

JK: A picaro above all. And here by picaro I mean the type or the character who is constantly in a stage of becoming. Picaros dot—rather highlight—literary history. Odysseus, Don Quixote, Tom Jones, Gil Blas, Moll Flanders, Felix Krull—the freelancers, the freebooters who played out their whims and caprices and lived their lives rather than considering their conditions. Now, there are no picaros in totalitarian countries. In totalitarian regimes, you can't even change your address. How can anyone be a picaro if he can't leave home?

GM: The protagonists in all your novels, from *The Painted Bird* on, are picaros.

JK: The picaro is the last champion of selfhood. And the notion of selfhood is on the way out. On a recent visit to West Germany, I was discussing various aspects of American life and letters with German writers. One German novelist described my fiction as dealing with "the imperialist idea of the self." In his view, each of us should be defined entirely in terms of the community. I assured him that his wish had already been fulfilled for a large part of mankind—led by the Soviet Union and People's China. But, frankly, I have little doubt that I am a marginal writer writing about marginal figures. In a current best-selling country-and-western song, the cowboy hero sings, "There's a lot of compromising on the road to my horizon." Good-bye, *High Noon*; good-bye, *Shane*. The whole genre has died.

GM: Writing as Joseph Novak in *The Future Is Ours, Comrade,* your 1960 nonfictional study of collective behavior, you stated, "There are some who will say that in an era of mass conflict endangering the existence of the whole of mankind, a small man with his individual experiences and his one-sided appraisal of them ceases to count. My answer is that these great mass conflicts count only so far as they affect the life, the thoughts, and the fate of the small man, the hero of grey everydayness." And writing under the same pen name in *No Third Path,* your second nonfiction book, published in 1962, you close by observing that "at such a time there comes a moment of reflection when, as Camus says, it is possible to have the courage to lose one's only life when so needed. But to look on while the meaning of that life evaporates, while our *raison d'être* disappears, that is unbearable." Do these two passages still reflect your opposition to what socialism has brought about in the Soviet Union and Eastern Europe?

JK: I left the Soviet orbit eighteen years ago. Those statements were written sixteen and thirteen years ago, respectively. Perhaps because of my exposure as president of PEN [1973–75] to the plight of writers in the socialist bloc, I find those beliefs even more true for me today. But even here, in the States, the mass culture dismisses the small man. It has taught him to turn away from himself, to believe that his fate is sealed. The small man who "made it" assumed that, because he had made it, life would take care of itself while he watched it the way he watches *All in the Family*. He lost the ability to redefine himself. He lost the ability to say no to the consumer society, to realize that he shouldn't have bought the house or the big car or the boat

73

that holds him in debt. In relying on MasterCharge, he proved himself to be neither master of nor in charge of his own existence.

GM: This defeat of the small man came about in Europe earlier than it did here. But it was already happening, I suppose, at the time that this country was born, was growing and expanding.

JK: With a difference. The European social disasters, the revolutions, the upheavals, the fascist and communist parties, the possibility of military invasion, the American military presence, et cetera, have been constant reminders that things are not perfect. In America, the middle class has experienced the benefits of being continually uprooted. In Europe, it was simply the threat of being uprooted.

GM: In the United States, the Civil War posed that threat.

JK: Yes, and then the Depression of 1929. Since then the Middle Class Intermission has happily reigned. But no longer. A great many people will be destroyed.

GM: Do you think that people writing now under conditions of extreme repression, in the police states—artists who really have to cope with that— have a better chance of developing perceptions about the necessity of defining and strengthening the self than writers practicing in the West?

JK: A writer is most useful and yields the most valuable truths when he writes what he has thought and felt and suffered. His social function is that of a detonator. He makes known what he thinks is critical and provoking, and acts under the assumption that because it is provoking to him—and he is *every man's Everyman*—it will also be provoking to others. He is driven to bring an awareness of that perplexity to the world at large. He feels the need to arm and rearm them, against apathy and self-defeat. If he cannot write what he thinks or feels, he fails. He doesn't exist as an artist. A writer who edits even one iota of his vision for the sake of being published—or for any other "practical" purpose—has already corrupted his calling.

GM: Do you ever change what you write?

JK: I edit it. I alter. I prune. I de-escalate. I make changes in almost all my galleys—to the despair of my publishers. But I do all this to ensure that the content reflects what I feel. You see, I am also everyman . . . that's why I write.

GM: As an agent?

JK: An agent in the service of counteracting the emotional suppression. But publishing a novel is the opposite of being a secret agent. One's work is open to everyone's scrutiny. My task as a writer is to turn a commonplace of daily routine into a dramatic arena, to transform mere experience into adventure. If I succeed, my novel will detonate a fragment of reality which had lost for us its detonating power. The explosive force is still there. A reader can see himself as a protagonist of his own story, a hero in charge of his life and his soul.

On the other hand, the servile writer who, for example, writes under the sponsorship of the writer's union in Czechoslovakia doesn't write at all. He doesn't aim at detonating; he merely aims at denying the presence of explosives. He is a *politruk*, a party hack. The Czechoslovak writers who now refuse to write, or who write knowing that they must guard against confiscation of their manuscripts, have experienced the essence of being a writer.

GM: Many have criticized writers who leave hostile environments, who defect or emigrate. It's easy to charge them with opportunism. If conditions are oppressive in their homelands, should they not stay and fight for change? How do you respond to this viewpoint?

JK: I think that this is utter nonsense. Take Solzhenitsyn—and some have accused him of cooperating in his expulsion—when Solzhenitsyn speaks to me or to you, he doesn't speak about the Soviet Union. He speaks about people like you and me who live in the Soviet Union. People are not divided by countries; they're divided by predicaments. The idea that he should have remained where he couldn't speak up is simply an idiocy.

GM: But he was having an impact in both the Soviet Union and the West by circulating his writings in the underground samizdat.

JK: An extremely limited one—and largely limited to people penalized for having read those samizdat sheets. Now he can reach millions in the Soviet Union through Russian-language radio broadcasts beamed in from the West. This is communication on a much wider scale, and there is little chance of the cautious listeners being discovered and penalized.

I saw Solzhenitsyn in the ballroom of the New York Hilton, addressing a gathering sponsored by the AFL-CIO. He delivered a very dramatic speech. Yet most of the audience saw him as a man from another planet, a total stranger announcing the arrival of destructive forces from outer space. Possibly that's how he sees himself. He does not address Americans as a commentator on an oppressive Cold War past that still grips the Soviet Union. He speaks to Americans about an American future which he believes they lack the courage or will to confront.

GM: You have something in common in that regard.

JK: All writers have this in common. Solzhenitsyn assumes that the American audience in the ballroom understood the notion of national selfhood. I assume that some of them, though not many, can still retrieve the notion of a private one.

GM: What will the world look like in the year 2000?

JK: A marching column. The State as in fortress—home.

GM: Nobody out of step?

JK: Who would dare? Those out of step would face various "treatments," and, in time, be brought back into the ranks. Possibly from an economic point of view, this situation is a necessity. Eventually, the industrial states will be run that way because they have failed to make provisions for an alternative future for themselves and for the starving nations. This militaristic, disciplined approach will be seen as the only way to ensure orderly distribution of limited supplies of food, fuel, medicines, accommodations, et cetera.

GM: The boy in *The Painted Bird*, pondering the Nazis' drive to power, wondered "whether such a destitute cruel world was indeed worth ruling."

Is that a question you ever ask yourself as a writer: whether such a world is even worth communicating with?

JK: I repeat: I am a marginal writer who attempts to communicate with a marginal group of readers. Imaginative fiction addresses a margin which is getting narrower. In time, the marginal novelist will disappear, since he himself is part of the margin. That is what happened in Czechoslovakia. The presence of such a margin is denied. It has been denied in the Soviet Union for many decades.

GM: Yet it exists. It may be officially denied, but it exists.

JK: For a while.

PARLIAMENT OF SOULS

In 1969, Kosinski won the National Book Award, the highest literary prize awarded in the United States, for his second novel, *Steps* (1968). For an event celebrating the National Book Awards in 1973, he prepared these remarks on the role of the writer and his commitment to his craft.

Having lived in two political systems which so differently approach the role of the writer, I am particularly aware of the value of the existence of the National Book Awards committee. I speak here for myself as a novelist, but I believe my comments may be extended to include all writers, who are by the nature of their work involved in a dual commitment, to their craft and to their readers. By commitment, I mean something more than a vigorous support of certain ideas or programs; it is not so much a stance or an attitude as it is a process, a reciprocal arrangement in which the writer is conditioned by his society and simultaneously influences it. Given the purpose of imaginative literature—the arousal and sustainment of the reader's self-awareness—I believe that a writer must continually be conscious of his potential impact. Through a response to poetry or prose, the reader may gain a sense of the dimensions of his own existence, and may perceive himself as a social animal as well as an independent being.

In this sense, a novelist's commitment transcends any historical or cultural definition. It is the organizing principle for the great social novelists of the nineteenth century as well as for the existentialists of the twentieth. Their work contradicts the notion that an artist creates for himself, that his art exists exclusively for art's sake. Only the diarist or the novelist who keeps his manuscripts in a drawer can be said to write for himself. But as soon as a novel, for instance, is available to the public, its author is connected to that public. For me, then, the writer's commitment depends not on detachment but on a primary attachment to his public, as he imagines it.

Yet while the writer's primary commitment does not seem to have changed, his audience's receptivity has diminished. The majority of contemporary society, trained by the mass media to expect the simplest situations and emotions, can no longer digest the novel, whose intent is the expansion of individual consciousness. The "normal" readership is continually bombarded by visual images and has been trained by television to observe without becoming engaged, to experience "art" as passive reception. Ironically, the only truly unaffected audience now is the blind, whose access to literature is wholly through the imagination. Thus, at a time when so much of the mass media—both visual and verbal—tends to retard individual and social awareness, the writer's ability to counteract fragmentation and isolation is particularly valuable. In the absence of any religious sustenance, the creation of an internal imaginative world is the only remaining means to emotional integration.

There can be no better proof that commitment to one's readership is extremely influential than in a police state. If a writer refuses to let the State define his commitment, he is denied the freedom to give shape to his vision. He is silenced or imprisoned. It is precisely this ability to address the unknown individual, to stir his imagination, that is feared by the agencies which seek to determine the individual's fate. From a nameless, faceless mass, the novelist or poet summons a parliament of souls, each man capable of self-affirmation, of resisting a meaningless fate in a bureaucratic vacuum.

Given the nature of the writer's commitment, any organization which seeks to single out, for award, particular works or categories of works could easily alter the writer's relationship to his craft or his public. But the National Book Awards committee has never taken advantage of this power, avoiding the inherent danger of manipulating the writer by having a broad-based selective process, whose judges reflect extremely differentiated literary opinions. Perhaps many of us in America take this for granted, but in any totalitarian state the first thing to be imposed upon is the writer's voice: it is directed away from the conditions of life which connect us all, and toward an official dogma which connects only those who are concerned with power. But by awarding its prizes according to a varied criteria of excellence, the National Book Awards committee reinforces the writer's instinct to find his individual voice.

Furthermore, precisely because of its enormous base and its non-partisan nature, the National Book Awards committee cannot help but influence publishers and booksellers by encouraging the distribution of a continually expanding range of imaginative work. Not only does this provide a wide selection of literature—alerting the public annually to the best new offerings in poetry, fiction, translation, biography, the sciences, history, philosophy, and religion—it also suggests that alternatives to a commercially predictable market may exist. The writer is freed from the notion that he must produce an economically viable property and may approach his work as a developing craft, extending beyond temporal and cultural limitations.

ON FICTION

In a lecture he titled "On Fiction" (1973), Kosinski examined the way that American writers approach the writing of fiction and demonstrated how their approach differs from that of Europeans, especially Eastern Europeans.

It occurred to me that because of my background, which is split between the so-called socialist countries and the United States—I grew up in Poland and studied in the Soviet Union—it would be unfair for me to talk about being a novelist or about the writing of fiction only from an American point of view. After all, the American way of life and of writing fiction is not the only one. There is another one, the one I left behind.

When I left Poland in 1957, I did not plan to write. Indeed, it would never have occurred to me to choose writing as a profession. Modern fiction writing was quite simply a very different process behind the iron and bamboo curtains. As you probably know, in the Soviet Union and throughout Eastern Europe, the process was much more structured than it is here in the United States. The prospective writer applied for a scholarship to the Writers Union and passed through a screening process. His work was very carefully analyzed by established critics and by senior writers in the Writers Union. Once admitted, the young writer was institutionalized, very much the way the Writers Union itself was. He was, to a large degree, an employee. His work was regularly discussed at meetings, and his scholarship was renewed every two or three months.

There was one additional difference. Just as the applicant's outlook was examined—can he become a writer? does he deserve to become a writer?—the notion of his destiny was clear. As a writer in the Soviet Union, you know very well what that destiny is: you are going to write novels, or poetry, or plays, or screenplays within a certain basic historical pattern. You must accept this pattern as the only valid and true one. You must accept the notion that the Communist Party knows the path of mankind; therefore, as a conscious artist, you must reflect only this path. Any attempt to do otherwise would mean that somehow you felt that history was not to be regarded as an intimate frame of reference, that you were ahistorical and, conversely, antisocietal. All of this was taken for granted. No one in his right mind questioned this notion of destiny but instead accepted it as such.

During the Stalinist period when I was growing up, I remember thinking that some of my friends who wanted to write would never be able to do so. Not because of political rebellion; this was not the case. They simply felt that the pressure of the writing profession—the meetings of the Writers Union, the constant scrutiny, and so forth—was something they would not really like to experience.

But very quietly, when no one was listening to us, when no one was around, we would joke that the most successful fiction writer in history was a man living at that time in the Soviet Union: Stalin. We recalled that whenever Stalin had his work published, all critics and potential critics disappeared the day before the book's publication date. This, of course, was a writer's dream! Somehow I cannot part with this metaphor, because whenever I have a book published—and you notice that I publish very few books—I have this same tempting dream: my book is scheduled to come out on Thursday, and by Wednesday the critics are already gone. And naturally the book is established in hundreds of thousands of copies, since it is obligatory reading. But clearly this was not the case with my friends or myself: none of us could actually have our critics removed.

At that time, outside of envying Stalin and his ability to eliminate his critics, we identified ourselves with the literary titans. I remember very well that whenever I would confront a particular situation in life—a situation like this one, for instance—I saw myself on two levels. One level was the level of my bodily existence, from which I could not separate myself. But then there was another level, a level of identification with a literary protagonist of some kind, someone who, I felt, reflected certain parts of my life, someone whom I understood very well and who understood me very well. It could be a protagonist from Balzac or Stendhal or Faulkner, although I do not think I was brave enough to use Faulkner. And then, whenever I faced a dangerous or threatening situation, I felt that I had faced it before, by reading about someone who somehow resembled me or with whom I identified. It was the source of a curious strength, and it did not matter how that strength was needed—whether it was in confrontation with another person (when I saw myself as a "lover" who needed reassurance, I would go back to romantic literature) or in confrontation with society (when I saw myself plotting against the system). Either way, there was a very clear feeling in my heart or in my mind that I had experienced the situation before; hence, in my real life, I was stronger. In such a way, literature performed a resounding function for my generation.

I recall a discussion I had one day with my father. There were very few occasions when we would actually talk to each other. My father belonged to the generation of those traumatized by the Soviet revolution, a man who withdrew altogether from active life to the point where he would not even confront the postman. A very remote and distant man, he went through the Second World War doing nothing but studying the ancient Greeks, because he felt that what they knew was enough to understand what was going on in Europe, and that knowledge eliminated the need for confrontation. After the war, however, we had one of those few confrontations. We pondered aloud—he and I—what I was going to do. I had some notions of my own private destiny, which he clearly would not understand and which in many ways he would condemn. Above all, I was determined not to be as removed from life as he was.

And I remember my father's recommendation: that the only way for a modern man to tolerate what was happening, to accept the absolutely irrational universe around us, to accept the separation, the atomization, the lack of contact, was to withdraw to something extremely abstract, some-thing which takes up the substance of life but does not deal with its actual forms. Mathematics, for example. But mathematics was out for me; I had had some unpleasant experiences in school. Music, another possibility, was disqualified quickly by my mother, who had studied at the Moscow Conservatory of Music and who knew for a fact that I could not repeat even the simplest tune. Then my father came up with the last available option for me: writing. He qualified it by pointing out to me and to my mother that while even animals react to music, they do not react to the printed page. Hence, the printed page—this was his superiority over my mother—had an undeniably abstract character since the ability to read and write was a purely human trait.

At that time, we left the question open. I would not write in the Soviet Union or in Poland. And although I could read, I could not read many of the books which I actually wanted to read and which my father had read before the revolution. Only when I left Eastern Europe and came to the States did that situation change. It slowly occurred to me that facing exis-tence directly was perhaps not the most ideal way of being, that maybe I should return to some state of abstraction, that maybe I should begin to write. When I arrived in New York, I again imagined myself as someone else. I saw myself as a protagonist from Balzac: the way he would face Paris, I would face New York. I saw the city as a city of literature. In every single corner I met someone else. There was a Hemingway expressway; there was a Dos Passos square; there was a little corner of Balzac; there was a heroic place in which I could be the hero of Stendhal; and so forth. I was the walking literature. And, in such a way, I wandered through the first few months, accepting various identities and surviving in a city which was rather hostile. For one thing, I didn't speak English, a language common in Manhattan. For another, I had some difficulty accepting myself; otherwise, I would not have developed this curious, almost vicarious identification with literary protagonists.

After a while, when I began writing, I realized that there was another substantial difference between Americans and foreigners like myself. For us in Europe—and here I speak as a European—the literary experience was always oriented and directed at the reader. If it was good literature, it would evoke in him some feeling, some fact. If it was bad, it would not engage him at all. Whether or not the writer actually experienced what he wrote about made no difference at all.

But here in the United States I noticed the attitude toward fiction was slightly different. I remember when I paid my first income tax, I tried to deduct some of my trips to Europe, which were clearly connected with my literary endeavor. The tax man asked me to point out the passages in my novel that corresponded to the trips. From the point of view of the IRS, the degree to which my travel was a capitalization toward a future novel was determined by its specific application to my fiction. And I would try to tell the tax people, in advance, what part of the novel would reflect a particular trip.

And then there was always the issue of autobiography: was what I wrote actually autobiographical? If I said yes, then I was a vicious man who wrote vicious things. If I said no, then I was a liar. I recall the insistence of my students: "Mr. Kosinski, that thing in *Steps*, you know . . ." "No, I don't." "Well, you know this page 122 . . ." "No, I don't know." "Well, that terrible scene. Have you actually done this?" I said, "No, but I intend to."

There was also the pleasant out-of-town editor who visited me just before *Being There* was finished. He asked me what I was currently working on—in addition to my teaching, of course, since teaching was considered to be the main path, the main destiny of my life. And I said I am writing a novel about a character who is, to say the least, a mindless man, perhaps—indeed—an idiot. As he sipped his martini, the editor said to me with all of his southern sweetness, "About an idiot? Fascinating. Mr. Kosinski, would this, like your other two novels, be directly autobiographical?" I pondered the predicament. On the other side of the Iron Curtain, my work was judged by whether or not it was directly political. In the United States, it was judged by whether or not it was directly biographical. Which was better?

At present, there is something even more important than the ideological differences or the tax systems or the political curtains that separate writing fiction here from writing fiction there. As I mentioned before, a printed page shows you nothing; you have to provide your own private theater. You not only have to subsidize the effort; you have to create the effort. And, by doing so, you actually live the experience you read about, since it is only from within that you empathize with the page. There are no drawings. There are no photographs. There are no moving pictures. When you read about a violent act, you have to stage it inside of you. By staging it inside of yourself, you become part of the violent act without committing it. You are purged of the dangerous emotion. Hence, the purging power of literature.

Confronting this effort is a new medium: television. Actually, that medium has been with us for quite some time—far longer than the actual screen and the actual set. It may have been with us from the very beginning of the human imagination and the human predicament. Perhaps there was a longing in us to get out of the psyche, so we would not have to imagine every condition from within. TV does it and shows it to us, and it frees us from the very uncomfortable notion that we have to do it for ourselves.

In 1968, in the United States, television outsold newspapers, seventy percent to thirty percent. The American case is an important one, because what happens in America will happen in a few years in central and Eastern Europe. In various public opinion polls, the question was posed: "When reports conflict, is television more believable than newspapers?" Sixty percent of the respondents said "Yes." Since I am also a teacher—or also a novelist—I know that, among the current generation, my students read one book for every twenty films that they see. Twenty films for every book—and I don't mean just novels; that includes textbooks. Yet there are eighty thousand students right now taking thirteen thousand courses in filmmaking at about two hundred colleges.

Today's students will, on average throughout their lifetimes, watch eighteen thousand hours of television; that corresponds to nine years of full-time employment. Now, nine years is a long time for any employment. Yet such is the generation that I meet daily in my classes at Yale and that I have already met at Princeton and other universities. To them, every encounter is reduced to a six-inch television screen. Everyone on that screen is the same: president, clown, politician, baseball player, even the occasional novelist.

What are the results of contact with reality when reality is reduced to a mere six inches? What are the implications of these encounters? They are staggering. There is no sense of hierarchy. There is no sense of gradation: nothing is of greater—or lesser—consequence. It is very difficult for my students to establish a range of priorities within their lives; for them, things are equally important or unimportant. Although, on the one hand, their exposure to the world is quite large, within this exposure the elephant and the mouse are the same size, and both produce a sound which is controlled by the TV set. This is the generation which somehow feels that it has the world at its disposal. They can turn it off. They can change to another channel. But whatever they do with it, it can never do anything to them. Unlike fiction, it makes no demands.

In contrast to the television viewer, the reader of fiction is not a blank screen. Because the images that fiction creates are limitless, the reader never runs out of channels or programs.

THE BILINGUAL VISION OF REALITY

Kosinski spoke often of the nature of language and the role of memory. Drawing on ideas he explored in his *Notes of the Author on The Painted Bird,* he examined the way that the two functions are combined in the creative process, particularly for a writer who is writing in an adopted tongue, and he demonstrated how the writer's perception of reality—the "remembered event"—becomes his "individual fiction."

Language, it can be said, is the translation of man's original weapons—fist, or rock, or club—and today it is still his most formidable weapon. A word has become the essence of a thousand objects, gestures, and dreams. In modern society, language serves man's mind as clothes serve his body: to hide and to protect, to seduce and to mislead. It is no accident, therefore, that it is as antisocial to emerge naked mentally as it is physically. But language is not just one human function among many; man doesn't speak in the same sense that he walks or eats or works.

The all-pervasive characteristic of language is that, through words, a human offspring confronts the reality of his self and the reality of others. What was once just a sound suddenly becomes an information, an instruction, a manipulation. The words create and expand the child's vision in ways that range from awareness of a part of his own body to induction into purely symbolic dimensions of past and future and otherworldliness. The child discovers that, more than the most magic of his toys, words allow him to stop time, to deal with reality at a distance, and to alter human situations in every conceivable way.

Thus, a very important part of our knowledge of ourselves and of others is given to us through language, which is as natural to our mind as metabolism is to our body. The words, the sentences, the syntax orient us not only to themselves but also to a realm of reality, whether actual, potential, or abstract. It is this power of language which makes the whole principle of literature as fiction possible. The printed page of a novel is strong enough to seduce the reader into participation in the fictive reality now accessible to him only via the symbols of the language.

Just as an actor playing Hamlet is neither Hamlet nor merely an actor but, rather, an actor as Hamlet, so is a fictive event neither an actual event nor a totally created fiction with no base in experience; it is an event as fiction. A symbol is both concrete and abstract. It is neither literal reality nor illusion; it is both illusory and concrete. Naturally, the stimulus that gave birth to it can never be fully known; if it could, there would be no need for the symbol. It can never be defined; it can, at best, be interpreted. Marcel Proust made this quite clear when he stated that the purpose of art "is to rediscover, grasp again, and lay before us that reality from which we live so far removed and from which we become more and more separated as the formal knowledge which we substitute for it grows in thickness and imperviousness—that reality which there is grave danger we might die without ever having known and yet which is simply our life."

The transfer of fragments of objective reality to this new dimension in which the literary work arises seems to have a logic of its own and requires the selection and condensation of a large number of phenomena, both real and symbolic. Through the use of language, the external world acquires for the writer a secondary importance; he makes use of it only to the extent to which it is already accommodated in the universe created by his imagination. It might be said that the writer takes from outside himself only what he is capable of creating in his imagination.

Thus, the indispensable prerequisite for the creative process is that the writer comes to stand outside the experience he aims at re-creating through his writing. He is consciously examining himself and the experience "from without," from a standpoint at which both he himself and his surroundings lose their concrete features and separate themselves from external reality to enter a fluid and less rigid reality of language which no longer obeys the earthbound laws of gravitation and where the minutiae of time and place cease to be important.

Since our minds conceive of creative situations according to fixed patterns which we were taught in the language of our growing up to perceive reality, certain fairly constant and verbalized fictive realities—everything drawn from the depth of our memories, or dredged up from our subconscious levels of mind, or wrought from our creative abilities—will lack the hard edge of total fact. These patterns are our individual fictions, created unwittingly to help along our own thinking and identifying. For we fit experiences into verbalized molds which simplify, shape, and give them an acceptable emotional clarity. The remembered event becomes a verbalized fiction, a structure made to accommodate certain feelings. Without these structures, literature would be too personal for the writer to create, much less for his readers to grasp. There is no art which is reality; rather, art is the using of symbols by which an otherwise and unstateable subjective reality is made manifest. Even film, the most capable of all the arts in portraying the literal, is edited; if it were not, it would be either entirely incomprehensible or totally indigestible to the viewers. This same editing process occurs in other art forms: remembering is the automatic process of editing. "Expression begins where thought ends," said Camus; this is creation, or, in this specific case, writing.

Therefore one cannot say that memory is either literal or exact. If memories have a truth, it is more an emotional than an actual one. It can be said that because of language, we cannot help but transmute all of our experiences into a mold for an emotion, into little films, always forming a situation in which the literal and the symbolic approach one another so closely that the meaning arises from the confrontation.

A writer writing in an adopted tongue which he learned in his adulthood possesses in the form of this tongue one more curtain which separates him from the spontaneous utterance, one more distancing device. The adopted tongue interferes with the writer's heightened perception, often suppressing or eliminating certain emotional phases of the writer's life grounded in his native tongue, in the roots of childhood, and in certain autonomous psychological experiences associated with and existing in his native tongue. The adopted tongue presents an opportunity for a vehement confrontation with all these mental processes so far realized only through the native tongue and responsible for introducing the individual to himself and to society and which thus were once the only ones capable of evoking the numerous feeling-states of hunger, of rage, of sexual arousal, of nervousness, of excitement, of shock, et cetera.

In such a way, the adopted tongue separates the writer from the culture of his growing up but equally efficiently prevents for a long time his emotional identifying with this adopted tongue and also the spontaneous encoding of the immediate experience which occurs and is verbalized in the adopted tongue. After a while, when a certain psychological balance between the native tongue and the adopted one has been established, the writer's visionary experiences, whether in dreams or in the waking state, will become more and more conditional on the dissociation that takes place between past and present. Such dissociations often come about precisely because a man's present state, in which he functions and perceives himself in an adopted tongue, comes into conflict with his childhood or adolescent state, personified by his native tongue. Or he may be confronted with the necessity to sunder himself violently from his original character—again, expressed only in his native tongue—in the interests of some arbitrary role more in keeping with his present ambitions, which has to be expressed only in his adopted tongue.

On this bilingual plateau, the writer's vision of himself can be neither an examination of the self nor a revisitation of the self, since the search for the self can be conducted only in the metaphor through which the unconscious most easily manifests itself and toward which the unconscious most naturally navigates. The bilingual writer has at his immediate disposal two sets of metaphors and therefore two sets of realities: one capsulated via the native language, the other via the adopted one. Each language directs him to different sensory identifications with different realms of his self, selecting the details within each selection. Not only is this process partly unconscious; it is also spontaneous and directs the senses to two various emotional levels in which the writer's specific emotional truths could be most strongly revealed. Thus, for instance, the same phrase expressed in a native tongue may lead the writer to the association of war and chaos and pain on a mountain in the middle of winter, while in an adopted one it may evoke within himself the peace and order and serenity of a beach during an invincible summer.

To summarize, it is not only the fact that languages differ as much from each other as do the cultures which they incarnate that prevents the writer who writes in an adopted tongue from alternating freely from one to the other in the creative process. It is, above all, that in his break with the wholeness of Self, the bilingual writer is constantly aware that reality rooted in one language is simply not conveyable into the other and that the idioms of one language turn into decoys that lead realities of the other to their oblivion. In this moment of choice, the writer who chooses to write in an adopted tongue is often both the master of this language and its most helpless slave.

CONFRONTING THE SELF

In this short interview originally published in *Le Magazine Littéraire* (1982), Kosinski explained to Bernard Mocquot how *Pinball,* his most personal novel to date, complemented his earlier cycle of novels.

BERNARD MOCQUOT: *Passion Play* was the last of the novels in your previous cycle. Is *Pinball* the first novel in a new cycle? Or is it an isolated novel?

JERZY KOSINSKI: *Pinball* stands vis-à-vis the cycle of my other seven novels, a cycle which began with *The Painted Bird* and ended with *Passion Play*. *Pinball* "confronts" the issues of visibility and anonymity, the two prerequisites for the social and moral consequences of being an artist—of Patrick Domostroy, the burnt-out classical composer, and Goddard, the rock superstar who is currently famous.

BM: Why did you choose music as a theme for the novel?

JK: Like language, music has to be written. And then, like language, the musical symbol must be decoded in the listener's mind, evoking, like language, emotional and verbal states. A proverb says, "words for the mind, music for the soul."

BM: What was your reason for including so many clues linking Domostroy to you—the Cuba Libres; *Octaves/Steps; Bird of Quintain/The Painted Bird;* the Hollywood film made in Spain; Domostroy's childhood and studies in Poland; et cetera?

JK: *Pinball* is a "mini-universe" of my own life—or, at least, of the last twenty years of my fiction writing, since the novel is about the spiritual consequences of public creativity, of being an artist. It is probably the most personal novel I have written. Maybe that's why I have committed to the pages of *Pinball* actual as well as spiritual profiles of people—my father, for instance, who influenced me the most. Even my own recent acting experience has become a part of the novel. As you noted, Patrick Domostroy, one of my fictional stand-ins, also once acted in an epic Hollywood film. For me, creativity is a supreme adventure. Maybe that's why I have also shaped *Pinball* as a psychological thriller, set in the wastelands of the soul, of the psyche, of the spirit, in a world dominated by hype and manipulation.

BM: Are there also other levels of meaning in the novel?

JK: On a personal note, *Pinball* is, for me, not only a meditation on the meaning of creativity but also an exploration of other issues—visibility, fame, failure, obscurity—that affect, that must affect, every one of us. I use the American contemporary music scene in New York, California, and even Mexico—an environment I know well—as a testing ground to find out whether or not it is still possible for an artist—be it a writer, a painter, a classical composer, or a rock star—to create a *human*-centered art and to preserve the creative intimacy such art entails. Or has art, by now, become by virtue of the place of the artist in our Western capitalist society an absurdist wasteland as burned out and as empty as the wasted, dehumanized, extermination camp–like urban environment of New York's South Bronx slums, where Domostroy now lives, and where I used to live and work shortly after my arrival in New York some twenty-five years ago? A parallel concern is what Western commerciality has inflicted on the artist. Reading *Pinball*, one has to ponder why Patrick Domostroy, a refugee from Eastern Europe who has survived the devastation of Hitler's Europe and its extermination camps, is now spiritually adrift in the free USA and cannot create new music anymore. Is Gerhard Osten, Goddard's father, right when he sees rock as totalitarian in spirit and fascist in nature? Or is Goddard right when he perceives rock as the embodiment of art for the masses, democratic in nature? What is Goddard after? Is his anonymity the reason for his creative life, for being sheltered from the fame that devours and destroys its stars? Or is his anonymity a prerequisite for being creative in music? Conversely, isn't being creative in daily life rather than in music a prerequisite for happiness—perhaps something that Domostroy had not realized when he himself was famous? And so on, and so on—like a pinball!

LITERARY INVENTION

During a visit to Amsterdam in September 1990, Kosinski was invited to the John Adams Institute, where he spoke about the process of writing, the pleasure of translation, and the special merits of his latest novel, *The Hermit of 69th Street.*

When I think about my own literary invention, I cannot help but reflect upon this particular Hermit in this particular Hermitage on this particular street. On the surface, it might appear that I appeared here accidentally. But I am not here by chance. From a purely novelistic imaginative point of view, in fact, I would compare this moment to a film in which a great number of things meet and refract at the same time.

I am a writer. Writing is not a profession for me; it's a vocation. I write in the mornings. And, when I write, I am the freest man of all. I can't wait to do it. By midday, the rest of the day invades.

Like all writers, I write in order to develop images. If the images can then be developed in other darkrooms—that is, in other languages—they become even bigger and better. But in this time of television, film, and other massive fast-moving narrative devices, writing is something very tough to sustain or even to explain. I learned this thirty years ago, when I went to an American bank to apply for a loan to buy a car. On the application, I was asked to list my profession. Of course, I was very proud, very European

96

about it: I wrote down "writer." The loan officer examined my application and said, "Yes, Mr. Kosinski. But what is it that you *really* do?" And, to this day, I've never had a loan. But I would like to believe that my most recent novel, *The Hermit of 69th Street*, answers the question of what I really do.

The reason that I am here tonight is because the first foreign translation of any of my books was published thirty years ago in Holland, by De Bezige Bij ["The Busy Bee" publishers]. Thirty years is a long time. I don't write often, and I haven't written much. But, over the past thirty years, all my books have appeared in Holland almost immediately after the American editions. In fact, one of them appeared ahead of the American edition, which threw my American publishers into a fit. At the time, if a book came out early overseas, it would lose its right to claim "first publication" in North America. That meant I had to rush to publish a few copies of the book myself and put them up for sale in the continental United States and Canada.

Foreign-language translation proves two things simultaneously: first, that a writer doesn't write in just one language; and second, that it doesn't really matter in what language he writes. Am I less of a writer in Dutch because of a novel that I originally wrote in English? Clearly not. The impact of my work is the same on a Dutch or an American reader; and it is the reader who matters the most to me. Yet as a novelist, when I create a fiction, I never know how readers will receive or perceive it. And, in some ways, I do not want to know. In fact, one of the reasons I would never write a play is that I would not want the director of the theater where it might be performed to call and tell me how many people had left the audience after the first act.

Since my first foreign-language translation was in Dutch, I have always been fond of Amsterdam, which I consider to be my European address. I feel very much at home here: I can speak in English without anyone being bothered by it, and I can wander happily through the many bookstores. Also, the architecture that I see from the boats on Amsterdam's canals reminds me of the architecture along the Long Island shore. I feel especially at home in this building, where so much important American history was forged. This is the place where John Adams came to secure funds for his young nation. Without financial support from the Dutch government, a decision that was undertaken in this very room, the fortress of Manhattan would never have been built. But thanks to that decision, today I am able to reside most of the year in the new Amsterdam, Manhattan, where I often walk along Amsterdam Avenue.

Last night, Alberto Moravia, a fellow writer, died. I never met Moravia, but I admired him. The critical obituary in the London *Times* noted that he promoted a certain notion of—let's be blunt about it—"sexual instinct." What's so strange about a sexual instinct that it has to be underlined as peculiar when none of us in this room would be here without it? Greed, appreciation of art—these things don't produce life. Sexual instinct is, in fact, the only authentic force left. Luckily, in Amsterdam, where the shop windows display both bank-o-mat and sex-o-mat, one is reminded that the sexual instinct still exists. According to the obituary, Moravia was one of the few who expressed that "obsession" in his writing. We will miss Moravia. But perhaps, because his books survive him, we will not have to miss him too much. He was a writer, which means he existed because of his books. And as long as the books are here, Moravia is here as well.

Every novelist relies on the writers who came before him. Without that literary heritage, no novel would ever have been written. That is a fact that we should not take for granted. After all, no architect builds a house without studying other houses. No painter invents all of his own paints, shapes, and colors but rather looks back to what other painters have used. No sculptor creates all new textures and forms but instead relies on existing materials. All good artists, therefore, realize that they must use the familiar media in new forms, in new designs, to create new ways of looking at the old. That refraction, that very refraction, is what I spoke about earlier, and, for me, it makes my evening here profoundly dramatic.

The other day, a pedantic critic told me that, in *The Hermit of 69th Street*, I quoted 999 sources and 1,012 books. And why not? I committed to *The Hermit* anything that I could or felt that I should. And I brought myself into the novel, too, not just as an author whose name and picture are on the cover but also as an independent character, since I have a right to be independent vis-à-vis my book. The result was a new form of narrative: an autofiction.

I have been asked why I chose the number "69." It is perhaps the only figure that is truly visual: 6 is graphically the exact reverse of 9. It is the only figure, of speech or number, that in some way graphically indicates something—although I won't explain what, since clearly you can look for yourself. In Amsterdam, that should be easy.

The Hermit of 69th Street costs sixty—not sixty-nine—guilders. That's a heck of a lot of money to pay for the average novel. But this book is worth the price. Maybe it should have cost even more, because it is not really a novel; it's a matrix, the result of a realization that one is always going Dutch (even if one is not doing so directly) when one creates whatever it is that one creates. In the paperback edition, I include a quote from a Dutch writer, which I will read to you in the English translation (because I wouldn't dare attempt to read it to you in Dutch): "Those who read this book, we beg them to correct anything that may seem amiss, for they who wish to understand such things know very well how hard the matter is." Writing is indeed a hard matter, since a writer writes in abstraction, so to speak, with nobody concrete in mind.

I am reminded of a beautiful phrase from F. Scott Fitzgerald's novel *The Great Gatsby*, about seeing with "Dutch sailors' eyes." By that, Fitzgerald meant to suggest a state of enormous admiration, specifically the ability of the early Dutch sailors to see a new continent, America, with fresh and admiring eyes. Fitzgerald liked the image and decided that he wanted to incorporate it into his novel, but apparently, throughout the various drafts, he was unsure to which of his characters it best applied. Ultimately he gave the phrase to the narrator, Nick Carraway, who likened the "fresh, green breast of the new world" that "flowered once for Dutch sailors" to Gatsby's great sense of "wonder when he first picked out the green light at the end of Daisy's dock." I hate to think how the *Village Voice* might misconstrue that process. But I do know that it is worthwhile to try to understand how it is that a writer writes the way he does, chooses the images that he does. We all try to determine where the punch should go, to decide if the leitmotif is indicated with sufficient clarity, and to find the best metaphor to express it. Fitzgerald's phrase is so powerful that I used it at the end of *The Hermit of 69th Street*, in which a different kind of murder takes place.

This brings up another point. I often hear that my characters are extremely manipulative, always in a state of relative defense or attack against the world. I would propose that the opposite is true: they are merely reacting. In *Cockpit*, for example, the protagonist, who is relatively strong, is totally traumatized when he becomes trapped in an elevator whose doors he cannot open. As a result, he falls to pieces. In *Being There*, the character of Chance may be the wisest man there is not because of the platitudes he utters but because he knows that watching the world passively is better and less painful than seeking it out. To some degree, therefore, my novels are about people who are profoundly weak, who are barely making it, who mobilize themselves the way most of us must in our own lives. Through their struggles, they bring to us an additional state of self-awareness. That is why I have written these books the way that I have written them.

Collectively, in the names of all of the writers and books I have included in *The Hermit of 69th Street*, I must thank you for inviting a writer to this institute. There are many other people whom you could have invited here today—movie directors, television hosts. But I believe that it is important for writers to have a platform to speak and to explain why people should read their novels. The work of the writer is vital to society and to the historical process. Storytelling, after all, is the only instrument that activates images from within. Television, movies, video, photography: all operate from without, from the outside. The images from those media present themselves to the eye and are, in a way, totalitarian: your only choice, your only freedom, is whether to open or close your eyes to the image. You cannot redo the image; it is not yours. But a novel activates you from within and forces you to create the image for yourself. When you do, it is intimately yours. No other artist, not even a photographer, has that power.

On Storytelling

In the Polish tradition as well as in the Jewish tradition, a storyteller has a very high place in society. It's the closest thing to being a shaman, a seducer. As a storyteller, you have all the advantages of being part of the community, yet you perform a unique function within that community.

I am a storyteller. There's nothing in my novels that isn't derivative [of my life] in some way.

But I have no right to impose my judgment on my readers. I'm not selling my point of view. I see myself as a storyteller.

LANGUAGE AS A FILTER

The English language, Kosinski told audience members at a "Meet the Author" session hosted by the *Jerusalem Post* (January 31, 1988), gave him the filter he needed in order to write, especially about the traumatic events of his youth.

Movies are fiction, regardless of whether one calls them documentaries or not. They are about editing. They are about selecting. They are about what Schopenhauer called exaggeration, about being an alarmist. Acting in a movie is an alarming experience: you get as many takes as a director will give you.

Writing means a pause. Writing means reflection. Writing in English was a useful experience for me since it allowed precisely that. Creativity is a filter. If, for example, a painter needs distance from what he paints, then the paint and the canvas offer that distance. But language is already a creative filter. I could never have written *The Painted Bird* in Polish—even though some papers in the United States once claimed that I did and had someone else translate it.

I wrote *The Painted Bird* in English because in Polish it would have been too close to my heart. It would have been just too complex, and probably too painful and too traumatic, because I am a Pole at the same time that I am a Jew. In Poland, my synagogue literally faced the church. Take a look at the photographs from centuries back: sometimes the synagogue was huge and made of stone while the Catholic church was small and made of wood; sometimes it was the other way around. But usually the two structures stood in close proximity to each other. And I stand here now, as witness to one thousand years of that presence.

The English language was useful in the sense that it protected me from a part of myself, the part that is too emotional, the part that wonders why all my relatives but one have died. What did they do to deserve their fates? They were good Poles as well as good Jews. In English, I didn't have to think about such things: the English verb and the English noun took precedence over my personal history, Anglo-Saxon objectivity over Eastern European subjectivity. In fact, if I were to make a movie based on *The Painted Bird*, I would set it in Canada, among the Canadian peasants, in order to create yet another filter to separate me from the events of the book. And remember: that book happens to be a novel. Don't you dare hold it up to me as a history book. If you want a history book, talk to the people from the American Foundation for Polish-Jewish Studies. They are here, right now, top Jewish historians, all of them—and top Polish historians—at the Hebrew University in Jerusalem.

By insulating me from my own sense of the past, from my own private past, the English language turned me into a perfect storyteller, a storyteller who tells a story in a language which evokes no emotion, a language which does not make Jews stand up and say, "Hey, Kosinski, I hate your guts. My relatives died in Poland, and I hate Poland with all my guts." I do not disagree that Jews died in the Polish house, but the fire was not set by the Poles. You want to blame the company that insured the house? So do I. The name of that insurance company happens to be Western civilization. Was it arson? Yes, it was. Were the Poles anti-Semitic? No, they were not—although individual Poles certainly were. The Germans, on the other hand, were clearly anti-Semitic: they believed that every Jew, no matter what his rank, no matter what his status, no matter what his accomplishment, should be gotten rid of. The Poles had nothing to do with that. They happened to die in the same house—not in the same way—but they died in it nevertheless. The English language gave me the filter I needed, the inner filter that could turn my story—and yours—into a universal one.

FICTION AS COMMUNICATION

In April 1988, Kosinski was invited by his friend Joachim Maître, Dean of Boston University's School of Communication and Journalism, to speak at the school's fortieth-anniversary celebration. Kosinski used the occasion to ponder the meaning of communication and the importance of storytelling.

I am honored and flattered to be here today, not only because this is the fortieth anniversary of Boston University's School of Communication and Journalism but also because the city of Boston has played a vital role in my life as a novelist. Novel writing is my trade. For a while, when I first came to the United States, I wrote nonfiction. But soon I started writing fiction.

Fiction is a different kind of communication. A novelist is free to move in any direction he or she wants, up or down the social scale, sideways, even below the ground. No other communicator, not even a social scientist—which was my profession in Poland—has this kind of freedom. The jump from nonfiction to fiction is therefore a profound one. It means abolishing the historical dimension. It means moving away from events, because events require documentation as they happen. It also means, as I have said before, the freedom of invention, which is a very important form of communication.

After my first two nonfiction books were published in New York, I decided that I wanted to be what my tradition had prepared me to be: a storyteller, not a recorder of events, not a communicator of any particular set of historical references, but rather a voice of fantasy, imagination, humor, sexuality—all of the things that a novelist can mix and fuse and propose in any fashion. A novelist can, in fact, retain his story exactly as he originally conceived it or he can turn it into an event—an entirely different event—a year from now. And none of you will have the right to complain. This is the freedom that only a storyteller has.

As a novelist, I produce movies in my head. They require no director, no investment of capital. They are re-created in the head of the reader, who does not even have to buy a ticket in order to enjoy the show. Some readers will see the things I have described more or less the way that I do, and so we communicate.

Boston was the city that published my first novel, *The Painted Bird*. Everyone in New York, I am sorry to say, turned this masterpiece down. And they turned it down the impersonal way New York typically turns things down. They said that I had established myself as Joseph Novak, which was an easy name to remember; Jerzy Kosinski was not. Novak had made an impact with his books, which were serialized by the *Saturday Evening Post* and condensed by *Reader's Digest*. Kosinski had not. So I was urged to keep writing nonfiction under the name of Novak.

But I said no. It had to be Kosinski because I wanted to be what I knew I always was: a storytelling Polish Jew. So I wrote my novel. And when all the likely publishers in New York rejected it, I asked a friend of mine for advice. He said that given the universal nature of the novel—made even more universal by the fact that my name was totally unpronounceable—only a publisher in Boston might understand my work. So I sent the manuscript to Houghton Mifflin, the oldest publishing house in the United States. And soon a letter came from Paul Brooks and Dorothy de Santillana, key names in my professional life. They said, "Dear Jerzy Kosinski"—they did not misspell the name—"we would love to publish your first novel." That was my first contact with Boston.

I have since made other notable contacts in Boston. One of them is Joachim Maître, the dean of this school. He and I share an important chapter in our lives: we are both children of the Second World War. Even though

I am a Polish Jew and he is a German—actually, a Huguenot, and, as any Jew would tell you, Huguenots were the Jews of the Christian world—we share a unique experience. We are both children of the same kindergarten, and that kindergarten was the war.

The war was an event like no other. It redefined society—in Germany, in Poland, throughout the world. The Jew, who had always represented intellectual thought, had, until that time, been a universal figure. He moved easily from one idea to another, from one language to another, from Hebrew and Yiddish to German and Polish. But suddenly he became an object of extinction and a symbol of the failure of communication that made possible the year 1939, one of the most powerful and devastating years in modern history. The four years that followed changed forever the pictures of Germany and of Poland. Historical towns like Dresden and Warsaw were destroyed, and Auschwitz was erected in their place. This is the war that I inherited, and this is what I have in common with Joachim Maître.

I am happy to be back again in Boston, celebrating this school's fortieth anniversary and reflecting on the real meaning of communication. Communication means the last free radio broadcast from France before the war. Communication means the exchange of information now occurring with Moscow. Communication means understanding how we face the world and explore the unknown. And for many Americans today, communication means television. The average American watches six hours of television daily. There goes the readership of my next novel! This, in fact, is the first pure television generation. No condemnation here: I know that television provides communication like no other medium. Secretary of State Alexander of Haig called television "the siege machine of the twentieth century." But I worry about whom it besieges. I worry that this generation, instead of communicating and engaging the world on active terms, will simply disengage and watch passively as the world goes by.

On this fortieth anniversary, we should take a closer look at the year in which this school was founded. In 1948, as the Communist Party took over the government of Czechoslovakia, the foreign minister Jan Masaryk, the son of Czechoslovakia's first president, Tomáš Garrigue Masaryk, jumped to his death from a window. And with his suicide, Czechoslovakia ceased

107

to be a free country. That same year, the Jewish state came into existence—and thank God for that, because there are only fifteen million Jews in the world. My demographically trained friends tell me that, without all of the pogroms of history, today the Jewish state could have been four hundred million strong. Apropos of that, I ask you, for the sake of communication, why was it that I was singled out by history to lose almost all the members of my family during the war? They were intellectuals, not businessmen. Like you, they were into communication. They wrote books on ancient Greece and on the battles between Sparta and Athens. They were chess players. They defined linguistic norms. They were educated in Heidelberg and Vienna. And yet all of them vanished—for the sake of what? For the failure of communication?

In 1948, the Nobel Prize for literature went to T. S. Eliot. Martin Buber, the product of the Polish-Judaic tradition, wrote *Moses*. Winston Churchill published *The Gathering Storm*, even as the political storm was still gathering. Jackson Pollock came up with new compositions in painting. The film *Hamlet* won an Academy Award, as did its lead actor Laurence Olivier. Arnold Schoenberg wrote an opera, *Survivor from Warsaw*. The price of uranium went up to sixteen hundred dollars and those who owned uranium fields were suddenly very, very rich. The atomic age was about to descend upon us, but at the time only a few people—like the friends of mine who lived in Katanga in Africa—were aware of the value of uranium. They became billionaires: uranium was the best stock of the day. Alfred Kinsey wrote *Sexual Behavior in the Human Male*, a volume which, many years later, allowed me to write my novels the way I do. (When anyone complains, I quote the appropriate page from the Kinsey Report.) Prince Charles, a fellow polo player, was born. And, in the United States, a federal rent control bill was passed; today, hardly any part of that bill remains.

How do we communicate the importance of those events? Do we base our communication on the events themselves or on their intrinsic value? And what values should we attach to any communication? For instance, in your college catalogue, there is a course on science and medicine reporting. We know that science and medicine mean life. If I were stricken by some disease that may or may not have originated during the Second World War,

I would probably need science and medicine to help me survive. For you as communicators and journalists, however, is it enough simply to report objectively on such illness? Is it not as essential, or even more essential, for you to grasp the content—the human content—of the illness?

When the novelist Charles Dickens came to this country in 1842, he visited various hospitals and lunatic asylums because he understood that insanity was itself "a matter of communication." After viewing the State Hospital for the Insane in South Boston, he wrote in his *American Notes* that the facility was "admirably conducted on those enlightened principles of conciliation and kindness, which twenty years ago would have been worse than heretical. . . . Every patient in this asylum sits down to dinner every day with a knife and fork; and in the midst of them sits the gentleman [the superintendent]." At every meal, "moral influence alone restrains the most violent among them from cutting the throats of the rest; but the effect of that influence is reduced to an absolute certainty, and it is found, even as a means of restraint, to say nothing of it as a means of cure, a hundred times more efficacious than all the straight-waistcoats, fetters, and handcuffs, that ignorance, prejudice, and cruelty have manufactured since the creation of the world."

In the news today, I read that at a certain Boston-area hospital, there are only thirteen psychiatrists assigned to help 3,899 patients. That's approximately one psychiatrist for every two hundred and forty patients. Only two months ago, the *New York Times* reported that at King's County Hospital, psychiatric patients were handcuffed to chairs or benches for days at a time while they waited for beds. This is in New York, one of the richest cities in America. That's communication, too—or, perhaps I should say, failure of communication. What would Dickens write about such contemporary events? What would he say about us as Americans?

In assessing the state of education in America, the most recent Carnegie Report claimed that many urban schools no longer educate at all; they serve merely as storehouses to keep young people off the streets. I have been to some of these schools, and I know that the report's conclusions are true. There is little communication anymore between the teaching body and the students. This is somewhat ironic, for what are schools if not places for communication? Apparently values, morality, attitudes are no longer routinely passed on from teachers to students. The Carnegie Report urges a crusade. But what kind of crusade? What new kinds of communication must we develop in order to reach these children? This much, however, is certain: if we fail, they will never learn. And all of us will pay the consequences.

The crisis in the schools will not pass suddenly—no more than the American unions are suddenly going to change their methods, no more than the Soviet Union is going to surrender its historical views and turn overnight into a democracy, no more than a deserving country such as Poland will suddenly turn into a state that is democratic and dependently independent. But there are things that we can begin to do. For instance, we can encourage young people to develop their concentration by teaching them the game of chess, and by helping them improve their concentration we can help them to learn. Chess is a great, democratic sport. It can even be played in the ghetto. Players can play against each other, regardless of their language or their profession or their financial status. But it takes a special kind of communicator to communicate the notion of chess, to explain to youngsters the values of the world that are inherent in the game—that is, that there are only a limited number of moves that can be made or that certain moves are final—and to propose chess as an alternative to the mindlessness of television, which has only minimal educational effect.

Think back to the hospitals. Have you ever seen those patients who are incurably ill and dying? They are left at the mercy of television. Nobody comes to visit the dying anymore. There is a fear of death in the United States, even though eventually all of us will die. That too says something about our values.

There was a time when men felt that they belonged to the margins. Now, we know better: we know that the margins belong to us. When we report to ourselves what we have seen or when we write a report on what we have seen for others, we rely on the values at our disposal. We must recognize those values and draw upon them. For instance, if I feel that teaching chess to young people might help them to stay in school, I must say so—even if my editor gives me hell for not simply reporting the news. Frankly, I think there is no such thing as "news": "news" is people. And people are what I feel most deeply about. Don't ask me, therefore, to write that the schools are overburdened. Ask me to connect myself to the problem, to speak with feeling about what I feel most strongly about. Of course, Dean Joachim Maître might add, you also have to know your subject: you cannot interview a defense contractor the same way you would interview a movie star. And you can't dilute the news. If you try, you will end up with reporting that is neither news nor entertainment.

This is your fortieth birthday. Forty is middle-aged. I am fifty-five, so I speak from experience when I say that communication after forty is difficult. Speaking for myself at least, I know that one tends to repeat oneself. In the past, I would routinely spend three years on a novel. This last novel took me five and a half. And I constantly ask my wife, "Did I say this in a previous novel?" I am no longer sure. The issue, therefore, for myself and for all of us, is how to rejuvenate ourselves, how to respond to changing conditions and to situations that at times may seem insane. Are we going to be at the mercy of the old message, going by the old textbook that requires a school to teach and a hospital to cure—and nothing more? Or are we going to develop new texts, new forms, new methods of communication? As you face the challenges of the future, the challenges of the next forty years, I—speaking as one communicator to another—wish you nothing but the best.

THE ART OF STORYTELLING

In this undated interview (ca. 1977), Kosinski discussed the relationship between his own life experiences and the art of his storytelling.

INTERVIEWER: How important are specific life experiences and life choices to your writing?

JERZY KOSINSKI: I think immediately of one choice that confronted me and was very important to me in terms of my life. I grew up in a Communist state and was trained to become a deliverer of others. In fact, as a political scientist, I was trained not only as a deliverer but also as an interpreter of the destinies of others.

I refused that role. I refused it because I knew how I felt when I was being delivered by the deliverers of destiny during my childhood and adolescence in the Communist state. I would like to think that my destiny was given to me for me to deliver, or for nature to take care of, or for whatever spiritual contact there is in our destiny—but not for anyone around me to interfere with. I learned that lesson at the age of twelve, when I was given my first Youth Movement uniform, which I refused to wear.

INT: With all the professions that were available to you when you arrived in the United States, how did you choose?

112

JK: I could have worked as a photographer, as an anthropologist, as a statistician—all professions in which language was less important and which relied more on the specific knowledge that I had. But I chose to write. At first, I wrote two nonfiction books under a pen name precisely because I did not want to be called to elaborate beyond my books. Nonfiction was interfering enough, and I did not want to increase that interference by bringing my own voice.

The reason that I moved to fiction, however, was because fiction is a democratic form of conveyance of ideas. It identifies itself from the outset as fiction, not as fact. What it says to the reader is this: "It is up to you. Take it or leave it. Project yourself or not. Turn the page or not." It does not seduce you with false promises. It does not tell you that it will change your life. I repeat this: it promises you absolutely nothing beyond what you want to get from it. It's a very democratic universe.

My name on the front cover and my picture on the back cover is in no way an admission of private knowledge. As a novelist, I come with no greater authority than you: no degrees, no research, no statistics. And you ultimately are the judge of what I have to say. It is the business of imagination that you as a reader and I as a novelist share in the act of your reading the book.

I love the fact that, in a society as free as this one, I could function in an area in which my freedom is additionally increased by the form it takes—the form of a fiction. Take it or leave it. No credentials. This was what drew me to writing fiction, and this is what still draws me to it today. I would rather write fiction than anything else, precisely because I don't interfere, because I do not seduce, because I do not promise, because I do not preach.

INT: So your fiction is deliberately free of moral judgment?

JK: I think that situations in fiction come to us the way they come in life: you have to judge them. I am not my brother's keeper. I am not his confessor. I am not his superior, or hers. We are both in the realm of things which are to be seen, to be perceived, and to be judged. And my reader is just as morally equipped and just as free to judge as I am. Therefore there is no reason for me to interject. Judgment is implicit in perception, and his perception is just as good as mine.

The protagonist's ultimate wish in *Steps* is to break from the collectivity which has been cemented by a bureaucratic frame of mind and bureaucratic frames of reference. And at one point in *Blind Date*, Levanter refers to the French mind as being bureaucratic because the whole French school system is based on Cartesian logic, which torpedoes emotions, torpedoes spontaneity. It is an omnipresent system from which no one in France can escape since, of course, the school system is public and state run.

I identify with the protagonist of *Steps* in his longing for a hypothetical situation of a hypothetical freedom in which he would be unattached, unjudged, bothering no one and being bothered by no one, locked in and yet free.

INT: Do you ever get upset when you are writing your work?

JK: Oh, yes, I get very emotional. I not only get upset; I notice that when I write certain parts of my book, I get physically exhausted. I noticed, for instance, that I normally do not perspire, even when I am on a horse in Latin America. But when I write I get absolutely soaked.

You asked before how important specific life experiences are to the writer. I like to think that the role of real experience in fiction has changed. Some of our nineteenth-century counterparts were basically storytellers, and a good storyteller ultimately felt free to tell any kind of story he wanted to. He was not subjected to competition in storytelling. He was like some of the peasant storytellers or Gypsy storytellers I have encountered. Remember that the Eastern European societies are very strong on storytelling. A storyteller is an important ingredient of a community. He is a pivotal point of entertainment. He is both the man of wisdom and the man of imagination.

Because he was a wanderer, the Eastern European storyteller gained a certain experience. He knew what he was saying. His storytelling, however abstract, however imaginative it was, reflected that experience.

By contrast, television and other plot-oriented media insist on elementary storytelling, in which the plot takes over the character and eliminates the ambiguities of life. These media are adversarial to the novelist: they are the spiritual enemy of self-knowledge, of self-discipline, of prolonged attention span. Therefore, the novelist must know what is on television, what is in the cinema, what is in the theater. He must know his enemy. And to know his enemy, he must be there.

INT: Is popular culture the enemy of the storyteller?

JK: Popular culture comes to us not as a preacher, not as a philosopher—at least not implicitly. On the most obvious level, it comes as an entertainer, and storytelling is part of that entertainment. *Kojak, Charlie's Angels*—these are exercises in storytelling. I perform as a storyteller in a medium which is more difficult, which is more demanding, which requires certain pre-knowledge—how to read, how to focus on a page, how to buy or get a book. These are efforts which visual culture does not require. Television sets are in every bedroom. All you need to do is to switch from channel to channel. But to reinforce my own position as storyteller, I like to think that I have to know as much as I can about what is happening around me.

I have to gauge this revolution which takes place, this state of permanent turmoil which society is in from day to day. I have to be able to gauge it in terms of what is old and what is new, what is coming up and what is about to depart. And I have to be very disciplined about it. I cannot afford not to know. I have to read magazines and newspapers and other books, see movies, and travel across the country.

INT: You write only in English?

JK: Yes, but I see myself as a novelist not only in the original, not only in the English language. Since my books are also translated, I like to think about my other readers, who read in French or German or Dutch or Swedish. But my primary responsibility is to the country in which I write and to the language in which I write. So this, the United States, is my spiritual home. This is the home of my language. This is the home of my fiction. This is the home of my typewriter. And this is the home of the freedom that I have to write what I want to write. The countries in which I am translated, I might add, would not give me this kind of freedom. They don't even give it to their own novelists.

Most of the people I meet when I travel don't know what I do. Very often, I test them to get their reactions to certain situations, some of which I include in my fiction. And very often, I discard large portions of my manuscripts because I have tested them on people who did not find them imaginative enough. I simply cross those portions out. If they weren't engaging enough for others, why should they be for me?

INT: Energy levels? How do you feed yourself?

JK: I feed myself with people. Society in its immediate form is what interests me most: the functioning of a restaurant, people on a train, people at work, people in the hospital, people in an emergency, people making love, people confronted by surprise and by each other, people cheated, made use of, betrayed, people in power, people who are strong, people who are bureaucrats, people who ride horses, people who ski, people who play tennis, who golf.

INT: Do you categorize? Do you feel you have to?

JK: I do not categorize. Very often you have enormous expectations for someone, but they are not fulfilled. You don't get what you expected. Then suddenly you spend ten minutes with a stranger and get more than you could have imagined. I spent fifteen minutes the other day with a woman who stuttered. I learned from her because, between stutters, she was the most articulate woman I have ever met. Between stutters, she could not afford to be inarticulate. So I decided she was a good metaphor for a novelist. I am a spiritual stutterer and therefore I have to be very articulate in the moments between my stutters. My fiction lies in that moment. So it was a very useful encounter. It began when I said to myself, "Can I go through this stuttering?" And then I said if she can, who am I not to?

You asked earlier to what degree a novelist can or should be involved in society. As you know, I was brought up in a collective environment, in which the State made almost every decision for the individual. My response to a free society has been to choose my own involvements. For example, I am and have always been involved in certain organizations in the United States, particularly those that safeguard human rights. On the one hand, I guard my privacy, my freedom to do what I do in the way that I do it. On the other hand, I feel I have a responsibility to others, a responsibility to be engaged in the events around me.

INT: What organizations are you involved with?

JK: My functioning as a novelist is basically a solitary effort, self-employment at its most extreme. At the same time, however, I devote a certain part of my energy and a certain part of my knowledge to social efforts such as PEN, the international organization of writers, and the American Civil Liberties Union, which for me is one of the most important organizations in American life for everyone, not just those who are involved in the business of the First Amendment, so to speak, or who benefit from the First Amendment. I also support the International League for Human Rights, an organization which increases American awareness of political prisoners and the state of liberty in other countries. And, of course, my teaching—I have spent seven years at Wesleyan, Princeton, and Yale—also reflects my belief that I should, at any given moment of my life, give at least a part of myself to others, that I should function openly and publicly and not just withdraw to the privacy of a typewriter.

In the United States, I have allowed myself to become a bit of a public spokesman. My role, however, is different from that of a writer in a totalitarian system, who is forced to serve as a spokesman—although not always for his own causes or beliefs. Here, I have opted to become a spokesperson. That is a crucial distinction. I choose the organizations with which I want to involve myself. And when I speak, I speak as a member of the community, not as a writer or a novelist. The characters of my novels have nothing to do with my commitment to my own social causes. In fact, I keep my fiction quite separate from this public effort that I make.

On Censorship

To reply [to the Village Voice controversy] would only be to prolong the matter. I welcome conflict, it teaches me to be a better man. They are free to say what they want. The essential freedom is the freedom of expression. I would rather put up with nonsense than have a state-owned press.

Whenever I learn of yet another journalist imprisoned, novelist silenced, teacher suspended, I feel implicated by their fate. Here I am, once a dissident myself, free to write, to teach, to travel—and they—men and women of my profession— are not. Their plight spoils my freedom—I have to do something for them, something that would improve their condition—and restore my peace of mind. Thus, I do it as much for myself as for them.

THE WRITER'S FOCUS

In a 1976 interview with Lorrin P. Rosenbaum for the magazine *Index on Censorship*, Kosinski spoke about the responsibilities of the writer and the role of PEN, Amnesty International, and other human rights organizations.

LORRIN P. ROSENBAUM: In this century of calamities, largely man-made, we've had the artist as suicide, recluse, troubadour, statesman, and talk-show performer. Given the past horrors and the unprecedented capacity for evil today, how do you view the writer's role?

JERZY KOSINSKI: The calamities are not only man-made but, far more important, they affect men, women, and children. For me, the writer's role—at its most essential—is to focus on man's condition and to illuminate it. Part of today's dilemma is that, in modern society, man's ability to reflect upon his true condition had been devitalized. Divided between his compartmentalized existence and artificially stimulated need to "succeed" and to acquire consumer goods, he has lost his ability and even his desire to perceive himself as he really is and to learn his true desires and his true destiny. In fact, he ceases to be aware of how cruel and exploitative his life has become even to himself; fewer and fewer people rebel against the most obvious infringements on their rights and well-being. Paid for eight hours of work, they are often forced to contribute four additional hours in commuting; for excessive taxes they receive minimal services, living in constant dread of major illness, violent crime, or even temporary unemployment.

A novelist, more directly than any other type of artist, can tap the roots of consciousness and trigger a reawakened awareness of what an individual life should be. Ultimately, each man's sense of self has to determine whether life has been passed in existence or in living.

LPR: How did you manage to combine your two-term PEN presidency with your vocation as a writer?

JK: When I left Yale University to take up my work at PEN, I moved to a very central two-room midtown Manhattan apartment, which I turned into a "President's Office." Thus, I relieved PEN's permanent headquarters of the disruption caused by a constant flow of visitors: American and foreign writers, diplomats, government and foundation officials, literary agents, lawyers, educators, insurance brokers, as well as PEN officers. Furthermore, this arrangement precluded any need on my part to commute. As I have always paid all the presidential expenses and used my own telephones, copying machines, and other office equipment, as well as hired part-time typists, et cetera, the drain on PEN's finances has lessened, making money available for more urgent human needs among our own writers and those in difficulty abroad.

For over two years now I have lived in this semi-office apartment, my bed flanked by the Xerox machine, the typewriters, the television set, and a library of foundation materials—grants and scholarships, of course, are very important to writers. I divided my day into three shifts: writing from 6 to 10:30 a.m.; attending to the immediate PEN business until 5:00 p.m.; answering my presidential and private mail from 5:30 to 7:30 p.m.; then sleeping and exercising—if night walks in Manhattan constitute exercise— in the rest of the day. I had to forgo vacations for two summers and did not attend the PEN international congresses or executive meetings, preferring instead to send as delegates other members of the board who were more qualified to deal with international issues than I was.

LPR: In *Cockpit,* your new novel, your protagonist Tarden refers to Amnesty International and to other human rights organizations. Why?

JK: *Cockpit* is a novel set in what can be termed our everydayness, in the most common regions of our life, areas so familiar that we have lost our sense of the roles they play. That's why Amnesty International is mentioned in the novel—it is part of our everydayness. For decades, novelists have used other social institutions. Why not become contemporary? Surely there's more human significance in Amnesty International than in plots dealing with small-town love affairs, absconding executives, and the activities of hoodlums.

LPR: What interests me on this point is whether you consider working for human rights a particular obligation which ever detracts from your writing.

JK: I felt that working for PEN was a natural extension of my everydayness. Ever since I escaped from totalitarian Eastern Europe, I have considered myself very lucky: I live my life as I want to. I am not used by any organization or political party to oppress others, and I manage to fend off any attempts to curtail my freedom. I write what I want to write, and it is published as written. I am free to change publishers; no publisher is forced to publish me. My novels receive many good reviews. They also receive many bad reviews. Neither sort alters my life or my relations with others. In how many countries in the world today can a writer like myself say that? Yet there was a time when as a student in Eastern Europe I was exposed to the very forces that PEN opposes today: the police state.

I can say that as a past citizen of a totalitarian country, not only do I hate these oppressive forces, but I also know how they operate, at home and abroad. The least I can do for my new country—I settled in the States in 1957—is to place this knowledge at the service of my fellow writers. The forces of oppression are manifold and their proponents are always among us. The American self-employed creative person is vulnerable to them; few social institutions are devoted to his or her protection. In the era of credit cards, bank loans, group insurance, and multipage contracts, creative individuals are a relic of the frontier—solitary men and women pursuing strictly personal artistic goals which they hope will later win public acceptance.

It was very symptomatic that when I was engaged in a yearlong struggle to set up a group insurance program for PEN, most of the insurance agents representing giant corporations believed that writers became writers because they had failed at everything else. Most of them believed that writers owned the books they wrote and thus could give away at no cost unlimited copies to friends. The majority of Revenue Service officials with whom I dealt did not realize that writers themselves did not translate their books for foreign-language markets. None of these officials could define the role of a publishing house editor or a literary agent; none understood the economics of retailing or the levels of sales or authors' incomes. Societal ignorance like this provides a good climate for the seeds of oppression.

LPR: What kinds of work does PEN do on behalf of writers?

JK: In principle, we have been a nonpolitical organization. There's a good reason for this stance as most writers' enemies are political—on the left or on the right. This position allows us to fend off assaults wherever they come from, without prior commitment to any particular ideological weapon. We have chosen to evolve toward being a service organization to the writing profession at large. American PEN uses the cumulative power of our membership, comprised of accomplished writers and editors—men and women of various economic, social, and ethnic backgrounds—to act as a shock group or lobby, as a force within the community for the benefit of the whole writing profession, but never, I repeat never, restricted to members of PEN. In fact, most of our services, which include legal expertise, copyright issues, prisoners' rights, financial help, translation and fiction programs and prizes, foreign exchange programs, testimony to the Congress, exhibitions, and dozens of others, have been extended to those who are not currently, and who may never be, members of PEN.

Take, for example, our PEN Prisoner Program in this country. It consists of four components: (1) an informal, four-month correspondence program between a prisoner and a writer, through which the writer provides the prisoner with a critique of his writing twice a month; (2) an exchange of letters between prisoners and writers; (3) general advice and referral to prisoners about possible publication of their work; (4) the PEN Writing Award for prisoners, expanded this year to include all prisoners in the United States. The response was excellent. PEN received over fifteen hundred entries. PEN will publish the winning entries in its quarterly, *The American Pen*, and will make all feasible efforts to attain publication elsewhere both for the prizewinners and the entries which received honorable mention.

Anyone who identifies himself as a bona fide writer is entitled to PEN's assistance, at home or abroad. PEN does not seek to confer privileges through membership, but to make available experience to those who can benefit from it. In this sense, it is not at all an elitist organization. And its president, other officers, and members of the board have always made certain that when they speak for the organization, they reflect its collective will rather than any idiosyncratic or private view. Depending, as PEN does, on donations from society in general and from interested organizations, all of us have this collective interest in mind when we speak for PEN. It is this very open, truly democratic aspect of American PEN that made the idea of service as a PEN officer attractive to me: I could no more infringe on PEN's identity than it could on mine. And I, like many other writers, have only one property to develop: my identity, my personal vision.

LPR: How does PEN help imprisoned writers? Could you discuss a few cases?

JK: Because of the international character of PEN, we learn rather quickly of arrests, detention, confinement, and other forms of harassment that the State can visit against the writer. When opposing these acts and working to bring relief to the victims, American PEN must act with prudence and not endanger its members in that nation. We employ a variety of means, among them financial help for a writer's family; retention of lawyers; sending observers to the trial; petitioning high officials concerned with the case; mobilizing prominent intellectual, sports, business, religious, and political figures on behalf of the prisoner or his family;

pressuring the American government as well as foreign diplomats and businessmen on the issue; and often involving international and local business communities.

The success of such intervention lies not only in our experience in dealing with such threats, but primarily in our strength in the community at home. Few events, however distant, are entirely removed from the United States. This country offers interested parties access to almost every significant event. It is the combination of the two—Washington, D.C., and New York as the poles of influence and PEN's place in the American and international community—that in most cases accounts for the success of our endeavors.

In recent years, when governments have become increasingly immune to mass opinion and able to outlast its manifestations, and when the public develops an even shorter attention span, we have more and more often employed a policy of individual intervention, syncopated by occasional editorials, letters to the editor, letter-writing campaigns, or TV programs. PEN designates individuals of renown to establish contacts with the diplomatic corps or in the business community to pursue solutions through intensive and persistent yet flexible negotiations on a narrow front. The principal ingredient of such intervention is face-saving reciprocity: the release of an imprisoned writer or the improvement of his conditions might lead to the opening of favorable commercial or other contacts. Conversely, the refusal to help would lead to the curtailment of such contacts and a certain ostracism in this country and abroad.

To give an idea of the results of PEN's efforts is this excerpt from a letter by an American writer imprisoned for many years abroad. PEN finally secured his release and now he is back home.

> The past five years have taught me some bitter lessons and there are more to come. But perhaps your swift and generous response to my emergency is a sign that my luck is changing. Would you be kind enough to thank Jerzy Kosinski and the Committee for their understanding? That is what is so astonishing to me: that there are still people who can show concern for another's problems,

particularly when these problems are largely self-inflicted. Why should they care? Could it be that as professionals, as artists, they remember the awful holes that we all manage to dig ourselves under at one time or another? Or is it something merely human—something that I still cannot allow myself to believe? I don't dare to believe in something as complex as goodness; that would be a lesson I wouldn't be able to survive.

I wrote to you as I wrote to others, expecting nothing. No fund or foundation has ever answered a letter of mine. And suddenly my mailbox is full of help and expressions of interest, warm and sincere wishes . . . the debts are suddenly paid, funds for a return to the United States are beginning to arrive . . . there is even a promise of rent-free quarters in New York . . . At this moment all this is a bit too much to cope with. It undermines the world as I've learned to know it. I keep looking for the hook, the hidden blade, the angle, and I can't see it anywhere. I hope you can understand my bewilderment.

Once again, thank you.

LPR: What are your own future plans?

JK: I hope to devote more time to writing. I will continue, however, to work with the organization as one of PEN's four vice presidents.

LPR: Judging from history, what is, in your view, the life expectancy of a regime that systematically destroys the artists of its country?

JK: The best measure of the repressiveness of a system is what it does to men and women who choose to speak for the condition of men rather than for political programs endorsed by authorities. What concerns me most is not the life expectancy of such systems but the life expectancy of artists struggling to work within them. In many oppressive countries, the artist's estrangement from society is reinforced by the society's drive toward material acquisitions. The products of poet, novelist, playwright, and journalist tend to give way to the products of the consumer society—the refrigerator, the motorcycle, the automobile, the television, and other gadgets. The government's hostility to the creative person is often reinforced by the indifference of the country's middle class.

LPR: What of the future?

JK: The trends are obvious to me. Further departure from the self, hence less ability to cope with the daily pressures, more giving in to society's institutions, and passive acceptance of what the great commercial, union, and political organizations provide. As a result, there will be fewer and fewer outlets for creative expression. It is not the voice of the poet that we will hear but the march of the armed column.

DEFENDING CHANCE

In 1988, the parents of a high school student in Crete, Nebraska, sought to have Kosinski's third novel, *Being There* (1971), banned from the curricular reading list and removed from the school library; several hundred parents eventually joined the effort to ban the book. On November 3, 1989, Kosinski accepted an invitation by the American Civil Liberties Union to respond to the criticism of his novel. (The following day, Kosinski addressed a town hall meeting of parents in Crete, where he reiterated many of the same points expressed at the ACLU dinner.)

I kept thinking what is it I want to tell you—not so much what will set the tone for the evening but what will reflect what I am really feeling at this very moment. And it occurred to me that since I have no children—an important issue in view of the children and parents I will be confronting tomorrow [at the town hall meeting]—if I were to name a group of people who think in a fashion that I would find close to my own, it would clearly be you.

I am a writer. I write primarily fiction because that is what I like to do and that is what I want to do. A writer of fiction depends on the freedom of expression to a far greater degree than anyone else does; therefore, he or she can easily be censored because both the freedom itself and the use of that freedom are so great. Fiction is above all a free flow of imagination which takes many directions, but every direction it takes demands a free expression of the imagination.

The irony of the situation is that, at the same time, fiction is not a mainstream of anything. Fiction, in fact, can very simply be gotten rid of. With nonfiction, you can always make the point that at least it teaches something, or feasibly that it can. With fiction, you can be very brutal. You can say, "Look, it is not even reality. What practical value does it have?"

At one point in my career, I promised myself that I would not speak in public, that I would be just a writer of fiction, which has its own voice. I would speak only through my characters, saying things that I would never dare to utter in public. As a writer of fiction, I can blur the distinction between my characters and myself. Through my fiction, I can invent as many selves as I want. I can make passes at people I have never met and they will never know. Believe me: it is a freedom like no other.

To a writer of fiction, the American Civil Liberties Union is a spiritual home. At the very beginning of the American chapter of my life, I was privileged to meet Roger Baldwin. After I came to the United States in December of 1957, I lived for a short time at the International House in New York, where I was one of the few arrivals from Poland. When Roger Baldwin arrived at the International House, I did not know anything about him, but we quickly began a friendship that lasted until his final days. In fact, it was Roger Baldwin who initially introduced me to the ACLU, which he founded. And then, thanks to him, I became active in the International League for Human Rights, which he directed. These connections are clearly very, very important to me; otherwise, I would not be here. After all, that is another freedom that a writer of fiction has. He does not have to travel: he can be where he chooses because he can write anywhere that he wants.

Being There is a novel, and it is a novel par excellence. I cannot think of anything more novelistic, in fact, than *Being There*. It is a novel par excellence because it has one thing which distinguishes it from a great number of other novels. I can say that because, at my age, one can praise oneself quite easily. It has probably—no, not probably, but *definitely*—the most innocent character in modern letters. He is so innocent that he has no drive of any kind. Not that he does not drive; he is not driven, and not to be driven in

America is a rare characteristic. If he has an appeal, it is an appeal he is not aware of. He is not self-conscious, and therefore he is doubly free. He is as free as one ideally should be, ought to be, could be, but nobody actually is. The temptation to create such a character was an obvious one. It was my private temptation—to be so free that I could be entirely myself, that I could say exactly what was on my mind, and to let others then make of it what they wanted. Little did I know what was going to happen as a result.

Being There followed two books, two novels of mine which were anything but innocent. *The Painted Bird* was about the Second World War, childhood, the state of war, a state of threat, the absence of innocence; *Steps* was about a man divided between different cultures and different languages, a complex man, not an innocent. *Being There* came as a reflection that if I were able to create a character in *Steps* so soaked in collective guilt, in collective crime, in collective apprehension, then I should be able to create a Chauncey Gardiner. Chauncey Gardiner is a creature of a natural dimension; he grows up in a garden protected by someone who is his benefactor. He exists in a condition of total security, with access to a world created only by television. If we think about it, to be able to live in a natural garden protected from the outside world and having access to that world only through the filters of television is not so bad, since television is neither art nor reality. Because television is very creative, you can make anything of it that you want. Since it is edited, television is clearly made to order. But it is not a natural order. So Chauncey Gardiner is a perfect creature of two dimensions, a natural garden and the unnatural world that comes to it filtered.

But when his time in the garden ends, when he is suddenly expelled, he has to come out into the world. When he tries to confront the reality which he would like to alter, the way one alters the channels of television, he cannot. What upset some of the parents in Crete is that in one particular chapter of the book, chapter five, Chauncey Gardiner encounters a man at a reception—encounters a situation in which he himself is totally innocent. He does not know what is happening in front of him, except that he has seen it before on television. The man introduces himself and sits down next to Chance, who is totally unaware. The man is older than Chance and looks like the men Chance often saw on TV. That is all. The rest is an act described in very objective terms.

I learned a great deal about television thanks to Johnny Carson, who invited me to his *Tonight Show* several times in the late 1960s. At that point, I had already appeared once on David Frost's show, which was then an extremely popular program. Frost was my first live encounter with television, and the reason I was invited is that I lived a couple of blocks from the studio where the show was recorded. My second novel, *Steps* [1968], had just been published, and when one of the guests did not show up as scheduled, the staff who knew me and knew I lived nearby called and asked if I would fill in. David Frost was very tired from his weekly commutes between London and New York. This was before the Concorde, so the trip was even more fatiguing. He was also dating people in both cities. That particular night, Frost was so tired that no matter what I said, he leaned forward and said, "Fascinating." I did not realize that he was exhausted, so I got braver and braver. Apparently he said "fascinating" more times that night than at any other time in his career, certainly more than at any time in mine.

Afterward, I was invited to the *Tonight Show*. Although that was a very important moment in my life, I was unaware of what would happen to me as a result of my appearances on the program. Occasionally, even now, twelve or fourteen years later, when I take a taxi, the driver turns around and says, "I saw you on Johnny Carson." Therefore it was appropriate that the innocent character I created would lose his innocence—although he does not know that he is losing it—by appearing on television, specifically on a program that in *Being There* I called *This Evening Show*.

Nebraska is listed in most of my dictionaries right next to the word "nebula," an appropriate association. Recently *Being There* was nominated for the Nebula Award, a highly coveted science fiction prize. This brought to mind the fact that, had this book been published as science fiction rather than as popular fiction—in fact, had all my novels, with all the sexual ambiguities, been published as science fiction—it might never have been banned. Adding the word "science" to fiction apparently makes quite a difference in terms of its reception.

Soon after *Being There* was released, my publisher called and said, "Jerzy, have you addressed any medical conventions?" I replied I had not and wondered why he asked. "Because suddenly a large number of orders for *Being There* are coming in from doctors and hospitals. Do you know why?" I soon learned that the *Journal of the American Medical Association*, in its March 19, 1973, issue, included an editorial entitled "Insane, Sane," which described a new condition that *JAMA* had observed in the United States. According to the editorial, there are certain aspects of average American life that can no longer be clearly defined as "sane" or "insane" and that a new category—"unsane"—should be created. "The line of demarcation between mental health and mental illness," *JAMA* suggested, is "defined by environmental circumstances." And on that point, as a supplement to scientific study, the journal referred readers to *Being There*. There you have it.

But that's just the beginning of my sermon. To a writer of fiction, there are no better works than the Bible and the Koran. These extraordinary narratives are also the most open-ended. They invite one to revise one's life and modify it; they invite one to another life if one chooses to believe in it. And sermons derived from such works are essential. "Being There in the Image of God" was one such sermon delivered by an extremely serious Protestant scholar in New York who used *Being There* as a vehicle for that very theme. Chauncey Gardiner, he proposed, is so pure at heart that he could in fact be considered a biblical prototype. And *America*, published by the Jesuits of the United States and Canada, once devoted an entire issue to my fiction. The issue focused on "The Moral Universe of Jerzy Kosinski." Imagine that! For once, someone wrote about my universe as moral rather than immoral or amoral! And he said, "It is quite legitimate to see Kosinski as a spokesman for a human capacity to survive." I liked that. "To survive in a highly complex, ambivalent and structurally brutalized social system." No doubt about it. "The relationship of the individual to the larger complex is explored, in different ways and from different perspectives, in all of Kosinski's fiction."

This brings me to an essential point: is there anything in my novel that eleventh-grade high school students in Crete haven't already learned from television? Significantly, that medium—unlike my novel—makes no provision for discussion and no provision for contextual analysis.

Before coming here, I took a look not only at what eleventh graders read in the magazines devoted to them but also at the materials that even fifth or sixth graders can buy at any newsstand. There are dozens and dozens of serious publications for young people their ages. So I began to wonder: do the parents even know what their children are reading? As I have said before, I have no children of my own, but I do have several godchildren and I have a great number of friends with children. I love children. I love them because they are ideal fiction readers. You say to a kid, "you are a parcel and I am going to mail you," and instantly they become a parcel. You wrap the parcel, you stamp it, and you send it by airmail; you throw it around. And the kid loves it. Children have an amazing ability to transform themselves, to imagine other worlds. I know many young people in their teens and even their early twenties who approach me and say, "Jerzy, you mailed me as a parcel when I was a three-year-old." That is the extraordinary thing about them. And that is the extraordinary thing about the classroom, the only place that I can think of—and a teacher is the only figure that I can think of—that can make a teenager use his imagination. The ability to imagine, to figure out things that might or might not take place, is precisely the ability that children need to go through the drama that is simply called life. When someone points a finger at you and says, "I don't like you, I want you out of here," you have to summon up that imaginative experience. You have to call upon *Macbeth*; you have to call upon all kinds of fiction that will allow you to be calm, to be cool, and to say, "What he thinks is not going to change my life. I am not going to kill myself over it." Because teenagers do kill themselves.

Now, let's go back to these teen magazines that I mentioned earlier. "Got a problem? Ask Alyssa"—that is, Alyssa Milano, star of the television show *Who's the Boss?*, who is thrilled by all the letters sent to her by *Teen Machine* readers. "Dear Alyssa, How are you? I am twelve years old and I am going with a fifteen-year-old guy. The past couple of weeks have been great but there is one problem. When we see each other, he just wants to hold my hand because he thinks I am too young. I don't know what to do because

I have to know if he really likes me, or is he just going with me because he doesn't want to break my heart? Please help, Nicole, Indiana." Alyssa replies: "Dear Nicole, If he didn't want to be with you, he wouldn't, but be thankful that the boy respects you. Enjoy the time you spend together. You don't want to rush through life. From Alyssa, with love."

"Dear Alyssa, I am having trouble with boys and fashion. I can't seem to get boys to like me except for the geek. How can I get boys to like me? I am twelve years old, and I'm in the sixth grade. I like this one kid, but he won't fall for me. I wear spandex pants to show off my figure, and I let him know that I am making my own money. Nothing seems to work. What should I do? Wendy, Pennsylvania." Alyssa replies: "Dear Wendy, Most boys in your age group really aren't interested in girls. Next year you will see that it will be a lot easier to meet boys." Next year Wendy is going to be thirteen.

In another magazine, teens write to advice columnists Davis and Crispy, and they write back. In fact, I intend to contact them myself with some of my own questions. They are ready for me, but I am not sure I am ready for them. "Dear Davis and Crispy, I am ten years old. Some of my friends at school are ignoring me. When people say I am fat, they just laugh. When I go to play with them, they either run away or tell me I can't play with them. What should I do? Angela B., Georgia." Davis and Crispy respond: "Dear Angela, These friends aren't your real friends. Make new ones." Do you know how tough it is to make new friends when you are ten years old? You are surrounded by a given number of people. You cannot just go to another neighborhood and pick up a new group of friends. What I am saying is that we—here I take the side of the parents, of course, since I am concerned about my hypothetical kids—want to keep them pure. But what does that really mean? In my view, to keep a kid pure is to prepare him to confront the impurities of life. Otherwise, he will not know what pure really is. By contemporary plane travel, Crete is only a two- or three-hour flight to almost any other part of the country—parts of this country that you know probably as well as I do, places that I would be terrified to send my kids. But one day they might go there on their own and be unprepared: unprepared emotionally, unprepared mentally, unprepared in terms of their fantasy. What I would be most afraid of, however, is who they might run into when they reach their destination. Not me; it is too late for that. Not a character from *Being There*. No, my fear is that they will run into the men and women whom I portray in my other novels, people who are creatively evil.

Evil has an enormous attraction. It is not something that you can easily disregard. Evil is very colorful. Nice and quiet, dances well, makes money, and behaves beautifully—probably one of the best behaved creatures on earth. That is why you cannot readily tell who is evil and who is not unless you analyze the hypothetical aspects of that evil in the classroom. There is no other place in America where you can do that. You won't do it in Las Vegas; there is no bar in New York or Chicago where someone can sit down with you and in forty-five minutes analyze the evil characteristics of the seemingly nicest man and woman on earth. The teacher, therefore, is the closest thing, the closest person, the closest agent to the parents. And the more the teacher recommends the most dreadful fiction, the most horrifying stuff, the better a teacher he or she is. But how are we going to convince parents of that?

Practically speaking, perhaps those of us who invest in imagination spend too much time on litigation. Litigation does not really accomplish that much: it mobilizes the very one against whom one litigates. In many ways, litigation creates a sort of endless battle. Maybe we should use our energies to develop a different kind of a model, in which free expression becomes the process that we cherish most, knowing very well that without such expression we will lapse into some morally ambivalent state. Instead of going to court, maybe we could sit down with the parents and ponder some of these matters. Read to the parents some of the things that they may not know. Kids watch television. Even if they watch only two hours a day, their television viewing totals seven hundred and fifty hours a year—and there is probably little that they have not already seen.

I think this approach may be much tougher to convey to Nebraskans since the state of Nebraska itself insinuates emptiness—a lot of living space, people uncrowded by others. But the issue that brings us together here—the printing of lists of books that are banned or are about to be challenged—is a troubling one. I don't think going to court is the way to resolve it anymore. A better alternative would be to go after those who challenge the books and talk to them, have a conversation—even though I was reminded recently that conversation is something one *watches* in America, meaning on the TV talk shows—perhaps try to bring about a different kind of community relationship, a relationship between concerned parents, who have a right to be concerned, and a medium which they may not fully understand. Is *Being There* really a book that parents should worry about? I doubt it. Why then is such an innocent book being challenged or singled out? Maybe what really alarms some of the parents is not *Being There* but the other media that influence young people today.

That is something to ponder: that we might in fact be spending our energies the wrong way—on an individual book rather than the free play of imagination. Here again, the classroom becomes the place where young people can develop the notion of what I call "life's spare tire." The spare tire is necessary when one of the original tires on a car blows up. And, just as flat tires happen to cars, terrible things happen to children, who find themselves broken and who need to know how to cope. Don't kid yourself about the letters to the editors of teen magazines. This is a code language, where the ten-year-old who says "I am wearing spandex" does not mean the harmless things you think she means; she means something far more dangerous, something you and I see every night on television's prime time. It is a very mature world—mature in the sense of what children have seen, not mature in terms of what they understand. Children need motivation. Children need the ability to become themselves in spite of seduction, the ability to say "I do not need spandex pants to be myself," the ability to say "I do not have to write that letter to the editor. I can write my own and answer it by myself, because I am an entity that can take care of my spiritual self the way my parents take care of their family. I can pick up my inner spiritual broker. I know how to represent myself. I learned it in school."

There is no need to praise a generation. Nevertheless, I will praise my generation, which went through life against staggering odds. We were facing a totalitarian system, and a great number of us were very individualistic, idiosyncratic, peculiar, perverse, obsessive. After surviving the Second World War we had a right to be. But the system kept saying, "You have no right to be different from what we allow you to be."

We survived because of those things that made us strong—things like the books we read. Speaking for myself, I survived by imagining myself as a character from Stendhal. At one point in Stendhal's *The Red and the Black*, Julien Sorel realizes that things are neither red nor black but somewhere in between. I too am somewhere in between the extremes; nobody can define me. And whenever I was confronted by totalitarian circumstances, I would fall back on Sorel, the character from Stendhal's novel. I would look at the face of my accuser, and I would say, "You think that you can break me? You think that you can threaten me? How little you really know. You do not know what I have read. You do not know how reinforced I am inside. Do you think I tremble? My hand does; I do not. You believe that you are in a position of power. But you are the weak one, and I am the strong, because I can imagine far more than you in this very moment. I know exactly what you can do to me because I read about it, and I have already defended against it in my head. Hence I do not care." This was the attitude against which even the strongest agents of a totalitarian system could not defend. This is what I speak for. Basically, this is what life is all about: a state of drama in which one defines oneself according to the dramatic circumstances, regardless of whether one does it in front of the podium and a group of people who are willing to listen or in front of the hostile crowd who scream, "Down with you, buddy!" It should not make any difference. The values that I cherish I carry within me. They were acquired in a classroom, no doubt about it. They do not come from parents; parents themselves, by virtue of their professional guardianship, are not always convincing. We know that, had I listened to my parents, I would have been far wiser than I am today. But while I did not always listen to their voices, I did listen to the voice of fiction.

If you read a nonfiction book today, two years from now that nonfiction may no longer be valid. Fiction, however, is different. It is the free play of the imagination, the First Amendment personified, free expression at its fullest and freest. That is the test. Suppress fiction and what have you got? Merely a how-to book.

NEW YORK FILM CRITICS AWARD

At the New York Film Critics Awards ceremony on January 31, 1982, less than two months after the imposition of martial law in Poland, Kosinski paid tribute to two of Poland's most prominent directors and pondered the implications of censorship for their work.

There is something tragically ironic in the fact that we are here tonight celebrating, among others, *Reds*, a film about John Reed, a socially conscious American artist and revolutionary who went to Russia to secure freedom and freedom of expression for the workers of the world, while in Poland, one of the largest countries of the Soviet bloc, the remnants of that freedom are being brutally suppressed by the Stalinist-fascist military junta sponsored by the Kremlin, in the walls of which John Reed is buried. Filmmakers Andrzej Wajda and Krzysztof Zanussi are no less socially conscious today in their work than John Reed was in his. Yet they have suddenly found themselves without a creative base.

Unlike a novelist or a poet who, when suppressed by the government, can still work for himself—and for posterity—a filmmaker like Wajda or Zanussi in his work is entirely at the mercy of the political system which owns everything he needs for his craft. Prevented from creating, he is banned for as long as the State chooses. If, like Wajda or Zanussi, he has committed himself during the brief period of Solidarity to the ideas contrary to those of the Kremlin and has expressed them on paper or on film, his situation is indeed hopeless.

That is why paying tribute to Wajda and Zanussi tonight is not only a matter of profound moral importance but also of practicality. It tells them that you are standing by them, and it tells the government which oppresses them that you will do your best here in America to rally the forces in their defense and in defense of others like them.

CENTURIONS AND

FREE EXPRESSION

In his remarks to the Century Association in New York City on October 1, 1990, Kosinski reflected on his debt to fellow Centurion Thornton Wilder and fellow novelist James Fenimore Cooper and on the importance of free expression, and he related an interesting and instructive anecdote about the photographs he had recently exhibited at the club.

I once read that a speaker should mistrust the microphone, since it will either connect him to his audience or separate him from it. But let me start with this notion: if, as a writer, I cannot be truly intimate and truly myself here at the Century Association, where else can I be?

There are a few things that make this place like no other. It is a place where you can exchange any kind of idea, no matter how outlandish—meaning from another land—or just plain outlandish. Imagine a place in the midst of Manhattan, the address of which is over a hundred years old, at a time when almost every five or six years there is a newly built skyscraper overshadowing your apartment window. Imagine a place which grew up to be precisely what it is today, a place for this kind of talk in which one can say anything to anyone else and in which one can be totally oneself.

There is a custom here which I tried to follow but could not. The custom is that, when a fellow of the Century Association arrives, he tries to secure a drinking cup marked with the name, the date of birth, and the date of death of another Century member. I requested Thornton Wilder's cup, but the captain told me that it was no longer available. Thornton Wilder is a figure who played an important part in my life—not my whole life, but a part of my life. In fact, my latest novel, *The Hermit of 69th Street*, which took more than five and a half years to write, was written almost entirely because of Wilder. I will not tell you why, but I will give you a few hints. And if you are truly interested, you can find any good biography of Wilder and figure it out for yourself. But, of course, before then you will have to know a tiny bit more about me.

In the current *American Scholar* [Autumn 1990], there is a beautiful article written by Paul Horgan. The article is entitled "Captain Wilder, T.N."—"T.N.," of course, being Thornton Wilder's initials. Wilder was a member here at the Century Association from January 1930 until his death in 1975. But since I don't have a cup with which to drink to him, I will instead dedicate these remarks to Wilder.

A few more things about the Century Association. In 1847, when the club was founded, Emily Brontë had just published *Wuthering Heights*; Charlotte Brontë had just published *Jane Eyre*; and William Hickling Prescott had just published *History of the Conquest of Peru*, a book that gave Thornton Wilder the idea for *The Bridge of San Luis Rey*, which was printed in 1927 and was one of the novels I read when I was growing up in Poland. Thomas Edison was born in that same year, 1847. Imagine the social changes that have taken place since then. Ours is an age of television, cinema, and the fax machine. Yet there are things that are the same now as they were then—most importantly, perhaps, the search for the meaning of life itself. The meaning of life, after all, is not defined by what one sees; nor is it defined by what one drives. It is defined by what one thinks about oneself.

I am eminently at home here at the Century Association. I live in the twentieth century, on Fifty-seventh Street and Sixth Avenue, only ten or fifteen blocks from here. But when I come here, I am thrust into a place that is absolutely timeless. And I am pleased to think that it will remain that way well into the future, long after all of us become dusty portraits hanging on the walls—portraits whose sale, I hope, might settle the debt to this institution.

Historically, when we Centurions moved into this building almost a century ago, in 1891, Gustav Mahler wrote his Symphony Number One. And at the same time, an American named W. S. Justin invented a form of the zither, which proved to be a difficult instrument to master. In fact, it did not come into practical use until almost three decades later.

Had I been invited to address the members of the Century Association a century ago, my talk would not have been much different than it is tonight. That's a very encouraging notion—and when it comes to notions, they don't have to wait, like zithers, to gain popular acceptance. They are instant. They are immediate. They depend on four thousand years of the development of an even more extraordinary instrument—creative expression—which this institution, I like to think, embodies better than any other in mid-Manhattan. This institution, where you can be as free as your creative expression allows you to be. Thomas Jefferson would know what I am talking about. Jefferson, who was a friend of Poland and who— some believe—would have felt quite at home at the Century Association, was a man who dared to do most extraordinary things because he imagined all men to be equal.

Intellectuals like Jefferson were influenced by the climate around them. And today part of the intellectual climate is influenced by the First Amendment. Yet intellectuals today have almost no influence over the First Amendment. Consequently, the First Amendment allows almost any kind of myth to become a reality.

At times, the intellectual climate can be private and intimate, as private and intimate as this evening is and has been. But at the same time there is no way we can keep it outside of the outside world. This microphone is hooked up to the electronic village. Anything that is said here this evening by you or by me belongs to the world at large, even if there is no actual television or screen in the room as I speak.

An American novelist once wrote that a great novelist—or, for that matter, a novelist of any kind—is to society what a heretic is to a tribe: he

143

introduces notions that people may not want to hear. Yet a novelist's fiction is an extraordinary instrument in other ways too. Because it must be formed within, because by itself it contains no images except those created or re-created in the mind, fiction is an instrument that can be envisaged even by the blind. Unlike film, television, or photography—all of which impose their imagery upon the viewer and demand that he take it or leave it, but only after actually seeing it—fiction evokes the innermost images. A blind person reading Kosinski in Braille, therefore, emerges as an ideal reader of fiction.

One of my great literary heroes is James Fenimore Cooper, whom Goethe considered the most talented writer who ever lived. At one time, Fenimore Cooper was also perhaps the most popular novelist in the world. He was popular in a fashion that we can hardly imagine today. He was popular solely because of his books, not because controversial photographs of him appeared in magazines. In Germany alone, there were ninety-nine editions of Fenimore Cooper's works. He was simply the most original writer who ever lived, an extraordinary storyteller like no other.

Many people immigrated to the United States because they were inspired not by the Bill of Rights but by James Fenimore Cooper's *The Pioneers*. The novel said to them that they too could be pioneers. In their own country, they were poor and no one paid attention to them. But Fenimore Cooper assured them that they could come to America and succeed. A pioneer, after all, is a mind; a pioneer is a man or a woman who says, "Look, I've got the gift of life. I must never forget where the gift comes from or that the gift can be taken away at any time. This is a country where I can explode. I can become a pioneer—of the Self, the self with a capital *S*, of what I think, not of what you think or what they think. There is no inquisition; no one can arrest me for my thoughts. I can protest—this is after all, a Protestant country." And pioneers do protest, just as the original pioneers protested the conditions in the countries from which they came. Fenimore Cooper told them to cross the ocean, to cross from the old self that means nothing to the new Self that can become anything one wants it to be. Even those who felt themselves to be insignificant could become the grandest of the grandees in a grand country, a country which is truly democratic.

Parenthetically, Morse, the inventor of the Morse telegraph, without which there would be no modern fax, gave Fenimore Cooper the authority to plug his invention. Morse observed that although the Indians had sounds by which they communicated, the forts that Fenimore Cooper described in his novels did not. So, after traveling with Fenimore Cooper, Morse invented the Morse signal through which one fort could alert another and prepare defenses against those who did not like pioneers.

For me, Fenimore Cooper was an authority like no other. To this day, in fact, in Eastern Europe he remains the second most popular writer— second only to Mark Twain. That is because Poles, thirty-eight million quite homogenous people, see themselves as pioneers. They are pioneering free enterprise, independent of Europe. Yet Fenimore Cooper, then the most popular novelist of his era, realized that there was a price to be paid for being an innovator and a pioneer. "Nobody is puissant in this country," he said. "A new name replaces the name of an old one so rapidly that one scarcely learns to distinguish who are the favorites before a successor is pointed out."

A few years later, in 1851, Fenimore Cooper died. He died, in part, because of the First Amendment, because he took the negative things written about him very seriously and very personally. And he made one terrible error which no Centurion today would make. He sued the press for libel.

By pressing his suit he made a great error in judgment. He felt so self-righteous, so pure, so pioneering, that he said to the press, "How dare you identify me with my characters? I am a writer. Effingham [a character in his fiction] is not me." The press retorted yes, it is. But Fenimore Cooper said it is not, and he sued them for that. He won in every court in the nation. And yet he lost because, as we know, expression has to be free: anyone should be able to make of it anything that he or she wants to make of it. Fenimore Cooper—a man as brilliant and as visionary as Thornton Wilder—was not pioneering enough to realize that. I mention Wilder for a good reason—not just because Wilder was a very distinguished Centurion but because when the same thing happened to Wilder, he knew better. Wilder said nothing. Centurions don't make waves. At least they never used to.

In at least three of my nine novels, I included characters who are transsexuals. Now, transsexuals are not readily found at the Century

Association—not yet, anyway. The association's guidelines state that "Because of the private nature of the Association but without interfering with legitimate scholarly or other interests, members shall unless granted permission by the Board of Management (1) refrain from using the name or address of the Association in any communication intended to be circulated among nonmembers of the Association or published or printed or released to any medium of public communication; (2) shall take all reasonable precautions to prevent public mention of discussions or activities of any characters including private parties that are held in the clubhouse and avoid assisting journalists who might do so; and (3) assume responsibility for the exclusion from the clubhouse of reporters and news photographers on assignment."

I have used transsexual characters in my novels—transsexuals, as opposed to transvestites. There is a crucial difference. A transvestite is a man who dresses the way his wife does. A transsexual is someone who makes a much more essential commitment, who—through surgery and the injection of hormones—tries to become a member of the opposite sex. Transsexuality is a condition that exists legally even though sex itself has never been defined in any court. Transsexuals are a part of our life. A great number of hospitals perform surgery for transsexuals, whose position in society is secure—secured not by me but by history. Like hermaphroditism, which Flavius Josephus documented as far back as his *Jewish War*—since hermaphrodites were active in the army—transsexuality is a very old tradition.

Thus I felt that it was perfectly fine to make use of transsexuals in another way—as the subject of my photographs. In addition to writing I am also a photographer; that is my hobby. And photography is a graphic art that is endorsed by the Century Association, which sponsors annual exhibitions of its members' photographs.

The association at that time was still open only to gentlemen. Women were not allowed to join. Being a faithful member, I tried to be as consistent and as kind as I could be to the rules of the house. So I decided that transsexuals, who are biologically men but physically women, would—by their presence—violate the association's traditions less than the presence

146

of real women would. I was not trying to make a demographic point. Nor was I trying to upset the all-male tradition, which I in fact like and have no opposition to. So I simply selected three transsexuals—not transvestites— to photograph as nudes and titled them "Wo Man 1," "Wo Man 2," and "Wo Man 3." The titles suggested my own hesitation: my typewriter, in fact, paused after "wo" and "man," as if to reinforce the fact that these feminine shapes were not those of biological women but of men who had become women.

When the pictures were mounted at the Century Association, I made no comment about them. Afterward, I came to the club and sat at a communal table in the main dining room. One of the nicest Centurions— someone who had once reviewed a book of mine—said to me, "Jerzy, we liked these women whose photographs you exhibited. Where are they from?" Quite truthfully, I said, "What women?" And the Centurion said, "Woman 1, Woman 2, Woman 3—these extraordinarily feminine members of the opposite sex that you photographed." There were a number of other members present at the table, so clearly I had to be truthful since lying would be against the rules. I repeated, "What women? There were no women." "You know, the pictures. The huge portraits of the three women at the exhibition." I said, "Actually, they are not women. They are men." There was a long pause at the table, and everyone said, "What do you mean they are men? They have all the attributes of women." I said, "Yes, attributes." But sex is decided above the belt, not below. In this particular case, the original gender of the subjects was masculine. In fact, had they deserved admission, any one of them could have become a member of the Century Association.

The story quickly leaked out: Kosinski's trio of lovely ladies weren't ladies at all; they were transsexuals. The members were shocked. But I was philosophical: the subjects of the photographs were perfectly beautiful and feminine. And, since even the law had never really defined sexuality, how could I?

Not surprisingly, especially since the Century Association is located so near Time Warner, the largest communications company in the world, the story made its way to a number of newspapers. In the heart of New York City, such a thing cannot be contained. So therefore, not only inside the club but outside of it as well, my photographic exhibit helped to generate discussion of what is normal and what is not—a discussion that is possible only in a climate of intellectual freedom. And without intellectual freedom, what other freedom do we have?

Intellectual freedom is what the Century Association represents, even more today than when it was founded in 1847. Members can share ideals and exchange ideas that are absolutely free. This environment fosters creativity and creativity knows no limits. We can only hope that this extraordinary place continues to foster creativity for the next one hundred years, into the next century and well beyond.

On Autofiction

I expose only what I want to expose, and I feel much stronger and in control. Besides, a novelist reveals himself whether he likes it or not. I call my book an "autofiction" and leave it to the reader to distinguish what is truth and what is fiction.

It's about a state of mind. It is about what takes place in a creative man's head when it sets itself to create a work of fiction—what kinds of associations a novelist enters with, by himself in life, outside of his typewriter and upon his tyrewriter, so to speak. In other words, what is the play and interplay of forces within his imagination? Where does he reach, both in his life and in his fantasy?

Why do I still have to write the way novels were written in the nineteenth century, when there was no telephone, video, synthesizer, synthetic materials? . . . I think frankly that a large number of ordinary readers are bored stiff with traditionally written novels.

MY PRIVATE FANTASY

In his lecture at the Smithsonian Institution in Washington, D.C., in 1988, Kosinski explained how he made the decision to shift from writing nonfiction under the Novak pseudonym to fiction under his own name, and he expressed hope that his readership would continue.

Before *The Painted Bird* I wrote two sociological books, a series of essays on collective society published in 1960 and 1962, under the pen name Joseph Novak. I chose the name Novak because the actress Kim Novak was the reigning screen queen of the day, and I thought if I were picking a pen name I might as well pick one that everyone would remember. The year 1959, when I sat down to write the first Novak book, was not the time to use the name Jerzy Kosinski. Before Brzezinski, before the Polish pope, Novak was perfect. Parenthetically, the advantage of using a pen name is that no one knows that you are the author; therefore, you can recommend your own work to others as the best book on the subject.

When I started writing fiction under my own name, my novels proved to be significantly less "commercially successful"—quote / unquote—than the Novak nonfiction books. *The Painted Bird* was, to some extent, an exception. At the time, I was married to my late first wife, an American woman. We had met after the first Novak book was published, and we married shortly after the second Novak book came out, so it seemed the right time to bury Joseph Novak. For one thing, I was no longer at Columbia University, and there was no one left to whom to recommend the Novak books. And for another thing, as I told my late wife, I wanted to write fiction because nonfiction ages so quickly. By 1962 the first Novak book—published two years earlier and serialized by the *Saturday Evening Post*—was already old hat.

So I decided to pursue fantasy instead. But since fantasy is private, I felt I had to write it under my own name. Moreover, in my fiction I wanted to convey to my wife, who was as American as I imagine anyone could be, an experience that was totally foreign to her. By this I mean the experience of occupation. For those of you who have never been occupied by a foreign power—and I see no Indians in the audience—you cannot understand how occupation by Others—"Others," with a capital *O*—feels. You suddenly realize, more than at any other time in your life, that the Other is in charge of you. You realize that, despite all of your laws and all of your constitutions and all of the contributions that you have made to thousands of years of history, from your occupier's perspective you are absolutely nobody.

What could I write for my wife and for our friends who have never been occupied? After searching my mind, I came across a book, *Polish Children Accuse*, written in Polish. It was a collection of recollections by Polish children—Polish, I would stress, not Jewish—about the years 1939 to 1945. The book was published in Poland in 1961 and someone had sent a copy to me. I said to myself that if I were to write about myself for my wife, she would need to know more about that aspect of my life. After all, I had access to her past. Her past was Minneapolis and Pittsburgh. Her name was Mary Weir. There was a town, Weirton, founded by and named for her late husband, Ernest T. Weir. I could retrieve her past. But how could she retrieve mine? How do you dig up the Second World War or the German Occupation? How do I explain that, when I dated her, I had only two living relatives—although until 1939 I had almost seventy of them? How could I explain to her that, in four years of the war, I lost essentially two whole clans—clans of people not unlike you, people interested in studying and chess playing, intellectuals who wrote books about Greek and Roman and Polish history? I had to write something universal, something that anyone—from Pittsburgh or from New York or from any other place—could hook on to. And that something universal was childhood.

The book I wrote—*The Painted Bird*—was published in October 1965. It received decent reviews but did not sell especially well. In fact, it sold one-sixtieth the number of books that the Novak nonfiction had. Three thousand five hundred copies: surely no major literary event, not even in the building in which I lived. But still I was delighted. Jerzy Kosinski had published his first novel—published his first novel under his own name and separated himself, wisely or not, from Joseph Novak. Then a paperback company said it would like to publish a paperback edition of *The Painted Bird*. I agreed but asked if I could pick out the cover. Since the name "Kosinski" meant nothing, I knew that the cover would have to say the rest. They told me to go ahead, as long as the permission costs for the artwork did not exceed three hundred dollars.

So I went to the painter whom I love most, Hieronymus Bosch. In a Doubleday bookstore, I found his triptych *The Last Judgment,* a fragment of which is called "Monster Carrying a Child in a Basket." In the basket, there is an innocent-looking child being carried off by the terrible-looking monster. I wrote to the Academy of Fine Arts in Vienna to get the rights to this particular fragment, for which they charged me $33.43—or maybe it was $43.33; I do not remember. This became the cover of the first, 1966, Pocket Book edition of *The Painted Bird.* The people at Pocket Books didn't necessarily like the cover but agreed that there was something to it.

Within weeks, the paperback of *The Painted Bird* was in every bookshop window in New York and in every place where I traveled. At first, I couldn't figure it out. I knew better than to trust my vanity. Although I'm vain enough, I realized something other than literary mastership was at work here. So I started visiting these bookshops and asking the salesmen and saleswomen, "Excuse me, I see that you have a book called *The Painted Bird* in the window. Why is it there?" And the young man or young woman—mostly flower children, it was 1966—would say, "It would freak you out. Did you see the cover?" Or else I would ask them to recommend some good reading, and they would say, "Do you want to read something way out? Get *The Painted Bird.*" And so, with all due respect, I must say I was launched as a literary figure not by a critic, not by another writer, but by a fellow man of fantasy, Hieronymus Bosch.

Ironically, what occurred just a few months after the paperback edition of *The Painted Bird* was published and became popular was something straight from Bosch. When I read in the *Smithsonian Magazine* that at one point Bosch's obsession with bizarre images had led to fanciful theories about him, including one that Bosch had been a member of the brethren of the spirit also known as the Adamites, a secret heretical sect, I could immediately appreciate his situation. It just so happened that in 1966 a major campaign was launched in Poland against *The Painted Bird*, even though the book had never been published in Polish and was not even known to most Poles. Nonetheless, *The Painted Bird* became a political cause as well as a cause célèbre. At the time, a small faction in the government had embarked on the idea that Jews should be removed from Poland, not because of any particular civilian sins they had committed but simply because they were Jews. This had never happened before in the thousand-year history of Poland: non-Jewish Poles and Polish Jews alike were Polish citizens, all part of the same country. So the articles about *The Painted Bird* in 1966 struck a very strange note: they all referred to the author as a Zionist, as a neo-Nazi, as someone who had written this strange book to slander the good name of Poland.

One day—I remember it was December 12, 1966—I was walking with my wife on a New York City street. I bought the *New York Times* and opened it routinely, only to find on the second page of the news section the text of an article entitled "Poles Are Bitter about a Novel Published Abroad." It said, "Kosinski's *The Painted Bird* is considered a slander" and a false picture of anti-Semitism. "Although Mr. Kosinski, who left Poland in 1957 and now lives in New York, made the book's locale no more specific than Eastern Europe and left uncertain whether his child hero was a Jew or a Gypsy, the Polish press and public assume that the book leads to Poland." And that, of course, had led to a furor in Poland.

Naturally, I was concerned by these charges. Poland was my country, and these charges were being written in my native language of Polish. Clipping services sent the articles to me. But there was one more reason that I cared. Even though I lived in New York, my mother still lived in Poland.

To be the mother of a neo-Nazi who happened also to be a Jew and who slandered the good name of his own country was to be a mother in trouble. Do I have to say more?

The irony is that at the same time the book was published in 1965, I also published *The Notes of the Author on The Painted Bird*. In those *Notes*, which were routinely sent to critics, I said things like: "the names used in *The Painted Bird* are fictional and cannot with any justification whatsoever be ascribed to any particular national group." I added: "the anthropologist could no more pin the facts of the lives of the characters of *The Painted Bird* to the printed page than he could those of the witches in *Macbeth*."

It turns out that, with *The Painted Bird*, I had created an interesting situation. I had written something quite fictional about something which feasibly could be nonfiction. Even then, I said to myself, it would be nice if there could be another dimension—a new literary dimension, in which I could do both. A new literary dimension—in which I could tell actual stories yet be fictional. A new literary dimension—in which I would preface my work by saying, "Wait a second. I am a storyteller. I am here as a storyteller. Take it or leave it." If I told the story convincingly, you would believe it. If not, you would disbelieve it.

I told myself it would be great to be able to do both: to be private and scream when I want to, and to be public and say I am angry and to argue with someone in a novel, and even to quote someone else directly in the text, not as a footnote but in the text, someone who perhaps would narrate my anger better than I do. There is always someone who has already described something better than I could. Why should I do it again? But how exactly could I use someone else's words or ideas in the text?

Six years ago, after I finished what I thought was the last Kosinski novel dealing with a single Kosinski protagonist, I asked myself why not sit down and come up with such a dimension, a dimension in which I could not only pick up something that would document my fantasy but also use it directly as a form for creating a new, more convenient method of expression in which I could be very nonfictional. After all, I am a sociologist by training. But then, if I did that, would I have to part with the "scream" of the novelist or the strange and bizarre Bosch-like sexual fantasy with the number "69"?

To put it in different terms: driving through a narrative literary terrain, could I feasibly come up with a new vehicle? Motor cars change over time. A four-wheel drive is quite different from a two-wheel drive; a rear-wheel drive is different from a front-wheel drive. Those are important changes in driving, aren't they? But do we make comparable changes in fiction? If Detroit is free to be so inventive—or the Japanese, for that matter—can't we novelists be inventive as well? Isn't it feasible that if I, as a novelist, am fed up with the old Kosinski novel, you as a reader are fed up too?

So I sat down to come up with this ideal literary vehicle—all-terrain, I would like to call it—even though I feared I might not even be able to drive it out of the garage. But still, an inventor is an inventor, so I said to myself: let's have the freedom of choice and the freedom of invention. Let's create an amphibious literary vehicle, a vehicle that skims the waves but also moves underwater, a vehicle that can handle the beach, the dunes, the city. And if it can deal with the beach and dunes, surely it can deal with the city traffic. That vehicle is *The Hermit of 69th Street.*

The Hermit of 69th Street is not autobiographical. By the way, I live on Fifty-seventh Street in New York City. The novel is what I like to call "autofiction." "Auto," not for the automobile, but "auto" for the parts which are mine—autobiographical or self-generated, so to speak. To a degree, that also means nonfictional, as in the choices I would make. But at the same time the novel is also total "fiction." In autofiction, when I want to use somebody else who utilizes literary vehicles better than I, I use him or her to strengthen the text. For instance, listen to Thomas Wolfe's description, which comes straight from my book: "And when he had worked for hours at a stretch, forgetting food and sleep and everything, he would rise from his desk at last and stagger forth into the nighttime street, reeling like a drunkard with his weariness." I could not do any better than that. Or writing about big New York, could I do better than Engels, who observed that "this colossal centralization, this agglomoration of three and a half million people on a single spot, has multiplied the strength of the three and a half million inhabitants a hundredfold . . . but the price that has been paid is not discovered until later." Could I say it any better? I could not.

But enough about the writer, this writer or any other writer. Let me for a second occupy you with something which has preoccupied me for quite some time. To prove that *The Hermit of 69th Street*, this all-terrain vehicle, is not a useless escapade, I need a reader. And in order to publish the novel, the publisher needs many readers. All of this raises issues about the importance of reading. In 1971 while I was working on *Being There*, I was a Senior Fellow of English at Princeton and I wrote an op-ed piece, an editorial for the *New York Times*, called "Dead Souls on Campus." The editorial did not make me any friends on the campus but, after all, life from time to time is supposed to be solitary. In that editorial, I wrote about an abstract student. I said that, at best, I find that students today share situations; they do not really live them. "They sit and watch films or television or listen to music in a group, thus isolated by a collective medium which permits each of them to escape direct contact with the others" or with their own imaginations. And then, also in 1971, I followed up that editorial with a far harder column in which I said that, after spending four years teaching at Wesleyan, Princeton, and Yale, I was struck by what I think emerges as the dominant trait of contemporary students: their short span of attention, their inability to know or believe or read anything for more than half an hour. I blamed television and observed that "during their scholarly and leisure pursuits, they [students] switch with exactly the same intensity and staying power from subject to subject, as if changing TV channels." Fifteen minutes is all a teacher can hope for—assuming the classroom is freezing and the students' chairs are very uncomfortable. Since reading is a solitary effort that requires imagination to translate a symbol into reality, young people do not venture beyond required reading texts. Worse yet, they limit themselves to a condensed page. And so, on college campuses, "the novel is not dead" but "its readers are dying fast."

Is there any way left for me or for you to change these patterns? Is it even feasible, especially when so many Americans spend most of their free time in front of a television? When I talk to youngsters, I see that they literally cannot concentrate. It is not their fault. Television is free; movies are free; video is free. They just have to sit and watch. Books, however, are tough. They make demands. So how do we get people to start reading again?

In my middle-class Polish-Jewish family, chess playing was considered to be both a royal game and the ultimate sport—a sport of high concentration. My father and my grandfathers played chess. At first, my father was not a very good player; he would always lose to my grandfather. But during the war, all the chess players in the family except for my parents perished in the ghetto of Łódź. It was a very distinguished ghetto, as large as the ghetto of Warsaw but less well known, since there was no uprising there. When the war ended I asked my father, who by then had become more skillful at chess—although by then he was also older, more tired, and more fatigued—to teach me the game. And my father said, "No, you are too obsessive. Why don't you write instead?" He said that paper was more patient than any opponent.

Even now, I don't play chess. I watch it, and I watch chess players. I've watched them in New York, where I am an honorary member of the Manhattan Chess Club. In fact, I am probably the only member who *watches* other chess players play. Yet I appreciate chess, which has played a very important role in literature. Almost every writer of distinction has written about it. One of the most popular writers of all time, Stefan Zweig, who is no longer popular—and quite possibly no longer in print—wrote excellent biographies of Joseph Fouché, who invented the police state, and of Balzac. In the early 1940s, shortly before he committed suicide with his wife outside of Rio de Janeiro in protest against what was happening to Europe, to the world of old Vienna, to the world of old Jews, Zweig wrote his last novel, *The Royal Game* [*Schachnovelle*], also called "the chess novel." The fact that almost every writer of distinction wrote about chess is no accident. Chess and writing have a great deal in common. Like chess, fiction writing requires concentration. It requires the novelist to imagine himself as somebody else. It has its own language. It does not speak in direct images.

People play chess on the streets of New York and in the ghettos of Detroit. Even kids play. They can't help it: it's addictive. It is an addiction that kills other addictions, because you get so high on chess that you do not want anything else, because anything else might bring you down. Chess is the ultimate kid's game. It offers an education and prepares kids for every other game in life. In chess, each move brings a consequence. Choices have to be made. Lessons can be learned from the moves that others make. The stratagems are universal. They are the same as those of big business: knowing which choice to make, and when to make it.

Poland was once a country known for chess; some of the greatest chess players came from there. Most were Polish Jews. One of them, David Przepiorka—in translation, his name means "quail," so we go back, once again, to *The Painted Bird*—sold his house in 1939 and took the whole Polish Olympic chess team to Buenos Aires. After his return to Poland, Przepiorka perished in the camps. But Mieczysław Najdorf, one of the players Przepiorka took to Buenos Aires, survived and became a great champion. Najdorf showed the Germans what a bright Jew could do, and he inspired the Jews in the ghettos of Europe by his success. He played masters and grand masters, sometimes while blindfolded. And when he won, even German-language radio had to report his victories, thus making the Jews of Europe triumphant at least once during the Second World War.

I consider all of you here today to be a secret society, not because of your number but because of the circumstances in which we have been introduced. And I believe that you can understand the secret of why I am fighting so hard, fighting for readers, fighting for the return of chess. I am not plugging my own novels; there is no chess in *The Hermit of 69th Street*. I have no children of my own. But my friends play chess. One of my closest friends, a man who is quite well-to-do, inherited money from his family, the result of many, many generations of the Protestant ethic and hard work. Since he could buy himself anything he wants, the only gift I could give him was the possibility of playing against Garry Kasparov in a simultaneous game in New York. My friend almost collapsed when I told him, because he is an obsessive, like so many other chess players. So he flew into New York and survived Kasparov for thirty moves, which—given Kasparov's previous simultaneous games with many other masters—was quite an accomplishment. Now my friend cannot wait to do it again, and he will contribute to making chess accessible to the public.

Imagine a time when chess really is a sport not just for masters but for the masses—a time when boxers or wrestlers are no longer considered fun to watch and when chess is a Las Vegas–style event. Kids would notice.

They would learn how to play it from television or the Internet. They could play with other people on video games or by themselves on computers. Playing against a computer could even help to raise their game. Perhaps the game that my father used to call a great Jewish game could become a national game. And the result would be a new generation of people who would know how to concentrate.

Concentration means focusing. It means making good choices. It means spirituality. It means knowing who you are, looking at yourself as if you were a chessboard, and assessing the options you have in life. Do you move to the left? Do you go to the right? The game of chess could open up other worlds—of creativity, of big business, of politics, of Wall Street—all of which require a similar level of concentration.

That brings me to the end of my private fantasy: that one day kids everywhere will be masters of concentration, not slaves to a television set. Instead of getting letters from readers who are over sixty-five, I will be getting letters from youngsters telling me, "Mr. Kosinski, you have made certain moves in your novel that could have been improved. Don't you think that it is time for you to sit down and learn the game of chess so that you can concentrate better on your next novel, so that it will not take six years to write?"

And that, of course, brings me back to *The Hermit of 69th Street*, my new all-terrain literary vehicle. It requires some concentration but I think my readers will enjoy the ride.

THE MAKING OF A NOVEL

The Hermit of 69th Street, as Kosinski explained to interviewer Joan Lunden in 1988, was a different kind of novel, an "autofiction"—that is, a novel about the making of a novel.

JOAN LUNDEN: This is a very different kind of novel, to say the very least; that's probably the understatement of the year. There's no real central plot. There are a lot of footnotes quoting everyone from Shakespeare to . . .

JERZY KOSINSKI: Well, it's a different plot. It's a plot about the plotting of a novel.

JL: Having to describe it: it's the describing of the process of writing a novel. Is that fair to say?

JK: Yes. I mean, there have been movies about the making of a movie and dramatic plays about the making of a play. This is a novel about the making of a novel and about what it takes, what happens here in this writing head when the head is trying to conceive of a novel, a different universe and yet the universe within this very head. What happens? Where do I go for the story? Do I look into myself? Do I look at you? What is the mixture, the fusion? What is the synthesizer? Then what kind of narrative boat do I create? Catamaran? One-man kayak? Speedboat? In other words, what will drive the narrative train of this novel? What kind of horsepower?

JL: I think anyone listening to that explanation can see it's a difficult process that you go through, and it's not a normal novel. I mean, this constantly going back to the footnotes—some of the critics say it makes the novel unreadable.

JK: Can we . . .

JL: But it's almost like a movie, where you go back in the plot.

JK: . . . can we call it an abnormal novel? That would be great.

JL: An abnormal novel.

JK: Read the abnormal novel by Jerzy Kosinski.

JL: I just wonder how difficult it is to publish a book that is so different because we live in a world where anytime anything is different, be it a movie or a book, people recoil. They don't want to take a chance. It must have been difficult to get it published.

JK: It is. It is difficult only in one sense, that you have to convince yourself that you want to design a different craft, a different narrative craft. It's no different than in any other area of life when you try to do something that is not quite common. I think it was far more difficult for Joyce to write *Ulysses* than for Kosinski to do *The Hermit of 69th Street*. And let us imagine what chances Joyce took designing an entirely different narrative story.

JL: Yes.

JK: Once you know this—that it can be done—look at Proust, look at Faulkner's *The Sound and the Fury*. I mean, it's not an easy craft to navigate, which means you . . .

JL: And this book took six years, right? Six years to make.

JK: Part of it was gathering bravery, gathering wind. Saying, "Yes, let's have something that will be different—overdesigned, almost."

JL: Was part of it also speaking back? I mean, this is the first book since the controversy of 1982, where there were allegations that you weren't writing your own material. Norbert Kosky faces that same kind of problem.

JK: Yes, it was. The whole idea of what is the role of all the writer's influences in a particular writer's life—the writers one reads, the writers one imitates. That gave the prompting to the book.

JL: And the usage of all the other writers and the quotations?

JK: Yes, whenever I feel that there's someone who says something better than what I could say. Let's say someone could describe a woman better than I. Why should I bother? Let Proust describe her. In the text, I clearly delineate what is mine, what is not. That's a novelty. There are many other novelties in the book, I like to think. It is a laterally written novel, not vertically. You move the way you move, the way you look at the screen, interrupted by commercials. As a spectator, you have at your disposal many other channels. As a reader, you have many other channels at your disposal on the pages of this book.

JL: What do you want the reader to walk away with?

JK: To be entertained. This is a reader who knows computers, who knows that a car built today is different from a car built twenty-five years ago. Am I going to imitate writers who write traditional novels, or am I going to write something different?

JL: For those used to a lot of information?

JK: Yes, exactly.

JL: Well, it makes you think.

JK: Exactly. That's part of it.

FUSING FORMS

In a brief comment to "Book Beat"s' Don Swaim in 1988, Kosinski spoke about his fiction as well as his most recent "autofiction."

DON SWAIM: As a child, writer Jerzy Kosinski survived the Nazi invasion of his native Poland. By missing an airplane that was to have flown him to California to stay at the home of Sharon Tate, he survived the Charles Manson murders. Kosinski also survived the efforts of two literary assassins from the *Village Voice*, who accused him of hiring other people to write his books.

JERZY KOSINSKI: The fiction written about me is very often better than the fiction I write.

DS: There was even a story in a Minneapolis newspaper that claimed that Jerzy Kosinski was holding a woman in literary bondage in his basement and forcing her to write his novels.

JK: There was another hoax, remember? There was a man [Chuck Ross] who submitted *Steps*, my second novel, as his own ten years after the novel was written. This hoax was even better than the hoax of the *Village Voice*. He submitted my novel under a different name to the very publishers who published the novel and to several other publishers, and they all turned it down.

164

DS: Jerzy Kosinski calls his new novel, *The Hermit of 69th Street,* "autofiction."

JK: There is no pure fiction, since clearly any invention has to be grounded in fact or at least in the head of a writer. At the same time, there is no such thing as autobiography, since if I were to recount our meeting right now, it would be an essence of you and me at these microphones. Hence, I decided to fuse both forms very openly, and I call it autofiction. Some of it is autobiographical. What's to pretend? Should Kosinski pretend that he doesn't exist?

SOCIETY AND DISORDER

In this excerpt from an interview in 1989 originally published in *Manhattan,* Kosinski analyzed his characters and literary methods and explained how his latest novel, *The Hermit of 69th Street,* simultaneously drew on and departed from the style and content of his earlier work.

INTERVIEWER: Many of your characters are outsiders. What is an outsider?

JERZY KOSINSKI: In my fiction, an outsider is someone who persists—in spite of himself and how society has defined him. At the same time, he is able to look at himself as if he were another person. Since he can be detached from himself, he can also distance himself from others. Conversely, with the knowledge he then gains, he can also be the ultimate insider. He can camouflage very well, appearing entirely authentic and spontaneous. But, in fact, he may be merely the best rehearsed.

INT: This also implies a perspective on morality between people, lovers, wives, and husbands.

JK: My situations are open-ended, since for me to propose any particular point of view would violate the rights of the reader, and fiction is a very democratic enterprise. It doesn't impose. It doesn't suggest. It merely says, "Suspend disbelief. My name is fiction." I leave morality to the reader.

Does this mean that I have no morality? Of course not. I do have it. Is the morality present in my fiction, even to the degree where it could influence someone's judgment? Clearly it is. But it manifests itself in the choice of incidents I deliver, in the narrative platform I offer the reader. The platform is my view. Any novelist has at his disposal an endless number of situations to illustrate any particular point. For instance, the situations I create often condemn totalitarian behavior, and that already implies a certain morality.

INT: In a very subtle way.

JK: The name of the game here is not so much subtlety as it is ambiguity—which is an essential element of any art. The art which lacks ambiguity becomes propaganda. Novels are premeditated. If they feel truly spontaneous and abandoned, that's where the writer is. But if he is really a good artist, where he is spontaneous, he may just be well rehearsed, the way a good tennis player is well rehearsed. It looks so easy, but you realize the work that went into it. In my case, I confuse the dimension even more, by openly integrating elements of my own life, in a distorted manner, into my fiction.

INT: You call your latest novel autofiction.

JK: The premise for autofiction was established with notes I wrote as an appendix for my first novel in 1965. In the notes, I said that the writer incorporated the fragments of objective reality into a new literary dimension, but took from outside of himself "only what he is capable of creating in his imagination anyhow." Perversely, I can also take from outside things that in my fiction can exist as a fact of my life, since clearly I exist only as a fiction writer. My personality, a certain version of myself, and therefore one I sell as a storyteller—is it a one-to-one conversion? It is not, since no such transfer can take place in literature. Is it a revisitation of my life? No, it is not. Rather, it's a vision. As I wrote back in 1965, *The Painted Bird* is a vision of myself as a child, not a reexamination or a revisitation.

INT: You also construct whole countries, like Ruthenia.

JK: Ruthenia was a part of Poland. There also is West Rutland in Vermont. In both *Cockpit* and *The Hermit of 69th Street,* Ruthenia is a nice fusion.

INT: So it is based on fact.

JK: Yes. Kosky, the hero of my newest novel, is, to a large degree, Kosinski without sin.

INT: If I read *The Hermit of 69th Street* like a regular novel I get confused. But if I just let myself be taken along by it, I become part of its flow.

JK: Any television kid is accustomed to having things interrupted. By sharing an entertainment with an act of life—we watch TV, go to the refrigerator, talk on the phone—we have become far more dispersed. I can no longer read a nineteenth-century novel, I admit, without a great degree of concentration. What I lack is the habit of thought that is horizontal and linear.

I do not have the patience to receive information which I already know or I am sufficiently able to imagine. I don't need a description of a bedroom; I know what it is. If you want to instruct me specifically, don't take half a page; make a footnote. Even include the size: "a studio with a kitchenette and a Castro convertible." *Hermit* makes the fullest use of the shorthand language of the video makers and composers. With *Hermit,* I am also challenging the existing order. I am telling the legions of American readers that I am creating neither a sedan nor a boat—it's a fusion. And I have introduced it into an area—fiction—where synthetics are not routinely used, where in fact everyone doubts the possibility of anything synthetic.

INT: Your book also reminded me of an MTV video as well as of writings from the Jewish prophets.

JK: Yes, the Talmud is also written like this. The footnote is one of the great narrative elements of history. And I have added what I call my Polish element—the confession voice—which is always present in my novels. It's not in any way filtered by psychoanalysis, like the American confession voice, which is mostly self-confessing or filtered by self-comment.

My confession voice comes from the Catholic confession, in which you are free from the necessity for a filter. You are free from apprehension, since you are excused from the very act of storytelling in the very moment the act takes place. Hence, so many great narrative voices in Jewish letters have come from the Polish Commonwealth or from Austria, since Poland was part of the Austro-Hungarian Empire. It's this Hasidic tradition which opens up the narrator and allows him to say anything he wants, and in fact permits him even to make fun of his own religion. The Polish-Jewish writers were armed with a weapon which no others had at their disposal—the new confession voice, the detached voice of the Austrian school.

INT: That inner voice.

JK: It's the American device of commenting on a comment. The inner voice in *Hermit*—K.—could be my initials, or Kosky's, which means I have far greater movement as a narrator within this book than I ever had in a novel.

I like to think I have more freedom of movement—which means your ability to say more and to entertain more—than just about any other novelist, given the dimensions. To be a larger storyteller, using this approach to narrative is far better than remaining faithful to the old form of Tolstoy.

INT: Where did you want to take the reader in such a premeditated novel?

JK: Technically, always into himself or herself, breaking their lives into creative components, to figure out the differences in their lives.

INT: In the book, you also talk about consecutive words, each beginning with the letter *S*. It's fun. But it gets beyond that. Words do have a magic.

JK: I see words as spatial trips that contain almost endless information. Going into a word is going into—a world. And you can start the trip with any word.

On Poland

*It is the totalitarian system which separates you from the human condition.
It insists that your place in society is measured by other yardsticks than your
actual life. The drama is imposed from the outside—the failure, the success,
the pain, the pleasure are all given to you by the state. There [in Poland and
Eastern Europe] I saw myself as an isolated cowboy.*

*Poland may be a poor country economically, but in terms of ideas it's probably
the richest country in Europe today. . . . What you have right now is what
you always had in Poland—an extraordinary explosion of creative ideas.
An ordinary newspaper in Poland today contains far more layers of thought,
imagination, confrontation with reality as well as departure from it, than any
Western counterpart.*

*The issue is not whether someone is an artist, but how to go about dealing with
life. You cannot dismiss any moment of your life by not making decisions, by
not knowing, because your life is the only thing you are entirely responsible
for. In a Communist state you are not free to say yes or no; your life is entirely
dismissed as not belonging to you.*

BEING HERE

Kosinski, who returned to Poland for the first time in 1988, shared with reporter Bert Quint his impressions of his native land and the feelings Poland evoked for him.

BERT QUINT: Jerzy Kosinski tells us how it feels "Being Here."

JERZY KOSINSKI: Poland is where it all began, where I started to cry for the first time and to be punished for the first time by someone, or by history. This is the place where I gained my freedom and sense of myself, and this is also the place where I lost some sixty members of my family, who were killed by invaders from the outside. But I also survived here, thanks to perfect strangers. Strangers came from Germany and killed my Polish-Jewish family. Polish strangers saved me during the war. This is my drama. This is what I am made of.

BQ: Why did you leave Poland?

JK: I collect life. I collect impressions. I collect being warm and being in love with things—and even being depressed by things. This is what I need. So I left to seek all of that. Nothing else. I was never a political person. In many ways, I think I may have been emotionally crippled, but I have been sentenced unjustly to an absence of thirty years.

BQ: You were exiled?

JK: Yes and no. I was exiled by circumstances which I found intolerable, which means that I was exiled in the most profound sense, because I exiled myself.

BQ: Because you were not allowed to write?

JK: Because the system has been such that it does not allow it.

BQ: Would you give me some of your impressions of your homeland?

JK: First, I think the Poles are extraordinarily outspoken now. At the same time, there is a markedly steeper depression. The country is substantially poorer than when I left thirty years ago. It is in very bad shape: people in my former hometown wait fifty years for an apartment. The country is sinking economically. You have an extraordinarily conflicting situation where you have both an explosion of freedom of expression and an old-fashioned economic suppression which literally suffocates the country. Poles are the freest people right now in Eastern Europe. I would never have believed that this sort of freedom could have developed from a Communist system—but at the same time there is still the stamp of the old-fashioned bureaucratic, autocratic totalitarian economic mind. What is so fascinating is that the political mind is almost Jeffersonian—at the same time, the people are starving.

BQ: What were you not prepared for?

JK: I was not prepared that I would cry again. I was not prepared to see the graves of my parents. I did not think that I would see them again because I was not with them when they died. I was not prepared for the sense of loss I would suddenly feel for the years that I lost. And yet I am back here, and I know that—as a Polish Jew, or simply as a Jew—this is where I feel the Jewish presence to its fullest. Therefore I feel very much at home. This is, after all, my spiritual home.

EUPHORIA

Upon returning from Poland after a thirty-year absence, Kosinski discussed with Charles Osgood his reactions to the new democratic process in his native land and shared his delight at seeing his novels published for the first time in Polish translations.

CHARLES OSGOOD: It must be nice to have your work available to the Polish people after all this time.

JERZY KOSINSKI: Euphoric. After thirty years, you go back and it's published in the language of your growing up, which means you are going back to that part of yourself.

CO: Did you make the translation yourself?

JK: No, no, I couldn't do it. But when I read it in Polish, I say to myself: "It's a great work of art."

CO: Exactly what you meant when you wrote it?

JK: Exactly.

CO: When you went back to Poland—you went back there in 1988 and then again . . .

JK: Yes, first time last year, first time in thirty years.

CO: What kind of reception did you get?

JK: I went as a private person. I went to see the extraordinary change that had taken place, in a country that I didn't expect to change that fast. In fact, most members of my generation are still in a state of shock, and it's a shock that's going to last probably for the next twenty years. It's unthinkable that you have right now in Poland, by central European standards, an almost ideal state that's protected from the outside. It cannot be invaded. Clearly, no longer. I think Gorbachev will take care of that. It's a country that speaks one language. It's a country of one set of values. And now it's a democratic republic where what . . . Let's not press our luck.

CO: Still, it's a country with a lot of problems, especially economic problems.

JK: I think these are the very guarantees that the extraordinary coalition will last. They now have to make the house profitable.

CO: But now there's a little trap in all of this for Lech Wałesa, isn't there? Because if the government says to him—if General Jaruzelski says to him—"Okay, Solidarity, you've done very well at the polls. Okay, smart guy, you help us run the country now."

JK: I think this is going to be a great challenge, and in fact I think Solidarity's ready for it. Keep in mind that they have been around since 1980. And it's not just a union; it's a multilevel institution in Poland which penetrates every aspect of Polish life. I'm almost certain that Solidarity has in its pocket hundreds of experts who will in fact put the house in order very quickly.

I think that Poland will follow the Finnish example. In a very short time, the country will actually become quite rich. Finland is the ninth-richest country in the world, and who would have expected it? In Henry Kissinger's memoirs, by the way, Finland appears only once, as a meeting place. Now it's the ninth-richest country in the world. I think Poland may offer that kind of incentive: center of Europe, thirty-eight million people, every one with a high school education, every one worshipping Jeffersonian America—your values and mine. If that's not political heaven, what is?

CO: If you were Solidarity, if you were Wałesa or somebody else in the Solidarity leadership, and you were offered the economic portfolio right now, would you take it?

JK: . . . a lot of headaches. I think that, in this case, the initiative would belong far more to people in Poland, who understand that the foreigners have to make an adjustment as well. Poland offers a country that is basically both very profitable and totally ruined at the same time. In other words, it calls for economic incentive, and a very original one, but there's an advantage to it. When you're as ruined as this and you start from the beginning, you may have only a fax machine, but you are already ahead of the other guys, who are still using a regular phone.

CO: And you have nowhere to go but up economically. You left Poland because of the situation, as it was. Are you and some of your colleagues tempted to go back now that it's changed?

JK: Keep in mind that there are, what, twelve million Poles outside of Poland, mostly in Chicago and New York. Eighty thousand right here in Greenpoint [Brooklyn]. I think a large number of Poles will be going back and forth. I think they will keep their place in the West but they'll be using Poland the way everyone else in Europe is using their countries—old countries. They'll go back and forth to rejuvenate and have a sense of the old culture. The monetary exchange makes such a trip a great, great bargain. For my authorial trip in Poland, I hired a taxi for a whole week. I couldn't do that here—not a limo or a taxi—but there, at the end of the week, I think I paid a hundred and twenty dollars, including the tip.

CO: Novelist Jerzy Kosinski, who apparently has a happy ending for this story that's going on in Poland right now.

SUPPORTING REFORM

In a brief interview with Faith Daniels in 1989, Kosinski speculated about
Poland's new freedoms and the implications of those freedoms for the
country's political and economic future.

FAITH DANIELS: President [George H. W.] Bush says it's important
for us to show our support for the democratic reforms in Poland. Beyond
the obvious symbolic message, what do you think the importance of the
president's visit is?

JERZY KOSINSKI: The importance is that he is visiting a different country. He is visiting a country as different from what it was as France was
after the revolution. That's what I think is essential to realize, that what's
happened in Poland is no longer a minor change. It is an entirely different
political system. Revolutionary, in fact. Hence, his visit is, in a way, the
first contact that the United States is making with the new Poland—this
time, with Poland meaning a great deal to the United States rather than the
United States meaning a great deal for Poland.

FD: How is that?

JK: Poland is almost forty million large, forty million people in the very
heart of Europe. Within minutes, so to speak, of all the important centers

of life. Think of Poland as the most valuable lot in Beverly Hills. Closed for forty years, now it is open. You can move in and secure for yourself the best address in Europe. So President Bush is right—he is looking at the property right now.

FD: Except that the economic situation in Poland is the worst it has been since World War Two.

JK: The Second World War contributed to the situation. But that's what makes the lot so advantageous. Had it already been built over, there would be no opportunity. The very fact that it is a system that welcomes any kind of change, and primarily American change, means the United States can secure for itself now in the very heart of Europe a position like no other.

FD: So now that they're open to us, what do they need from us?

JK: What they need from us is what we do best—and thank God for that. That means construction, equipment, things which could help Poland turn the corner and make the country productive.

FD: And money as well?

JK: Banking, banking, I think more than methods, more than anything else. And probably equipment, again, which would revitalize the industries which are already there. Before the war, Poland used to be a very free enterprise–oriented country. Keep in mind that what happened in Poland over the last forty years was not done by the Poles. It was done to the Poles. The Marshall Plan rescued Germany and Japan, America's greatest enemy. Poland could not be rescued by the Marshall Plan because Stalin was standing at the gate and Poland was handcuffed. This is the first time that the country is no longer handcuffed. And this is why the United States can do practically anything it wants in Poland.

FD: Forty years later. You raise an interesting point. How does Poland view the United States versus the way it views the Soviet Union?

JK: There's just no comparison. Poland is probably—no, Poland *is*—the most pro-American country in the world. There is just no other place in which the United States means more to the population. One, because the values are the same. Two, because of the history between the two countries. Every important Polish intellectual visited Jefferson. It was an essential thing to be part of the Jeffersonian myth, in a way.

Poland is a country of profoundly free people, people who value freedom perhaps even more than the Americans do. Many Poles live in this country. Hence, the Polish diaspora in the United States is part of the relationship between Poland and the United States. There is also an economically important element here: the United States is entering a country that is already very American.

FD: In the few seconds we have remaining, I wanted to ask you what you think will come of the elections that will take place for the [Polish] president after President Bush leaves.

JK: I think the fusion between the opposition and the government will be even greater. The new government will be in charge of a very important economic change. To what degree the change will succeed will depend greatly to what degree the United States will want to become part of central Europe.

THE IMPACT OF WAR

Upon being awarded an honorary Doctorate of Humane Letters from Albion College in April 1988, Kosinski spoke about the repercussions of the war on himself, on his life, and on his fiction.

Let me qualify who I am. I am not a historian. I am not a recorder of events in any objective sense. In other words, what I know comes from the things that I remember.

Keep in mind that I was just twelve years old when the Second World War ended. After a war like that, you are, in many instances, much older than the typical twelve-year-old and, in many others, much younger. My perceptions, therefore, are very varied. They are the perceptions not only of a child but also of an undergraduate student confronted by the very powerful force of the Communist state. When a war like that ends, you are grateful that you are alive. Almost everyone you know has lost someone. In my case, more than one-fifth of the country was gone. Imagine the United States, over four years—the period between elections—losing one-fifth of its population. Losing it, not to the sea, but through butchery, killing, hanging, and mutilation in every conceivable fashion. That would be seventy million people gone in four years. Had that happened here in the United States, you would be in far different shape today.

This would be a far different class. Because of what happened to you during the war, you would have no relatives left. You would be afraid to look me in the eye. You would not be able to talk. I myself was virtually unable to speak after the war. My father feared that I suffered from a serious speech impediment which bordered on muteness.

When you talk about what happened to a country that in just over four years has undergone a disaster like no other disaster in history, you have to take all of the horror into account. No movie can re-create it. No teacher can evoke the image of it. The reality is far beyond the scope of what Americans can imagine. And rightly so: there was no occupation in this country. You do not understand what it is to be occupied. Yet occupation is the cardinal experience that every European has known at one time or another. "When was your foot broken?" "It was broken when we were occupied by the Nazis" or "When we were occupied by the Russians." "Why doesn't your friend speak Polish any more?" "Because he lived in the part of Poland which was occupied by the Austro-Hungarian Empire. So he doesn't speak Polish. However, he speaks German."

This is what we are talking about. Any artifact, therefore, be it a novel or a photograph or some other object that survived the war, has to be considered in the context of that disaster. This disaster was unique— unique because of the method. The bombers wiped out whole cities, regardless of who lived there. Anonymously. You could not even tell who the bombers were. Russian bombers? German bombers? At the same time, there was civil war. When there is rioting in a neighborhood, all kinds of people want to profit; they simply seize things and walk away with them. During wartime, the rioting occurs on an even larger scale: home owners leave and others move in and try to ensure that the original owners never come back.

The reality, nevertheless, is hard to convey. I feel very much aware of it, because I was there. And I am much more aware of it now than I have ever been, because I just came back from Poland. It was my first visit to Poland in more than thirty years. I left when I was twenty-four and returned at the age of fifty-five. Thirty years is a long, long time to be away from home. You can't just call your old friends and say, "Hey, I'm back. How about a cup of coffee?" The friends have not read your books, because the books have never been translated. And they have not heard from you—or else they have heard things about you that they can't quite understand. Yet we still had one thing in common: the state of war and all that happened to us after the war ended.

During my visit to Łódź, the city where I used to live, I had the chance to bring together some of my friends from the postwar years. My poor American wife was part of the evening there, but she ended up sitting like a deaf-mute! These were friends from my childhood, from the time I was twelve until I turned twenty-four. The ashes and the diamonds. Six men and six women who had seen each other every day and who knew each other intimately. I remembered things about them which perhaps no one else had ever known, and they knew things about me which no one else had ever known.

Even though we were all now in our middle to late fifties, we still shared one thing: our experience of the very complex postwar period, which in many ways was worse than the war itself. Now, you ask, how could this be? Because after the war ended, we had to start healing our wounds. But our relatives were no longer around. In my case, that was a hell of a sudden absence. Then, after the new government decided that the eastern part of Poland was going to be given to the Soviet Union and Poland was going to inherit part of Germany, we were moved from one part of what used to be Poland to another.

Even after the war, the war doesn't really end. Migrations take place; people are resettled; so the war goes on. The Soviet Union, which won the war, was technically the owner of this whole territory. They set up a satellite government—although not too quickly, since things had to be done with care. They brought back to Poland people of Polish origins who had lived in the Soviet Union. Many of them were Communist Jews. That was a very menacing mission. A Communist Jew returning from a Communist country to a Catholic country to become a member of the government might want to pay others back for some of the more unpleasant moments in Polish-Jewish history. The picture was further complicated by the fact that some of the fascists wanted to be in power too.

The Church was the single most powerful force in the country, but what could it actually do? During the war, priests were killed. Many of them became martyrs, and many just plainly died in the gas chambers because of their opposition. They died like the Jews, which means that the Church proved itself to be very vulnerable. It could be bombed and simply made to disappear. Its priests could be shot or put in concentration camps. It was subject to the vagaries of the Soviet Union. Especially after the war, it tried to mobilize—but how? And against whom? Such was the climate of the postwar in a country as brutalized as Poland.

Even in the classsroom, the war continued. Some of the returning Jews—because of their background—suddenly became important. Their families were workers, and the new government felt that workers were on their side. Conversely, if you were the daughter or son of a doctor or an engineer, you were viewed with suspicion. You might be swayed in a more cosmopolitan direction. You might be reading the wrong books. The new government believed that a worker's son or a peasant's son knew nothing because he had had no chance to learn; therefore, he was committed to the new education. But that did not apply to those with a middle-class background. We found ourselves being pushed back. That was the new social justice. Oftentimes, teachers had no degrees; they got their jobs because they too were the sons or daughters of workers. Many real teachers, in fact, were no longer allowed to teach.

In these kinds of ways, the system reinforced itself. Imagine, for a moment, if this country was suddenly turned upside down. Do you really think that this college would still be the Albion you know? Maybe even the name would be changed. All of that would depend on the township committee, a committee entirely different from any township that exists today. It was precisely such confusion and upheaval that made the postwar period even tougher on us than the war had been. During the Second World War, things were clear: you knew that you and your friends had nothing to do with it. The war was a bomb falling from the sky. The war was a Nazi, whose mechanized aggression was entirely foreign to the Polish character. The war brought death to a Catholic country which was basically life-oriented, unthinkable destruction, with concentration camps, in which hundreds of thousands of people died, and transports to the gas chambers. And the postwar was a further radical departure from previous history, however bad it had been.

No film can convey what occurred during those years. Let me be straight on this: I am not a film lover. In fact, I am not a lover of the visual image. I write. I think of the images which I create without the help of a studio or an actor. I like to think that even though I am a novelist, I am in charge of a large production, a huge assembly of images which are cheap to produce. My production requires no company to insure and no extras to compensate. And, of course, I don't have to pay myself. I can change the script from day to day, and what's more I can recast as I go along. I can even bring out a new version of my production by making changes in the paperback edition, or in the next edition in another country, and so forth. Therefore, I feel that writing fiction allows the best image creation in the world. Almost godly, in fact. After all, "in the beginning," what was there? Not a movie. "In the beginning was the word."

Fiction depends on images. If I describe a classroom, you see a classroom. But if I describe a situation of the kind I already described—that some students are advancing because their parents are uneducated while, conversely, others are brought down because their parents are well educated—it sounds contrary to everything you are familiar with here and now. So you must use your imagination. "What do you mean?" you ask. "A kid brought up in a well-educated family is the one now being held back, and the one who knows little or nothing is advancing?" But don't dismiss this form of social justice too readily. After all, someone can say that the kid who had a doctor for his father and a schoolteacher for his mother is already educated. That kid knows where Portugal is located, knows the difference between *Hamlet* and *Richard the Second*. The son of a peasant, however, makes no such distinction. Say *Hamlet* to him and he thinks of, say, a little structure, a small village. Socialist social justice.

Actually, I am not making any judgment here. I am merely portraying the complexity of the situation that I experienced in Poland after the war. It was complex in every conceivable way. The only simple thing, particularly for someone such as myself who has lived through a war, is this: there should never be another war.

On the Holocaust

No one can make me a Jew and no one can unmake me a Jew.

How can I make them understand [the Holocaust] if I am not graphic? . . . The Holocaust was, in one sense, an experience of the future, in which the individual may be totally unimportant and is labeled as something inhuman. None of my relatives were singled out. They were labeled as "negative elements," potential enemies to be eliminated. The idea of eliminating whole groups after dehumanizing them was inherited by the Nazis from the apparatus of Soviet dictatorship. The Nazis modified it—political labels became social labels.

Remembering the Holocaust and financing Holocaust-related projects that help to make certain that—never again!—such an atrocity could be repeated is clearly one of our most challenging obligations. But that task must not be carried out at the cost of failing to remember—and to make others know—what preceded the Holocaust and what had come after.

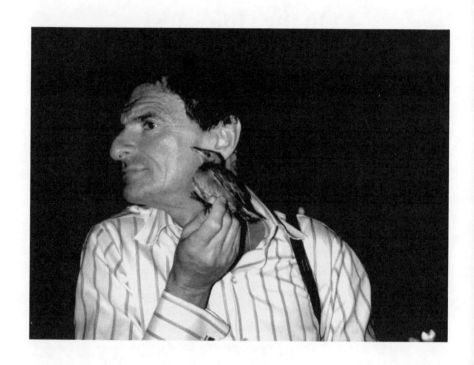

A MONUMENT TO HISTORY

In his 1990 address to Congregation Emanu-El in New York City, Kosinski spoke about the importance of remembering the experience of the Holocaust, not only in monuments to those who perished but also in celebrations of past and ongoing Jewish achievements.

Thirteen years ago, one of the first municipal monuments to the Holocaust was erected by the city government of New Haven, Connecticut. It was an important monument meant to commemorate an unprecedented moment in history, during which—for no reason at all—people who could have been university professors, people who could have been musicians, people who could have been actors, people who could have been Modiglianis and Pissarros or who could have invented vitamins that we could feasibly use today were exterminated. For no reason at all. That monument is discreet, not very big at all. But then, nothing could be bigger than Jewish presence in history. What could you possibly build in stone that could be more enduring than our presence in the human mind? No stone could be bigger than Jewish thought or more melodic than "White Christmas," written by Irving Berlin, a Jew, no idea bigger than the Ten Commandments. The slab of stone erected in New Haven reminds us that the Jewish universe is so huge that there is simply no way to describe it.

I was living in New Haven at the time and was invited to speak at the dedication. Among other things, I said that the memorial would serve "as proof of our grief and sorrow and mourning that would never end." Clearly, I meant those words. How could I possibly not miss having my family, not miss being part of routine procreation—I who historically, as a Jew, was always pro-procreation? But my mission in history was not merely to procreate. It was also to create something larger than myself and to take a stand—a stand that perhaps I wasn't even expected to take since, in Mark Twain's words, as a Jew my hands were tied behind my back. [ed. note: The reference is to Twain's essay "Concerning the Jews," originally published in 1898 in *Harper's Magazine*, in which Twain observed that the Jew characteristically succeeds by beating the odds against him: "He has made a marvelous fight in this world, in all the ages," Twain wrote. And he has "done it with his hands tied behind him."] An inquisition complete with instruments of torture was upon me long before Auschwitz-Birkenau, and my mission and my destiny were defined as being much broader than just myself. Yet while I will mourn forever the events of the Second World War, I don't really believe that anyone capable of thought will ever forget them. Ultimately, all that matters are people who think; the opinion of those who don't think doesn't really matter at all.

After that memorial was erected by the community of New Haven, I wrote a brief piece which no one, so far, has wanted to publish. Since I write by hand, I don't know how long the piece was, but my wife transferred it to the computer, which automatically counts my words. I don't like the idea of my words being counted. But, in any case, in that piece I proposed the idea that what happened to us during the Holocaust—the extermination of one third of the world's Jewry, of five thousand Jewish communities around the world in twenty-two countries—has somehow, over the last twenty or thirty years, led to something which I called "a Second Holocaust." By the Second Holocaust, I mean the most aggravated persecution complex in Jewish history. Instead of renewing ourselves spiritually through the Jewish ethos that celebrates life, we have allowed ourselves to be defined by Auschwitz-Birkenau and by death.

The Holocaust has become not only a way of defining a historical moment that, in fact, defies all definition but also, as I noted in my article, an event that many Jews have canonized long after the actual cannons of the Second World War went silent. But such canonization absorbs an extraordinary amount of energy. By now, in most communities, we have Holocaust memorials, Holocaust museums, and Holocaust study centers. Certainly, they ought to be there. But what else do we have to establish our identity in our own eyes as well as in the eyes of the others?

My father once warned me never to listen to anyone who tried to count the number of Jews in the world. He said we are not countable. We are not even accountable. Since we have given so much to mankind, counting us would be very unfair. But I have to mention one account—actually an accountant whom I know, an American Jew who volunteered to do pro bono work for the Polish-Jewish Presence Foundation that I chair. He wondered about the way that some of our history was being taught. His two daughters, who attend a Jewish school, were required to do a project for their class. That project was to build a replica of a concentration camp. The students had seven concentration camps to choose from.

When I heard that, I thought to myself that at this very moment, Dr. Goebbels must be raising a glass of German champagne. If we Jews— we American Jews, of all people—are teaching our children to focus on the concentration camps, then Goebbels has won. We are not in a ghetto. We can express ourselves freely, in any fashion and in any manner—the manner of Broadway, the manner of Wall Street, the manner of the Forbes 400. Why then should we now go back to a period which was not designed by us? Auschwitz-Birkenau is not my monument. I had nothing to do with it, nothing whatsoever. Not once in my four-thousand-year history would I have come up, historically, with the idea of something like that—the idea of being exterminated like a rat. There is not a single metaphor in the Talmud that links a human being to an animal. And yet the designers of this monument tried to reduce me to destruction, to collective extermination, to a manner of liquidization usually restricted to animals.

Auschwitz-Birkenau belongs to those who are united right now: it is their monument. It is an integral part of the German-Austrian history, and it should be called by its German name: Auschwitz-Birkenau. Don't you dare call it by any other name, especially not a Polish one. Oświęcim [the town

outside of Kraków in which the Auschwitz-Birkenau death camp was built]
was an innocent village. Jews lived around Kraków for a thousand years.
Some of the best Jewish thinkers, who were published in fifty languages,
lived only kilometers from Oświęcim. Some of the largest synagogues still
stand in Kraków, too big even for the Germans to have destroyed. Nearby,
cemeteries not just with tombs but with obelisks almost as large as this
room still serve as a reminder of the Jewish presence.

Back to these two girls who are building the replica of a concentration
camp. Why not a replica of a statue by Man Ray? Why not a dissertation on
that other Jew Modigliani? Why not an essay about Jews in Hollywood, which
two Jewish writers recently described as "the kingdom of our own"? Frankly,
I disagree with that description. Calling Hollywood a kingdom of the Jews is
as mindless as calling "White Christmas" a Jewish song. Hollywood, in fact,
is the most universal kingdom on earth. With television in practically every
home, there are few places now that Hollywood does not reach.

When I speak about Jewishness to my polo-playing friends in other
parts of the United States—some of whom have never physically met a Jew,
although clearly they have encountered Jews mentally, in the Ten Commandments and elsewhere in the culture—they look at me and say, "My, my, are
you Jewish?" I say, "Yes, for all practical purposes I am." One of them even
asked me if I met Hitler when he visited Warsaw in 1942. Somehow, in my
friend's mind, Hitler and I were personally connected. Poland is a large and
diverse country, over sixty million people. And yet, interestingly enough,
most Poles are connected to Jews, even if they do not necessarily know it.

Yad Vashem is also an extraordinary place. So is the Museum of the
Diaspora in Tel Aviv. Such places must exist, and they must be enriched
because their lessons are essential. The account of what happened to the
Jews is clearly part of a universal history. There is currently in print an *Encyclopedia of the Holocaust*. Two volumes long with over two hundred and
forty contributors, the encyclopedia lists every place where the physical
body of a Jew was exterminated. But where can I find an *Encyclopedia of Jewish Achievement*? If I wanted to enlighten my Gentile friends, where could
I locate a *Jewish Hall of Fame* book? I don't mean the yellow pages, with
the yellow Star of David on the cover. If you know of such a book, tell me.

And then I wrote something else that upset some editors, most of whom are non-Jews. After getting angry that no one wanted to publish my original little piece, I enlarged and reinforced it. In the revised piece, I said, "It is a wonder that, at this very moment, thousands of American teenagers and adults cannot find Jewish tradition inspiring enough to let them remain or become Jewish." I explained that today, many American Jews regularly gather in America's crystal-laden ballrooms in order to lavish funds on one more Holocaust monument to be erected in one more community of North America. Yet "the countless Judaica, Jewish thousand-year-old spiritual pyramids and cultural citadels, perish worldwide because no funds are forthcoming for their recovery, rescue, restoration, or preservation."

Someone asked me for an example. I will give you one that technically should blast you off your feet, one that the Jews have no right to lose because we are a people of oral tradition. We lost a language. I don't mean Esperanto: Esperanto is alive and well. Some three million people speak Esperanto, a language invented by Dr. L. L. Zamenhof, a Polish Jew. I don't mean Hebrew: Hebrew is very much alive and well in the extraordinary state of Israel. I mean Ladino. No, Ladino is not a new restaurant or nightclub downtown. Nor is Ladino related to the popular dance the Lambada. Don't laugh. This is no joke. Ladino was a language we spoke for a thousand years. It is a language in which we wrote millions of books and songs and philosophical works. It is a language like no other. It is a language spoken not just in the Iberian Peninsula, not just in Portugal and Spain—although this in itself would be enough. Take a look at the historical map of mankind. At one time, Spain was the size of the United States and Europe combined, many times over. Ladino is part of our Jewish civilization and also of universal civilization. Yet do you know of a prominent university with a chair of Ladino? Holocaust studies abound. But there are no departments of Ladino.

Some evening, take your car and drive to New Jersey. That's not too far—not the Middle East; not Iraq; not Morocco; not Madrid. Look there at the Jews who used to speak Ladino. Most of them live quite well. Any one of these families, in fact, could redeem Ladino for the next thousand years. My accountant tells me that the cost of redeeming Ladino would equal the cost of buying a studio in SoHo. But so far no one has done so.

Over the years, we became polyglots who speak all kinds of languages; we changed our names; we gave the first Berlitz course in history. And we had three languages of our own. Now, one is dead. And even the second, Yiddish, may already be dying. The fact is that we have done this to ourselves. The Second Holocaust, which brings even greater damage, is also self-imposed.

Last week, I was in Amsterdam, which is an extraordinary place. When John Adams, the second president of the United States, was the first American ambassador to the United Provinces, as Holland was then called, he sought a loan for a country to whom nobody wanted to lend money. Even then, Amsterdam was quite an enlightened place, a place where Jews could—for the first time in their history—serve as members of Parliament. It was the Sephardic Jews of Old Amsterdam—Jews originally from Spain, who at one time or another advised the mightiest monarchs on earth—who urged their Dutch colleagues that they could not go wrong subsidizing a new Amsterdam. And so the Dutch gave the loan, in tribute to these Dutch Jews who spoke Ladino.

While in Amsterdam, I visited the Portuguese Synagogue that stands in that city. With all due respect, there is nothing like it in the New Amsterdam. That synagogue was built in 1675, at the cost of 186,000 guilders. That is, relatively speaking, probably three times as much as the hundred and fifty million dollars the Holocaust Memorial Museum in Washington, D.C., will cost, eighty million dollars of which has already been collected. This synagogue, however, is a sanctuary like no other. Since photography is my hobby, I brought with me a twenty-four-millimeter lens with which to photograph the interior. But my lens was not wide enough for that amazing sanctuary of Jewish treasures. The reason the synagogue stands there intact, as it was in 1675, is because—during the Second World War—the Germans decided to keep it. They had their own reason: it was to be a museum of Jewish absence, a very different kind of Holocaust museum. Yet today, it is still what it used to be, a synagogue—a testament to Jewish presence. And it took my breath away.

MIND POLISH

In this lecture (an early version of his essay "The Second Holocaust," which appeared in the *Boston Globe* in 1990), Kosinski suggested that the Jewish preoccupation with extermination and annihilation during the Holocaust creates a kind of "Second Holocaust." He urged Jews to define themselves not by wartime deaths and losses but rather through celebrations of life, including Jewish accomplishment and achievement, and to focus not on Jewish absence but rather on Jewish presence throughout history.

The twentieth century enters its last decade to the march of newly forged national freedom. Among the many losses, wounds, and still-opened graves that have marked its passage—all of which are immune to this march—one loss remains higher than all others. To this loss, the Jews have given the irrevocable name of the Holocaust.

But the Holocaust must also be seen as the loss of memory, the loss of mind—a loss far greater than that of life, the primary and most dramatic measure we attach to it. This dimension both adds to and transcends the numerical-historical record—the record of who and why, the record of how and where.

In "Concerning the Jews," Mark Twain noted that the Jew's contribution to "the world's list of great names in literature, science, art, music, finance, medicine, and abstruse learning [is] also way out of proportion to the weakness of his numbers." In spite of this contribution, which has continued at an accelerated rate, the trauma of the physical loss of the Holocaust has now virtually paralyzed the Jewish psyche and soul for nearly half a century. This paralysis is so far-reaching that it has brought almost to a standstill preocccupation with life, once the most formidable characteristic of the Jewish presence worldwide. In his fondest dreams, Dr. Joseph Goebbels, who dreamt of a Jew-free world, could not have dreamt up a period in the Jewish chain of tradition in which Jews themselves would insist en masse on defining themselves as being cursed by history to an everlasting damnation. These definitions have fixed upon the nonstop wallowing in every exile, every eviction, every mass slaying, every butchery, every carnage, every bloodbath, every pogrom, every concentration camp, every gas oven—a veritable fixation upon every conceivable form of Jewish death as caused by non-Jews. Fixed upon death, instead of being fixed upon what the Jews have always been known for: the celebration of life.

This Jewish self-excommunication—this turning away from Jewishness perceived as a perpetual source of life, to insistence by so many Jews themselves on Jewishness understood to be an unending state of death dealing—has consequences for Jews and non-Jews alike. Those consequences are far more deadly than all the decimation inflicted upon the Jews throughout history, not excluding the Holocaust, the greatest pogrom in history symbolized by Auschwitz. A Nazi-erected state-of-the-art monument to human annihilation, to human absence, Auschwitz has become for many Jews synonymous with Jewish fate.

Paradoxically, the preocccupation with absence, with asphyxiation, and with the fear of being extinguished continues to be shared by millions of Jews, so many of whom flourish in every conceivable way and who—alive and well, though commemorating liquidation—contribute far more to mankind's well-being than any other culturally cohesive group. But they do it silently, timidly, always on the lookout for yet another murder or future atrocity.

Hence, the Holocaust that aimed at the physical annihilation of the Jews which ended over a half a century ago has been succeeded by a Second Holocaust: the virtual elimination of knowledge of historic contributions of the Jews to the human mind. The Jews—not only those who survived the Holocaust but also those who remained safely outside of it—are doing all too little to stem this loss. All too often, they see themselves not as victors over the forces of organized death but as mere chance survivors of some past, present, or future anti-Semitic fusillade.

Fortunately, we can't live by Holocaust remembrances alone. And, while the physical substance of the brain, whether Jewish or non-Jewish, could—as the Holocaust proved—be pulverized and reduced to ash, the collective memory cannot. This memory must acknowledge what until now the Second Holocaust has wiped from it—namely that, while since biblical times the Jews have resided in many places, none save the United States or the state of Israel has been more hospitable to their autonomous cultural and spiritual development than the great swath of the territories which once formed the Polish-Lithuanian Commonwealth where Jews first settled long before America or Israel became states. There, free to remain themselves, Jews devoted all their energies to family life, self-enlightenment, and the ethic of productivity.

Within the Polish-Lithuanian Commonwealth, sufficiently aware of the wealth of thought as well as of the industrious qualities of the Jewish character, the overwhelmingly Catholic state let the Polish Jews develop the widest range of trades and crafts, whether in villages or in towns, whether working for themselves or for others, whether managing the estates of petty squires or of great nobles. There the Jews achieved a uniquely favored status seldom matched in the rest of Europe. It was there, in Poland, that the Yiddish language—in translation, the word means "Jewish"—gave the Jewish mind and soul its greatest vehicle for artistic expression until the emergence of modern-day Hebrew. Even today, the dominant cultural forms and achievements in Israel and among the Jews of America and Western Europe stem directly from the Polish-Jewish heritage, one of the richest heritages ever endowed by a single ethnic group. And it is not an accident that Eliezer Ben-Yehuda, the creator of modern Hebrew, credited a member of the Polish nobility with encouraging him to pursue the idea of a Hebrew nation.

In this context, so easily verifiable by historical records, the Holocaust of Jewish memory tragically gained the greatest momentum when it succeeded—at least in the American-Israeli Jewish popular mind—in turning Poland, the very territory where Jews accomplished so much for themselves and others, into a spiritual no-man's-land. This turning away from a rational assessment of the past meant that, no longer secure in their perception of themselves as the most alive of peoples, the Polish Jews became accountants of death bent on counting their dead rather than on praising their deeds. The culturally victorious march of Polish Jewry throughout history was spoken of as though it was an endless funeral procession of so much of the Jewish psyche. Accordingly, in order to accommodate such mental disorder, a new brand of Jewish topography was construed. It blamed Poland for the crimes committed against the Jews by the Nazi-Stalinist occupiers and blatantly disregarded the fact that more than one fifth of the entire Polish nation was slaughtered by the Nazis—with help from Stalinist Russia—in less than five years of the war, in one of the greatest, if indeed not the greatest, wholesale national massacres in history.

The results of the Second Holocaust are here to see: with so large a chunk of Jewish heritage thrown into nothingness, it is more natural today to encounter a Jewish child in Brooklyn building a replica of a Nazi concentration camp for a Jewish history project than being taught the glowing Jewish contribution to human achievement by, say, the musical genius of Aleksander Tansman, a Polish-French Jew born in Łódź in 1897, who enjoyed unrivaled acclaim in the thirties and forties in Europe but who remains virtually unknown in this country today.

And why not analyze the miraculous prose and graphics of Bruno Schulz or the art of Man Ray? And who, if not the Jews who originated in Eastern Europe, gave the world new forms of entertainment? Ask Broadway. Ask Hollywood. What must go on: the audit of horror or the honor roll of Jewish achievement? Must Dr. Goebbels succeed by injecting spiritual Zyklon B into the galaxy of the human mind where Jewish presence has been anything but marginal and nebulous?

Generating pride in one's victimization is an unhealthy task. No matter how many times the trip is made to Auschwitz and back, no matter how many monuments are built to the Holocaust, however dominant their size, the net result is that Jews keep on surrendering their spiritual pyramids and cultural citadels to the darkest forces of the Holocaust.

As a result, the missing image of the Jew has been supplied by the ignorant and the prejudiced who, never having traveled into the depths of their own mind where so much of Jewish-made inspiration could be found, instead mindlessly draw upon pejorative notions of the Jew picked up from sensationalist news rags and revisionist propaganda, festering worldwide in pockets of irrationality. No longer reassured by their daily achievement in every area of human endeavor, unable to find self-affirmation in the record of mutilations afflicted by morbid preoccupation with the role of disaster in Jewish history, Jews turn from history to hysteria. For example, the emergence of a single anti-Semite or even an anti-Semitic group testing the limits of free expression in Eastern Europe seizes the Jewish imagination more forcefully than the extraordinarily creative role of the Jews in contemporary America.

Similarly, the confused utterance of an otherwise well-meaning though utterly confused Polish Catholic dignitary receives more attention than the recent Polish debates on the Holocaust—the most thorough debate of this sort ever conducted by the largest and most enlightened pro-Jewish Catholic forum in contemporary history. A publicity-seeking French revisionist dominates the Jewish psyche for weeks upon weeks at a time while the most spectacular contributions of French Jews to science, technology, and intellectual discourse pass without comment.

The never-ending stream of Holocaust images in which Jews, the ever cited six million, are shown either in mute herdlike surrender or in heroic but doomed resistance have saturated and derailed the mind to the point where we no longer care how many people in the British Commonwealth know the work of Isaac Rosenberg. Nor do we tell the camera-wielding Japanese of the immense contribution of Jews to image making and the art of photography. The list and the argument could be continued indefinitely.

This Second Holocaust has truncated the Jewish tree of life in many other ways. In Poland, Jews, who made up more than half the population of world-famous textile centers such as Łódź and Białystok, helped to develop some of the world's largest textile industries. Should not their descendants

199

be returning to initiate joint ventures in the rapidly privatized environment, making use of age-old economic skills and technical expertise to reestablish themselves where they once flourished so strongly? Must pilgrimages to Eastern Europe be devoted solely to visiting death camps, cemeteries, and memorial plaques? Must initiatives be limited to the preservation of Eastern European Judaica and exclude investment in the production of goods, once so successfully accomplished by Jews?

The verdict is clear. As this century, the most tragic century in Jewish memory, is about to end, the Jewish voice must be heard in defiance of death as it celebrates life. Celebrates it, as Jews have done for so many years—in family life; in education and scholarship; in science, technology, and research; in literature, art, music, and drama. The remembrance of the Holocaust must never again be allowed to still the voice of memory.

DEFINING MYSELF

In a session sponsored by the *Jerusalem Post* while he was visiting Israel in 1988, Kosinski commented on how the Holocaust shaped his own identity.

What am I defined by? Am I defined by the Holocaust? Am I going to be defined as one who has lived and survived? Am I a soul which has been around for a great many centuries, a soul which inspired every single belief that surrounds me in this city of Jerusalem and in all other cities too? Am I a collective being who has sustained the very best in every aspect of life, be it music or technology or religion or architecture or media? Or am I going to be defined as a victim? Am I going to look at myself again—and again and again—on American television, being killed by people in Nazi uniforms? Is this my history? Am I going to pass on, to the child whom I don't have or to the friend whom I might have, a definition of myself as a victim or as a survivor?

As a Jew, I have been around longer than almost everyone else. I have contributed nothing but the best to this civilization: the best values, the notions of mercy and understanding and human rights, the belief in a supreme being—"being" meaning being here as well as being there. Am I now going to be defined by four years during which a group of people, however large or small, armed with machine guns, ran me down? Am I going to accept this as the definition of myself? Am I going to erect a monument to every single Jew who was burned, who was killed, who was pogromized in the last two thousand years? Or should I erect instead a monument to those living Jews like me, those who wrote a book, who wrote a tune, who wrote a poem, who contributed to science, who invented a microphone— or a human microphone, meaning an inner voice? This is the issue that is at stake. The minute I see—here I speak only for myself—anything to do with what is known as the Holocaust, and what is known to me instead as the period between 1939 and 1945, I turn this particular microphone off.

The Holocaust had nothing to do with me. I did not design it. I did not write the screenplay for it. I did not participate in it in any way. There is nothing, nothing, in my whole history that would contribute to the notion of the destruction of another human being. Nothing whatsoever. I may have moved from the extreme left to the extreme right; I may have been Rosa Luxemburg at one time in history or Karl Marx in another; I may have been Zinoviev or Trotsky. But I have never proposed—*never* proposed—the destruction of life.

The Holocaust had nothing to do with me. It doesn't belong to me, and I am no part of it. Since I am not didactic, it is also no business of mine to tell those who were responsible for it that it is their business. They know it. They suffered in it too. Some of them died in it as well, and they died pretty tragically.

The question, therefore, is how I am going to define myself. I remember looking at the Holocaust monument erected by the New Haven community, which was well designed out of barbed wire and stone, and at those remaining members of the Jewish community, some of whom came from Europe and some of whom did not. And I asked myself if we, the chosen intellectuals and the chosen "spirituals," if there is such a noun, were now going to be in the business of erecting a monument to every victim of the Holocaust. In that very moment, as we were consecrating the monument, we were in fact saluting Goebbels. We were paying tribute to the fashion in which we as Jews died, even though that fashion had nothing to do with us.

Each time I see a movie about the Holocaust, I hear a German voice. And each time I pay tribute to my own relatives, almost all of whom vanished in the Holocaust, I ask myself am I going to pay tribute to that disappearance? Am I—the most alive of all people on earth, the most spiritual of all of them—going to say I salute those of you who have died? Of course, I do salute them, and of course I cry that they are not around. Apparently, I once made a terrible error when, in the spirit of emotion, I said to someone from the American Foundation for Polish-Jewish studies that my relatives would have died anyhow. He replied, "Don't say that, because they would not have died in the ovens." And that was a good correction. They would not have died in the ovens, but eventually they would have died. So I say it is tragic the way they died; it is tragic that their children died; and it is indescribably tragic that they died simply because they were Jews. But they would have died anyhow. There is one thing that should not die with them, though, and that is the way I live—the way I sit, the way I write, the way I think. My tradition should not die with them. It is one thing to erect a monument to the victims of the Holocaust and quite another to feel that the tradition in which I have been raised and which is part of me should be part of this death. If this tradition is going to die with them, then who am I? Where do I come from?

ON THE FILM *SHOAH*

At Albion College, where he was awarded an honorary doctorate in April 1988, Kosinski offered a comment on the film *Shoah*.

The American Foundation for Polish-Jewish Studies [chaired by Kosinski], through the Oxford Institute, financed Claude Lanzmann's film *Shoah*. And I will tell you what I think about it. *Shoah* was presented as a documentary. Clearly, it is not, and it should not have been presented that way. Mr. Lanzmann, however, was free to do *Shoah* as a work of fiction. Fiction is a work in which the creator documents his own prejudice. Nothing wrong with that. Any artist can do that. In fact, being an artist means documenting your own prejudices. You pick up on certain aspects of the universe and then select documents that justify the outlook you have adopted. Lanzmann adopted a particular outlook. And there is nothing wrong with that.

Let me give you a clear example of what I mean. I am very fond of Switzerland because I love to ski there. Yet Switzerland is also a land of many lakes—and I don't like lakes. They threaten me because they are cold and forbidding; they are neither buoyant nor life giving. You can't swim in them because they are full of floating ice. They are not truthful. If I were to make a movie about Switzerland, I would portray it as a country of mountains, but I would not show its lakes. That is the outlook on Switzerland that I would adopt.

Lanzmann adopted a view of Poland that was similarly selective. He seemed to suggest that the preponderance of concentration camps were situated in Poland because of Poland's anti-Semitism and not because of German hatred. He neglected the fact that, during the war, many non-Jewish Poles suffered as much as the Polish Jews. His *Shoah* is therefore a picture of amnesia.

Similarly, to say that the Jews in Poland were not helped enough by the Poles is to say, in the same breath, that the Jews abroad, in America, did not help the Polish Jews enough. Such a view neglects the fact that there is such a thing as war. There is such a thing as the viciousness that the war brings about. There is such a thing as fear.

The film *Shoah* is as biased as it can be. It is a portrait of a psyche which demands hate as its mission. Nothing wrong with that. I am who I am because I was despised by others; I am who I am because I had to overcome that. And so I accept hate as part of the human condition. I am not here on this stage to be liked. I am here to stimulate thought, to prompt. Prompt—but to what? To pogrom? No. To action? Yes. But to what kind of action? To mental action, to concentration.

That is not what *Shoah* is about. *Shoah* is about bias. Pauline Kael, writing in *The New Yorker*, called *Shoah* "a long moan." By that moan, I believe she meant the feeling that we have always been oppressed and that we will be oppressed again. Kael also said that the film "is exhausting to watch because it closes your mind, the way hate does." Again, nothing wrong with that. A creative man, after all, can create a portrait of hate; he can even sell hate. But this is what *Shoah* is. It surely is not history.

On Jewish Identity

I am hardly a didactic character, but I think the best thing we can teach our children is an understanding and appreciation of the past. Let them define themselves by what we, the Jews, have always defined ourselves by—our tradition. Tradition is the key to the Jewish Self, with a capital S. Who were we? Where did we come from? What have we done? What are the pyramids that we have left behind—in Eastern Europe and in every aspect of life? We must teach our children that we cannot leave those pyramids unattended.

Can we be vulgar, brutal, unkind? Is one supposed to hint at something rather than name it? What is the level of confronting one's past when it is the past of six million people?

In the Jewish tradition, language, the word, is the repository of tradition. . . . I only want to be a tale bearer among people.

OBSESSION

In a session hosted by the *Jerusalem Post* in January 1988, Kosinski spoke about how his Jewishness defined his storytelling.

I was asked this afternoon if I was "obsessed" with finding my Jewishness. Obsessions are a difficult subject to talk about. Being Jewish was never an obsession. It was a state, an inner state, which I felt defined me, so there was no need for me to define the obsession. One was Jewish, as my father said, simply because of the way one moved, the way one talked, the way one laughed and made fun of things. My Jewishness is something that has grown over years and years and years; therefore, I was never detached from it. It came not necessarily as an obsession but as a preoccupation.

What matters most to me as a novelist are my books. I am defined by little else. Over the last six years, I wrote a novel that was different from all my other books—a novel in which the content was not so much the issue as the form. I felt that the traditional novel, the novel with a plot, had basically run out. At the very least, it had run out of me. I no longer felt that I could tell a meaningful story, a story that would attract my attention, much less anyone else's. The idea was to find a different form, a different narrative form. And I remembered that the Jewish tradition is about narration, about looking at the world not directly but in a mediated form—one's own relationship with the world mediated through language. Language allows a pause, allows a reflection. Maybe that is why it is a Jewish condition that somehow one does not go into the world directly; one meets it through the book.

During those six years, I looked for the new narrative form—not for the new religion, not for the new state of being. I know exactly where I stand and what happens within me. But what I missed was how I could rejuvenate a form that was boring to me. I did not want to write another Kosinski novel, a ninth novel in more or less the same vein that I had written the other eight. Being worldly and confronting an audience? I had done that. Nature? I love nature; I already knew my own relationship with it. But I kept asking whether there was any other part of myself into which I had not yet looked very closely—and that part was the inner cast, the soul. What is a soul? Soul—not soil. What is the state of a soul? What happens in the brain of a writer who sits down to write a novel? What is he after? Is he after himself? Is he after an obsession? Does he want to please an audience? I started wondering if I really even know who my readers are. In fact, when I met Philip Roth this afternoon in the King David Hotel—he has a new novel coming out—I asked him if he knew who his audience is. He said, "Do you?" I don't.

The idea, therefore, was to find the new form within myself. The idea was to go to the very place my father had once identified when he told me not to write too readily because paper is patient. My father said, "Eventually you will have to define yourself in terms of what it is that prompts you to go through life." I have no family. I have no estate of any meaningful sort. I do not own anything really. So I realized that I had to look deeply into the cast of my own mind in order to understand what makes me feel, believe, act the way I do: why do I sit *this* way as opposed to sitting *that* way? Is there, I wondered, a formula somewhere? Is there a background? That is why I decided to look into certain aspects of Jewish history. The whole of Jewish history is too vast to know: it would fill this room, and even then no one could fully appreciate its scope.

The aspect of Jewish history that particularly fascinated me was this: narrative drive. What is it that makes me a storyteller? Why do I want to tell a story rather than do something else? Suddenly my past became open to me. Even Poland allowed me to come back. But to come back—as who? As an American? How American am I, really? I have spent over thirty of my fifty-five years as an American. But what about those first twenty-four years? What happened to me during those years? I had to ask myself many questions: How did the war shape me? Am I a survivor? Do I see myself as a survivor or simply as someone made stronger by my wartime experience?

Most importantly, perhaps, I realized that I had to go back just so that I could understand what it was that made me *want* to go back. Was it vanity? No doubt about it. But what kind of vanity? Polish vanity? Jewish vanity? Was it some sense of community? Was it the fact that I enjoyed spending time with people who did not know me and whom I did not know?

I love people, and I connect with them through my fiction. I have no other reasons to be around. So I went back to the Polish-Jewish past— particularly to the narrative aspect of the Polish-Jewish tradition in which I was raised. My novels may be written in English and they may project universal characters, but they are profoundly grounded in the Jerzy Kosinski who came to the United States when he was twenty-four. In searching for a new form for my latest book, I returned to an old form and to my Polish-Jewish origins.

BEING THERE AS A POLISH JEW

In his 1988 lecture to the Van Leer Jerusalem Institute, one of Israel's leading intellectual centers for the study and discussion of issues related to philosophy, society, culture, and education, Kosinski explored various questions of identity. Specifically, as a Polish Jew, he discussed what it meant to "be there" in the Łódź ghetto and what it means to "be here" as a survivor and as a writer.

My first novel, *The Painted Bird*, was not entirely original. Clearly no work of literature really is. In fact, some one hundred and fifty years ago, a book called *The Painted Vulture* was published in Hebrew; I decided that it would have been a better title for *The Painted Bird*. But that's what happens: somehow you always get these ideas when it is too late.

"Being There as a Polish Jew" is a contextual title. By itself, the phrase "being there" is a contradiction—that's why I picked it initially—a contradiction in terms, since if one *is*, one is a being; one is here. Yet "being there" also suggests a sense of division. The phrase works much better in English than in any other language I know. When the novel was translated, it lost that particular contradiction. It became "Wystarczy Być" in Polish, "La Présence"—the state of external being—in French. It occurred to me that to convey the state in which one sees oneself as contradictory to oneself, "being there," that is, being divided, being an exile and yet not an exile, being one's self and yet one's Self with a capital *S,* could best be illustrated the way a novelist illustrates these things: with an act of self-revelation.

Some years ago, around 1969, I was invited to teach English for a year at Princeton University. My wife and I arrived in Princeton, a big school in a small town, a place which I didn't have any real sense of. After I met the members of the faculty and the head of the Department of English, I was introduced to a young man who was responsible for taking me to the apartment where my wife and I were to live. As we drove toward our destination, he said to me, "Oh, Mr. Kosinski, you know there is an extraordinarily interesting woman who lives in the apartment next door." Kiki and I were not married yet, so it seemed a perfectly reasonable comment. He added, "She's a fascinating woman." As a courtesy, I replied, "Really? What's her name? What does she do?" He said, "Well, she came from abroad. She's Khrushchev's daughter." I said, "Khrushchev's daughter? Do you mean she's Stalin's daughter?" He said, "That's right. She's Stalin's daughter."

Now, of course, before coming to Princeton, I had read that Svetlana Alliluyeva Stalin lived somewhere in that area, and I only hoped that it would be as far away as possible from where I was going to be. But what was fascinating is that, to our escort, there was no conflict in the situation. Khrushchev's daughter, Stalin's daughter: it didn't make any difference to him. The difference to me, however, was enormous. For the rest of the trip, I felt completely shaken. There was in me a sense of trauma—trauma, not because the name of Stalin carried any particular implication at Princeton but because I suddenly found myself challenged by history in a very unsettling fashion.

Here I was, a Polish Jew living in the United States, already pressing my luck after the Second World War. And now I was going to live next to—*literally* next to—Stalin's daughter. I had visited Moscow after the war, when I was a university student, and the idea that, through the strange working of history, something like this encounter with my Russian past was possible terrified me a great deal. Needless to say, afterward, each time I had the pleasure of meeting Svetlana, I felt torn, divided. It was as if two of me walked with her—maybe three of me, maybe even four. Without a doubt, I could never speak to her in Russian. I wouldn't dare. Whenever she pronounced a verdict upon my books, I didn't dare to argue, although normally, with anyone else, I would have. I remember being in my office with one of my American students when Svetlana rang me up by phone. As soon as she said, "Hello, Jerzy," in English—that's the language of mediation between myself and history that I imposed—I automatically stood up in a kind of salute. In fact, I was not saluting Svetlana. I was not saluting myself. I was saluting an extraordinary event. I was brushing elbows with an extraordinary history. That's what "being there" really means.

Judging by the average age of the audience, I assume most of you will be just as traumatized by the proximity to the Stalin name as I was. But there is another name I should mention, since it also belongs in my spiritual vocabulary and because, whether I like it or not, he is a kind of spiritual kin. The second name, of course, belongs to Adolf Hitler. To a large degree, Hitler was responsible for who I am; for how I think—about you, about myself, about the state of Israel; for the way I tell stories and for the kind of stories I tell, or do not tell. In his book *Symbol, Myth, and Culture*, Ernst Cassirer, a professor from Yale University, wrote that on the eleventh anniversary of his National Socialist regime, Hitler—that other kin of mine—changed his tone. No longer promising the conquest of the world to the German race, he began to see his defeat and feel its consequences. But, even at such a critical moment, Hitler did not speak of the innumerable evils which his aggression had brought to the German people, to Europe, to the whole world, or of the defeat of his armies and the destruction of German cities. His whole attention, Professor Cassirer writes, was still fixed on the fate of the Jews. "If I am defeated"—he says—"Jewry could celebrate a second triumphant Purim festival." What worried him was not "the future destiny of Germany but the 'triumph' of the Jews."

Cassirer concludes that, by this utterance, Hitler "proves once more how little he knows of Jewish life and Jewish feeling. In our life, in the life of a modern Jew, there is no room left for any sort of joy or complacency, let alone exultation or triumph. All this has gone forever. No Jew whatsoever can or will ever overcome the terrible ordeal of these last years. The victims of this ordeal cannot be forgotten; the wounds inflicted upon us are incurable."

I love *Symbol, Myth, and Culture*. But I do not agree with Professor Cassirer that the ills are incurable. I like to think that, for the most part, they have been cured. I don't suffer from them at all; I have transferred them to something else—fiction. What better way to get rid of anything? I do, however, agree with Cassirer that, in this combat, the modern Jew had to defend not only his physical existence or the preservation of the Jewish race; he also had to "represent all those ethical ideals that had been brought into being by Judaism and found their way into general human culture, into the life of all civilized nations. And here we stand on firm ground." On this, I definitely stand firm as well.

In his own quiet cabalistic way, my father had tried to teach me an important lesson. "What will eventually matter to you," he said, "is not the outward expression but rather who you really are, how you see yourself, what you think of yourself when you get up in the morning." To do that, I had to go back to Poland, where—historically—I resided for some thousand years. Poland—a place from which I can never extract myself since the place resides within me. It is located somewhere between "being" and "there," in that never-ending inner contradiction, the fusion of the confusion—as I like to call it—that every one of us represents.

Poland, during the war, was—one could say—an inferno. During the war, it lost some twenty-two percent of its population, a number that includes its Jewish citizenry. By comparison, the Soviet Union, although much larger in size, lost four percent of its population. Yugoslavia lost ten percent, Greece seven percent. All in all, however, in Poland, some twenty-nine percent of all intellectuals and twenty-seven percent of all Catholic clergy—important figures, after all—disappeared between 1939 and 1945. Out of three million and five hundred thousand Polish Jews living in Poland before the war, only five thousand children remained in 1945. Thus, as you can clearly see, it was not an ordinary place. In fact, the place was so extraordinarily unordinary that one of my kin—the man I mentioned before, Adolf Hitler—felt that only in Poland, because of the proximity that the Jewish soul shared with the Jewish soil, certain laws had to be enacted and maintained. These laws were very simple. They were posted on every tree, on every house, on every auditorium, and they said—in Yiddish, in Polish, and in German—that anyone who harbored a Jew would be sentenced to death. That's all. And anyone who refused to denounce those persons who harbored a Jew would be sent to a concentration camp. And that's death as well. This was the case only in Poland, not in any of the other countries which were incorporated, one way or another, into the Third Reich.

Imagine for a moment that you are harboring a Polish-Jewish child like me. Where do you hide him? In a basement? In the wall? Behind a chair? Suppose that child becomes ill. What do you do? Call a neighbor? A doctor? Do you wait for a night without a moon, so no one can see what you are doing? Imagine just how many people would have to be involved in saving a single Jew. Thirty-five? Forty? Fifty?

There is always someone in my audience who stands up and screams at me, "You don't realize what the Poles have done to us, the Jews! They didn't help us." And to this person I say very advisedly, not because I was advised by anyone in particular but because just as much as I brushed elbows with Svetlana Stalin I brushed elbows with history—and I say with all respect for the pain and trauma and tears that come from an authentic disaster—that the reason the Poles did not help the Polish Jews during the Second World War in Poland is no different from the reason the Jews in Poland during the Second World War did not help their fellow Poles. They did not take the inflammatory posters down from the walls because of fear: even the smallest act could destroy a whole household.

Fear is not something that historians know a great deal about; there is no such thing as a historical definition of fear. To know anything about fear, one has to read the novelists, who can best describe that state. Historians at most can speak of the absence of visual action. Statistics, for example, can show that I was being beaten up on this stage and none of you came to my rescue. But statistics won't offer any explanation for your response. Maybe you were afraid to come to the stage. Maybe you feared for your own life. Or maybe you felt, as apparently I am supposed to feel, that you should not come to my rescue, since you had no right to believe that my blood is more red than yours.

This brings me to literature and—whether I like it or not—to my own work, *The Painted Bird*, which was kindly mentioned in the introduction.

When I sat down to write the book, my idea was to convey something which is quite common to us as Jews, and that is the folklore of superstition—not the civilized state of destruction, not ideology, not any particular historical trend, but something the Jews have always been very good at believing in: the inexpressible. But the Second World War was about much more than just superstition; it departed very substantially from what happened before. It was actually a war launched against a child, any child. It was no longer a war where the people who were fighting actually knew each other.

When *The Painted Bird* was first published, I did something which novelists are not supposed to do and which in fact they very seldom do: I wrote the *Notes* on my own novel. I did so not because I was secure about the book, but because I was insecure and felt that it might be misrepresented. And the publisher sent the *Notes* to every reviewer along with the book itself. As I wrote in the *Notes*, "The anthropologist could no more pin the facts [of the lives of the characters of *The Painted Bird*] to the printed page than he could those of the witches of *Macbeth*." As a novelist, I was not trying to pin facts; instead, I was trying to describe a very real state of oppression. Superstitions are real; blind fear is real. And the Second World War was certainly about blind fear.

Not too long ago, a newspaper wrote first in German and then in English that the Holocaust did not occur; it was just revisionist history. Imagine that: it never happened! Your speaker tonight was therefore a Holocaust swindler and a Holocaust macher. I don't speak German, but some of you might know what that means in English translation. According to the paper the Holocaust was merely a myth. That made me wonder. If I could magically remove the Holocaust from my life, simply wipe it out, would I do that or not? Would I like to see myself in 1939, a middle-class Jewish child spoiled by his parents and eventually by his children—because my parents would have wanted me to have children, even though I don't have any? Would I want that or not? Of course, I would, that's only natural. Had there been no Holocaust, I might have retained my family, all sixty-three or sixty-four or more of them.

But there was a Holocaust, and I was a part of it. So how do I see myself now? Am I a living memorial to the victims who suffered and died? Or as one of the monuments that celebrates what Jews have contributed to civilization?

Personally, I would love to see a monument to Bruno Schulz, a great novelist who wrote only two novels and a great master of drawing who died at the age of fifty. From his small town of Drohobycz, which was then in Galicia [now Drohobych, Ukraine], Schulz corresponded in German with Thomas Mann. At one point, instead of a funny, moving letter, Schulz sent Mann a whole novel that he wrote in German, just to please Mann. For a man who had written only two novels in his lifetime to send a third one, in German, as a kind of act of courtship was truly a formidable thing to do. But there is no monument to Bruno Schulz. Even his books are largely unavailable today.

Or Stefan Zweig. I love Stefan Zweig. Part of my ability to stand in front of you and talk comes from the extraordinary mixture of biography and narration that I learned from Zweig. With his biographies and his novel about chess playing—one he wrote shortly before committing suicide in Petrópolis, Brazil, in 1942, the same year Bruno Schulz was killed in Drohobycz—he had a hold over my whole generation. Yet there is no monument to Zweig. When I ran into a young Austrian recently, he informed me that, while Zweig's former home in Vienna still stands, it is now a private residence, and he confirmed that few people even know who he was.

So the question remains: how am I to see myself? Should I see myself in terms of *Every Day a Remembrance Day*, a book that reminds me that on this day in 1614 the Jewish quarter of Frankfurt, Germany, was attacked by a crowd led by Vincent Feldnich? Is Feldnich part of my spiritual history? Should I remember that, on this day in 1941, the Nazis shot seven hundred and sixty Jews, among them sixty Jews in a certain Latvian city? Am I going to see myself as a never-ending figure of horror? Am I—someone who historically left nothing but spiritual pyramids behind me—somehow supposed to erect daily monuments in my selective memory to those who are after me?

I was born in Łódź, Poland's second biggest city, which was almost evenly divided between some two hundred fifty thousand Polish Jews and three hundred thousand Polish non-Jews. In 1939, the year that Adolf Eichmann arrived in Łódź, my family of Weinrichs and Lewinkopfs [the original name of the family before Kosinski's father changed it during the war]

218

numbered more than sixty. But under Eichmann's supervision, a ghetto was established and a thousand Jews were killed in a "test"—a sample, one could say. Although my parents decided it was time to get out of the city, the rest of the family stayed.

And they all died.

They died in the ghetto of Łódz that Eichmann had engineered. No, not the Warsaw ghetto—although the Łódź ghetto was only an hour and a half away. The Łódź ghetto was an international ghetto, which housed Jews not only from Łódź but also from other cities and countries—Vienna, Luxembourg, Cologne, Frankfurt, Düsseldorf. Sixty-two-year-old Mordechai Chaim Rumkowski, a solitary man, was chosen to run it.

You must understand that Łódź had long been a very literary town. In fact, the best Polish-Jewish writer—I should say Polish writer—Julian Tuwim, a poet who manipulated language like no one else, hailed from there. Virtually every child in Poland learned the sound of Polish through a poem by Tuwim called "Lokomotywa" ["The Locomotive"], the most onomatopoeic poem in the Polish language, a language which is far more about sound than English.

Even in the ghetto of Łódź the Jews kept writing. They were writing because writing preserved their tradition of oral pleasure. To a Jew, writing is essential to chronicling the past, our past, a past that is being made as we go along, just as we go along because of the past. Some sixteen or seventeen or eighteen prominent Jews in the ghetto, maybe even more—maybe some of them members of my own family—kept a detailed account of daily ghetto life, which was just published by Yale University Press as *The Chronicle of the Łódź Ghetto*.

Łódź had also long been been a textile town full of working people. And the Łódź ghetto was a working ghetto: it produced uniforms for the German army. Jews were expected to keep on working. Work meant that they would be needed by the Germans, and as long as they were needed by the Germans, they had the prospect of longer life. And to a Jew, life is what mattered—not the ritual of life, not the memory of the past, not the hope of the future, but the gift of life, which is what I believe being Jewish was all about. To me, being a Jew meant worshipping life in every aspect, soul and soil, spirituality and sexuality, preconceived ideas as well as the ones about to be conceived. Life. Life is what we are all about. If every German uniform produced meant one more day of life, one more day of Jewish life, then let it be.

Since the ghetto in Łódź was run differently, it lasted longer than any other ghetto. And the Jews of Łódź lived longer than the Jews in any other ghetto. In fact, when the Łódź ghetto was liquidated in 1944, the Soviet army was only some sixty-nine kilometers away. Had the army rushed to Łódź, a great number of Jews might have survived.

Within the ghetto was a semblance of normalcy. The residents of the ghetto performed the obligations and duties of life that they would have performed outside the ghetto. Although people suffered and felt over-whelmed by fatigue, they continued to observe the Sabbath and to fast on Yom Kippur. Even those who grew sick or died were allotted a place—a permanent rubric, an identity, in the *Chronicle*. In other words, life in the ghetto of Łódź was more or less a replica of normal society for as long as the Germans would allow it.

But the moment inevitably arrived. In 1942, the Germans—who, until then, liked the way the Jews of the ghetto of Łódź made the uniforms—approached Rumkowski and said, "Look, Rumkowski, the uniforms are made by adults. What about the kids? They can't work. And what about the sick and the elderly? What are you going to do about them?" Feasibly, old Rumkowski tried to please the Germans and replied that he would try to use them in some way. But the Germans said, "No, you can't. You have to get rid of them." Perhaps this is why so many of you are not aware of the ghetto of Łódź and of our spiritual history, which seems increasingly selective these days. We select certain aspects of history because they are more powerful and more heroic, and others we neglect. Perhaps we question the rabbinical notion that one should collaborate with the enemy for the sake of life rather than give oneself up in flames because of Maimonides. Perhaps we ask ourselves: Is it the Talmud and life? Is it the notion of heroic death? This is certainly a question that a novelist must ponder. As for me: my mental ghetto is a ghetto devoted to life, to the life that ran through the ghetto of Łódź until July of 1944, the life that ran through the veins of my family. They lived longer than many other Jews. And life, after all, is a sacred gift.

In September 1942, however, Rumkowski had to stand in front of microphones that the Germans had installed for him. I imagine that he must have taken a drink before addressing the inhabitants of the ghetto of Łódź. He said:

The Ghetto has been inflicted with a great sorrow. We are being asked to give up the best we possess: children and old people. I was not privileged to have a child of my own and so I devoted the best years of my life for the sake of the children. I never would have imagined that my hands would deliver this sacrifice to the altar in my old age. I must stretch forth my arms and beg, brothers and sisters, yield them to me. Fathers and mothers, yield me your children. Yesterday afternoon, I was given an order to deport some 20,000 Jews from the ghetto. If not, they would do it. The question arose, should we take over the responsibility ourselves, or leave it for others to carry out? We—that is, I and my closest colleagues—concluded that, however difficult it would be for us, we would have to take over the responsibility ourselves. I have to carry out this difficult and bloody operation. I have to cut off limbs in order to save the body. I have to take children because otherwise, God forbid, others will be taken.

I have not come to comfort you, nor have I come to set your heart at ease, but to uncover your full grief and despair. I have come like a thief to take your dearest possessions from your hearts. I left no stone unturned in my efforts to get the order changed. But when this was impossible, I tried to mitigate. I succeeded in one thing: saving all children beyond the age of ten. Let this be a comfort in our grave sorrow.

Perhaps this plan is devilish, perhaps not. But I cannot hold back from uttering, "Give me the sick, and in their place we can rescue the healthy." I could not think over the problem for long. I was forced to decide in favor of those who are healthy. I can understand you, mothers. I see your tears. I can also feel your hearts, fathers, who tomorrow, after your children have been taken from you, will be going to work when just yesterday you were playing with your dear little children. I know all this and I sympathize with it. Since four p.m. yesterday, upon hearing the decree, I have utterly collapsed. I live with your grief, and your sorrow torments me.

I must tell you a secret. They demanded 24,000 victims, but I succeeded in getting them to reduce the number to 20,000, and perhaps even fewer. But only on the condition that these will be children up to the age of ten. Children over ten are safe. We have to meet the quota by adding the sick as well. You see before you a broken man; don't envy me. This is the most difficult order that I have ever had to carry out. I reach out to you my broken and trembling hands and I beg you give into my hands the victims. Hand them over to me so that we will avoid having further victims, and a population of a hundred thousand Jews will be preserved. The part that can be saved is much bigger than the part that must be given away.

In 1942, I would have been nine. Had I been in the ghetto of Łódź, clearly I would not have survived.

And so we come back once again to the question of memory. Is my memory going to be selective? And, if so, who is going to do the selection? Am I going to be trained by history, brainwashed by history, in terms of one particular act or another? The acts we face in daily life do not come spontaneously; they are the result of our cast of mind. We react out of certain fear because that fear is historical. The image of the Jew can be the image of one who runs away. Americans have seen that image for years and years and years: a Jew is one who has been killed by history. Not a program I would like to watch any longer. There could be, of course, another image—the image of a Jew who worships life to the very end. But that depends upon where we turn to look for our history. Is it going to be exclusively biblical or is it historical—or both? Is it going to be Warsaw or Łódź?

Earlier this evening, I was asked another question—why it took me so long to come to Israel. The reason is that I was not ready for Israel. I carried within myself my private state of Israel, which was a totally fictional one, and I did not think it should be matched against this concrete one. But after wrestling with my Self—after looking deeply into my history and into the Talmud, whose extraordinary narrative form mixed commentary with fact, and folklore with being Jewish, with being a folk—I felt that I was ready to come. And that is why I am here tonight. And that is also why I will be back again soon.

WRITERS AND ARTISTS FOR PEACE

IN THE MIDDLE EAST

In his opening remarks as moderator of the conference "Writers and Artists for Peace in the Middle East" in New York City in 1988, Kosinski shared some of his personal observations on wartime suffering and on Jewish statehood.

I am here today to moderate this conference in celebration of the fortieth anniversary of the state of Israel. I am doing something which my students at Yale University would say I should be disqualified from doing, since I am not objective, as a moderator should be. An objective person is one who has not been a participant in a particular event. And since I was "there"—there, meaning the war which some of us were fortunate enough to survive and which none of us can deny when we talk about the state of Israel—I am clearly not objective.

The state of Israel is a state of dreams. For one thousand years in Poland, where I came from, the state of Israel was a narrative dream, part of the great Polish-Jewish oral tradition. In contemplating my role tonight, I had to recall all that which I had experienced firsthand—and to recall the hand, as well as the soul, with which I had first experienced it. In fact, to be a moderator of anything having to do with the state of being a Jew, with the state of Jews' having their own state—and stake—in the world, I felt compelled to research the moderator's traditional role.

A moderator, I discovered, should be able to be reasonable. But I cannot be reasonable. When it comes to the question of being a Jew or to the existence of the state of Israel, I am not at all reasonable. I am historical, and history was not reasonable. History took away from me much of my self, historically speaking.

A moderator should also be rational. I cannot be rational. You have in front of you a man who is fifty-five years old, who loves Cynthia Ozick [one of the conference participants] with all his narrative heart—and maybe not only his narrative heart. But how can I be rational, when, in just four years, all but two members of my family were gone? Gone—but to where? On my recent trip to Poland, I could not even visit their graves. Sixty family members of mine, give or take a few, all suddenly gone. Yet I don't know how they died, or why, or exactly when, or by whose hands. Is Auschwitz my cemetery? It is not a Jewish cemetery; Jews did not design it. Even the name is not Polish.

According to the dictionary of synonyms, a moderator should also be average and unassuming. Can I be average? Can anyone who survived genocide possibly be unassuming? On the contrary, a survivor must make a lot of assumptions. He must assume that mankind is not necessarily kind to man, especially if that man happens to have a Jewish-sounding name. That is why I kept my Polish-sounding name—as a tribute to my survival.

That same dictionary suggests that a moderator should be mediocre. Do you really believe that anyone with an Eastern European background suddenly planted in the spiritual history of the years 1939 to 1945 can feasibly consider himself to be mediocre? Clearly not.

A moderator should be able to appease. No way could I appease, because I know that when the chips are down, as they say in this country, so are the Jews. In fact, as Jews, we have been considered some of the most valuable currency of history. We have been the chips that others have played. The history of central and Eastern Europe proves this fact.

Finally, a moderator should be able to coordinate. That I might actually be able to do: to coordinate and to confront. After all, we need to confront

224

the state of the view of the state of Israel, because the media is not sufficiently addressing the state of Israel itself.

When I was in Israel in February, I saw not only an extraordinary
strength but also an extraordinary state of restraint. I saw a democratic,
compassionate, yet troubled forty-year-old state. But even a forty-year-
old man is not yet a man of wisdom. And I saw a state baffled by what
you might call a civil disobedience, if you are kind to the state of Israel, or
a civil strife, provoked by the civilians, if you are not so kind. That state
must define what it is going through; otherwise, someone else will try to
provide that definition. And what right do others have—even those of us
in the United States who are sympathetic to its plight—to speak to the
condition of Israel, the condition of being surrounded by people who are
openly hostile to it? Mind you, even in 1939, not everyone was openly
hostile, as so many are today.

If you are in the state of Israel, then you know that history is something
very perishable, something that can condense overnight. So tonight we are
attempting to confront, from an American perspective, the options that
Israel faces today. Can we be moderate about something so important? As
a Polish Jew, I believe that we must look at this issue with all the objectivity
that history affords and all the subjectivity that our tradition allows.

SEIZING EACH MOMENT

At Congregation Emanu-El in New York City in 1990, Kosinski spoke about his Jewish identity and discussed how he defines himself "by each moment."

I noticed in the invitation statement for tonight's gathering that I was to make a major statement "regarding Jewish identity." That would be an awfully ambitious task, especially since I have great difficulty identifying myself, even in my own eyes.

What actually is identity? It is certainly more than an ID card. Identity is how we think of ourselves, how we define ourselves to—and for—others. Identity determines how we go through life, how we worship the gift of life itself.

As most of you already know, I am a Polish Jew. My mother, whose family name was Weinrich, initially came from Wilno. My father's family—the Lewinkopfs—came from Łódź, Poland's second largest city. These cities were the fortresses of Jewish identity in Poland. Łódź, in particular, was a well-known textile center; that, too, was a part of Jewish identity in Poland, especially before the Second World War. But most of the members of my family—more than sixty, in all—lost their identities very suddenly, when they lost their lives. Their presence once helped me to define my identity. Now, their absence does.

The extraordinary experience of the Holocaust is not unique to me. The Holocaust left in its wake unspeakable horror. It left the organized extermination of millions of different people, people as different as people can possibly be, simply because they were identified by the Nazi state— German-Austrian, to be exact—as enemies of a particular doctrine or targets of a particular hatred.

One particularly tragic and particularly nondeserving group lost half of all its population: the Romany, also known—unfairly—as Gypsies. One out of two Romany perished in four and a half years. I mention the numbers since occasionally we do deal in numbers rather than identities, in numbers rather than books. The Romany rarely stayed in one place long enough to become guilty of anything. But they were exterminated by gas and by execution simply because they were defined as nomadic.

Then, of course, came the Jews, one third of us murdered—one third of the whole collective body, in perhaps the only program which successfully served the purpose of the Nazi state. For all practical purposes, however, we remained very firmly present in the human mind. Despite their efforts, there was no way the Nazis could remove us from there. But physically, at that particular moment in history, one third of us were asphyxiated by gas and destroyed by other means specifically designed to make death as inhumane as possible. These were not deaths by execution. These were not deaths by a verdict. These were not even individual deaths; they were collective. The German law was a specific one: "We do not deal with an individual Jew." And, as Jews, this difference is important to us. We were singled out simply because we were Jewish. No other qualification was needed, not even an arbitrarily created definition, for instance, that said we were nomadic or we disobeyed the State or we didn't pay taxes or we didn't serve in the army or we misbehaved in some other way. Nothing else was needed: it was enough just to be Jewish.

Of course, others died as well—millions and millions of others, including some three million Catholic Poles and four and a half million Soviet prisoners of war, whom Stalin would not exchange for German prisoners of war. Four and a half million young Russians, Lithuanians, Bialy Russians, and others in Soviet uniform were captured by the Germans and asphyxiated by mobile gas units. Gas is gas. It kills regardless of whether it kills in a gas chamber or in a mobile gas unit. But for Jews, the Holocaust was unique, essential in the sense that our extermination was different from all the other war deaths.

I recently received the galleys of a soon-to-be-published book entitled *Holocaust Testimonies: The Ruins of Memory.* The book is divided into five chapters: "The Buried Self," "The Divided Self," "The Humiliated Memory: The Besieged Self," "Tainted Memory: The Impromptu Self," and "Unheroic Memory: The Diminished Self." I immediately began wondering how my personal experience reflected these categories.

Am I to see myself as "The Buried Self"? No way. I am perfectly alive—I ate my dinner, had my drink, looked forward to the evening. I will be buried only when I am dead. Am I a "Divided Self"? Clearly, I am divided, as divided as I can possibly be. Because I am a human being, I am divided between myself, my private self, which I won't discuss with you—although I may hint at it—and my public self. I am divided between my novels, which are flights of fancy, and the things I think. I am divided between all sorts of things, which means only that I am a complete human being.

Am I "The Impromptu Self"? Do I make myself impromptu? Of course, I do. As a novelist, I make up things as I go along. In fact, I enjoy that kind of impromptu creativity probably more than I enjoy anything else. Even my favorite sports demand an instant action from me; they demand that I act so that I will not be buried or beseiged. And I am diminished only to the degree that all of us are diminished by life and by time. But I do my best to cherish life and to appreciate time. In fact, my self is the very last thing that I will let die.

Conversely, for years now, many Jews have allowed themselves to be defined by the persecution they suffered. They have chosen as their identity not their historical identity but an ID card with Auschwitz-Birkenau written on it in capital letters as large as we could possibly imagine. They have been unable to find—or even to seek—their own spiritual renewal in the Jewish ethos, which is vibrant and ongoing, a celebration of Jewish life no less than the life of others.

The Holocaust became for some Jews the easiest—and maybe, at the same time, the most difficult—way of finding themselves in a historical moment that defies explanation. When I first came to the United States, someone asked me, "Are you a survivor?" I said that I was not. I don't speak Survivaleze; I happen to speak English. I said that I was not a survivor but a human being. Like anyone else, I could be killed at any time—perhaps by a taxi that is leaving a garage this very instant. But there is one sense in which I am indeed a survivor: I am fifty-seven, and there are not that many fifty-seven-year-old people of my generation still able to get up and speak. The Nazis can answer for that. So in that sense, yes, I survived until this very moment.

And that is how I define myself: by each moment. Each moment is to be enjoyed, to be fulfilled. Basically, *that* is what I am all about.

CELEBRATING JEWISH LIFE

In 1987, Kosinski addressed the Polish-Jewish Foundation in Boston, Massachusetts. He impressed upon his audience the need not only to remember Auschwitz, a site of so many Jewish deaths, but also to preserve places like nearby Kazimierz, which celebrated Jewish life.

A novelist is born not only in a country and not only to a language. A novelist is born when his novel, especially his first novel, is published. Therefore, to a certain degree, a publisher's address is a novelist's place of birth. I was born at 2 Park Street, in a hospital or clinic, depending on how you want to see it, a literary clinic called Houghton Mifflin. Thus, my coming to Boston is in fact quite significant for me because it allows me to revisit the city where I began as a novelist and where, to be honest, I would not mind ending up.

Recently, I returned to another place of great importance to me—my country of origin, Poland. I was born in Poland in 1933 and I left there thirty years ago, in 1957, when I was twenty-four. When you leave a country at that age, you take the country with you. You take the language with you. And frankly, you take with you a formation I once described to someone as an inner sculpture—since the person I was speaking to was a sculptor—an inner sculpture which you can modify later. No doubt about it: you can chip things off and maybe even add things to it. The cast of the sculpture, however, is already there.

Over the past thirty years, I have often examined this part of myself, this inner sculpture of mine. And I have looked at my very formidable past. Historically speaking, we—the family of Polish Jews—have been in Poland for more than nine centuries. A millennium is a very long time to reside anywhere, even under the changing conditions of historical apartments. You know how tough it is to have a place for that long in history, especially when you are a Jew and the apartments are difficult to find because the tenants are not always welcome.

Therefore, going back to Poland—and going to Israel, for the first time, shortly before that—meant that I had to ask myself questions which feasibly I could be asked by one of my own kin, perhaps by my own child, if I had one, although I do not. That American-Jewish child might wonder just where I go when I travel. But he probably would not know much about my mental trip. How could I begin to tell him about the changes that have occurred in Poland since I left? My mother was buried—and my father, too—and I wasn't there. My adopted brother grew thirty years older, and in all that time I never saw him, either. Because I was at one time persona non grata, anyone connected to me one way or another was persona non grata as well.

But what then was "grata" in all of this? Before the war, some six hundred thousand people lived in Łódź, Jews and non-Jews alike. Today, only two hundred or so Jews remain. At least that is what I was told at the local museum of art, and they should know, since by now any remaining Jew in Poland is almost as rare as an art object. There are very few Jews left, and most of them, I must say, are quite antique by now. Nevertheless, what was striking to me when I returned to Łódź is the fact that even though the Jews were not physically present in any significant numbers, they were still there in the culture: in the names of the streets, in the local newspaper, which was founded a hundred years ago by a Jew. So was the Kronstadt funeral home. And the largest Jewish cemetery in all of Europe is in Łódź as well.

I also visited Auschwitz. I took that trip because I thought my American-born wife, who does not speak Polish but who speaks history—her family came from Germany and Austria—should take a look at the language with which history spoke in Poland. The language was not Polish; that has to be clearly stated. It was German. And it was German from Germany, not German from any part of Poland. I went to Auschwitz to pay tribute to the place where my philosopher relatives died, even though none of their graves was marked in any way. My tribute to my relatives was a tribute to a detached death. Perhaps their luggage was there, in one of the barracks now used as a museum. Perhaps their hair was there, after being cut by the German barbers soon after their arrival. Perhaps their rings and jewelry were collected there. Perhaps, though I hate to say, some soap or other utilitarian object was made of them. And as for the medical experiments conducted at Auschwitz, perhaps some of my relatives qualified for those, too.

Yet Auschwitz itself is not the issue. Instead, the issue is that not far from Auschwitz stands an extraordinary place which you ought to see; it is only a forty-five-minute drive from the gas chambers. Those gas chambers speak a language that is not mine but which pays tribute to my martyrdom—no doubt about it—and to the martyrdom of Poland as well. In some remote fashion, they also pay tribute to the architect of the monument. The architect of Auschwitz was not a Pole; nor, for that matter, was he a Jew. But clearly there was an architect, wasn't there? Now, when you visit a home that has been turned into a museum, you must wonder whose home it once was. But despite its very personal connection to my family, Auschwitz was not my home. Near Auschwitz, however, is precisely such a place—Kazimierz, a spiritual home for me, only a slow forty-five-minute ride away.

Kazimierz is a place where Jews settled in large, large numbers. It is located right in Kraków, which was the home of Polish kings. Even after the four or five years of war and occupation that ravaged Poland like no other place on earth, today in Kazimierz—with Auschwitz so nearby—ten synagogues still stand, mighty and high. You should see the quality of the stone. Overall, those synagogues, some of which date back to the fifteenth and sixteenth centuries, are in no better shape than the rest of our history. But they are still there.

Among the saddest sights I witnessed in Kazimierz was in one of the more modern synagogues, which is falling apart; in fact, only a few of its extraordinary windows, originally made in the nineteenth century, remain. In that synagogue, I saw a closet which, like everything else in the building,

232

was rather substantial in size. The door was ajar, and when I opened it I discovered that the closet was filled with books. However, they were not neatly arranged, as they might be in a library. Rather, they were simply thrown in—old and rare books, from the seventeenth, eighteenth, and nineteenth centuries, written in Yiddish and in Hebrew. Some of them were wet, and most of them were disintegrating, like the synagogue itself, because there was no money to restore or to preserve them. The only caretakers of the synagogue and of the Remuh, one of the oldest Jewish cemeteries in Poland whose tombstones go back to the sixteenth century, were an older woman and an elderly man.

On top of everything else—on top of the years of war and occupation by the Nazis—there was a period of our absence, the postwar absence of Jews in Poland. During that time, the acid in the air from the steel plants in Kraków had begun to eat away at Poland's historic documents, including the irreplaceable Jewish documents in that particular synagogue. Now, there is hardly any time left for the necessary restoration and preservation.

When I look at my own life, I find it quite unthinkable that here I am at the age of fifty-five, going back to my own country where I was a nonpolitical figure, where I was a remnant of a civilization very badly hit by war. But I can no longer retrieve those years. Imagine how useful it would have been for me had I had access to my past. My past could have triggered all kinds of emotions within me. Ask any writer: we live off impressions, not off collecting Impressionists. I am what I am and I do what I do only because something has stimulated me. When those things no longer stimulate me, I must find others. And what could be more stimulating to me than my own history? Had I been a free man, I could have packed my bags and gone back to Poland. But for thirty years I was not free.

A French writer who writes in English and lives in America can go to Paris any time he or she wants. An American can travel anywhere. But for thirty years, I was not able to revisit my past. Who knows what damage that has caused or how many things I have lost by not being able to know my past—for instance, the books written by my relatives. I am ashamed to say that even now I don't know the exact titles of those books, some of which were published at the turn of the twentieth century, some of which were published as late as the 1930s. Although I keep trying to research that information, much of it is lost to me.

Now, imagine the civilization that was left behind by the Polish Jews, many of whom moved to the United States and to Israel. And imagine the remnants of that civilization, of that culture, that still could be retrieved and restored. That whole closet of books that I saw in the synagogue in Kazimierz, for example. According to one official, at the current rate of exchange, those books could probably be saved for a mere two or three hundred American dollars—since, in terms of currency, the American dollar is still king; in the words of the American ambassador Richard T. Davies, Poland remains "the most pro-American country on earth."

One purpose of the Polish-Jewish Foundation, therefore, is to restore the things that still can be restored, because one day someone like me may want to go back to revisit his past. Someone writing about the humor of Mel Brooks might want to try to figure out why this particular kind of humor originated in Poland and moved to Hollywood, where it has flourished. Someone listening to an all-American standard such as "God Bless America" written by Irving Berlin might suddenly realize that the song was composed by a man not from Berlin but by a composer from "Balin" in Poland, whose name had once been misspelled by a printer. The foundation, in its historical capacity, could help to remind all of us that much of the humor, the theater, the other entertainments that we ultimately think of as American in fact came, as historians can prove, straight from the old Commonwealth of Poland.

That brings me to another point, that the culture which was left behind was neither Polish nor Jewish; it was universal. The books written by my relatives, the Weinrichs and the Lewinkopfs, as well as the chess games, the matrix of which they left because many of them were well-known chess players, are not just part of my own personal historical chessboard; they are part of the chessboard of history. That is why, for my hypothetical children, I would choose to photograph myself not in Auschwitz but in Kazimierz, to show them that I am not a creature who is bent on death but rather one who has always worshipped life.

In other words, if I were to turn away from humanistic values—the values of being stimulated and prompted by life, the values that hang on to more than the ear perceives or than the mind can decode—and insist that American children, as part of their curriculum, know the names of the concentration camps but not the Polish and Jewish names that form so much of American culture, then I am performing a terrible disservice to cultural free expression and to this heritage which makes me free enough to be at the same time parochial if I choose to, as parochial as Jewish humor in America, let's say, or as universal as Universal Studios. The foundation, as we envisage it, fuses the spirit of the present with the sense of the past, because the past under no condition is dead. It is very vibrant and very alive. It is alive right here. And precisely because it is alive *here*, we must preserve what is still left of it *there*.

My dream is this: to transform Kazimierz, with its ten spectacular synagogues which so proudly face the castle of the Polish kings, into a center of Jewish life—a monument to the way Jews lived and not to the way they died a mere forty-five minutes away at Auschwitz. The four and a half years of war which resulted in Jewish absence must be measured against the thousand years of Jewish presence, a very monumental presence in central European history. That is what the foundation purports to do. And that is why, with great pride, I hope to launch this new effort.

On World Affairs

I have gone through the experience of the twentieth century. I have seen the war machine of the Germans and the Soviets at its finest. As a Jew, I experienced that machine during the war and also, in a curious way, in the war after the actual war. . . . My past is part of my being. . . . But just as the past is part of my being, the Germans also in some way have incorporated their pasts in their presents. To keep them hostage to their past would be to keep my being entirely a hostage of my past. And clearly I do not see myself as a hostage of my past. I speak a different language than the one I spoke at the time. I can do things now that I could not have done in Poland then.

So we have the freest people right now in Eastern Europe.

ON A UNITED GERMANY

At the Yale Club in 1990, Kosinski shared his delight over the reunification of Germany and spoke of that country's role in his own life and in Western culture.

The Second World War, which I survived, was certainly a crystallizing event in my life. This evening is another such event. As I realized on my way here tonight, at no time over the last thirty years did it ever occur to me that Eastern Europe would become a place where I might be able to travel freely or that Germany would be united again.

Let me be very clear on that point. I was delighted when Germany united, and am ready to drink a *bruderschaft* to the reunification. For many years, I have longed to be on a first-name basis again with Germany. After all, as a novelist, where would I be without Germany, with its poetry, music, and other extraordinary intellectual apparatus? And now, with the two Germanys united, I am finally at one—since if Germany is united, so is a part of me. I will no longer have to try to figure out whether Goethe or Schiller or Hermann Hesse or Rilke belong to East Germany or to West Germany. I will be able to dwell only on the quality of their minds, which is what really matters.

We have with us this evening a representative of Mercedes-Benz, a very distinguished motor car company. His presence makes me wonder about a different kind of vehicle, the vehicle of history. Where will that vehicle drive us? On what kind of a blind date will it take us? And what kind of vehicle will it be—a Russian-made tank or a pleasure car? At my small residence in Switzerland, I drive a 1968 Volkswagen, which never fails me. In this country, I drive a 1970 General Motors Buick. I tell you this to show you that I am well balanced and have no prejudices at all when it comes to cars and therefore can speculate on the types of vehicles that history can provide.

The name Kosinski, by the way, was forged by my father from Polish folklore and German literature. The original family name was Lewinkopf, a Polish-Jewish name of German origin. But, as you can imagine, this would not have been a very good model to drive back in 1939. So the name Kosinski was born. "Kosinsky" was the name of a robber in *The Robbers*, a play by Schiller, a German writer whom both my mother and father loved.

For many years, Germany suffered the terrible threats of Communism. And now, in 1990, Karl Marx is back—as a kind of philosopher, and sometimes even a funny one—although, unfortunately, millions of people suffered as a result of his beliefs. Today, we can quote Karl Marx freely again. Marx once said that, when it comes to government, there are single days in history that are more important than entire twenty-five-year periods, and there are twenty-five-year periods that matter less than a single day. This short day will, in some ways, be of greater significance than the twenty-five years that preceded it because of the change that has occurred in Europe.

Europe has become an entirely different continent: it is now a continent without passports, without borders, without dangers. Germany is no longer a power to be feared. Just the opposite. It is a profoundly humanitarian country in which the notion of humanity is essential because the memory of inhumanity is still so fresh. I would like to think that Germany will emerge as a prime bastion of humanity, a central point within the European community. I even tried to come up with a new word for this concept that I envision for Europe: sodality. Sodality—not Solidarity—or *sodalité* in French means fellowship, although it sounds more as if it derives from soda, which is found in headache remedies, or sodalite, which is a mineral found in certain igneous rocks.

Speaking of minerals, there is also a metallic element called germanium, which takes its name from the Latin word *Germanica,* meaning Germany. Discovered in 1886 by German chemist Clemens A. Winkler, germanium is a metalloid that conducts electricity; consequently, it is important in the electronics industry, where it is used to make transistors and semiconductors, and in the fiber optics industry. Germanium also has properties that are similar to silicon.

To me, the connection between germanium and Germany is very interesting, because in many ways nations are like minerals. I like to think of the United States as a mineral, and the Bill of Rights as a mineral, and figures like Washington and Jefferson as minerals. They are all minerals of the mind, vital minerals that nourish the spirit. And within the new European sodality, which will include Poland, Hungary, Czechoslovakia, the Scandinavian countries, France, Germany, and other European nations, there will be similar rejuvenation—and perhaps even a new "Silicon Valley."

Germanium, by the way, is commercially retrieved from coal and ash. The European sodality that I have in mind will be similarly refined by the decomposition brought on literally by time and symbolically by history. It will take its new form from the ashes of the past. Europe, which is still rising from its own ashes, could certainly use such an infusion of mineral at this moment. We can only hope that it will use that mineral wisely and not misuse its properties, as it did in the past.

Going back to the *bruderschaft* that I mentioned: one day in 1949, my father told me about Aspen, a place I had never heard of before then. He said that Aspen was a ski resort, an extraordinary place that was serving as the site for an important festival, the Goethe Bicentennial. Albert Schweitzer, a man who viewed life with enormous reverence, had been invited to be the festival's main speaker; other participants included the great Polish pianist Arthur Rubinstein and the Spanish philosopher José Ortega y Gasset. This fact made a great impression upon my father, who believed that, four years after the end of a war that had turned one fifth of the Polish nation into ashes, it was time again to celebrate the great German contributions to mankind. People needed to be reminded that Goethe should not be confused with Goebbels. So, my father said, if you ever make it to the United States, the first place you must visit is Aspen.

Many years later, I arrived in the United States and met my late wife, Mary Weir, who was very wealthy. Knowing that I had lived so long exclusively in Eastern Europe, she wanted to show me the world, and she had the resources to do just that. I told her that there was only one place I really wanted to visit: not Bangkok or some equally distant and exotic locale, but Aspen. When I told Mary, she doubted that there was even a motel in the town. This was in the very early 1960s. I said maybe not, but there is a spirit in Aspen that hangs over the mountains. It is probably the most essential spirit that can guide a person, be it a skier or a writer. And so we went to Aspen, as I once promised my father I would.

Clearly, in many fundamental ways, my own private history has been shaped by Germany. My blood relatives in Łódź—known during the war as Litzmannstadt—who perished during the war spoke German; most of them were educated, in one way or another, in Germany, Austria, or part of the Austrian-Hungarian Empire. On a larger scale, German culture has long influenced historical thinking: *Deutschland, Deutschland, über alles.*

The tragedy that the Germans experienced during and after the war has been our tragedy as well. That is because, as I keep reminding my friends, the tragedy of a totalitarian system is not only the tragedy of the victims of that system; it is also the tragedy of the system itself. But the system is changing, and that is what we are here to celebrate tonight.

One hundred years after the initial unification of Germany in 1871, the first four-wheel vehicle traversed the moon. That vehicle was the moon rover, an invention of American-Polish scientists. Notably, it was an American vehicle—not a German vehicle, or a French one, or, for that matter, a Polish Fiat. Each time I look at the moon, I can hardly believe that vehicle was there, and I wonder if anyone, in 1871, might have even imagined such a thing. Yet the speed of change is remarkable. Some of us here tonight are old; we are very much grounded in history. But the very young, those who are seven or nine or ten years old, view the world much differently than we do. They are accustomed to seeing image and music at the same time in a three-minute video. They assume that the world is moving and changing much faster than we do. Theirs is an entirely different time line that neither a novelist nor a diplomat can imagine.

If the speed of change continues as rapidly as it has in recent months, who knows what kinds of real and economic forces we can expect in the future. For now, though, we can only speculate what kind of language those forces might speak, what kind of currency they might use, what kind of automobile they might drive. We can only imagine what changes we will be celebrating at this time next year.

One of the best things for me about this evening is the fact that I have lived to see such an important event and that I can offer a *bruderschaft* toast to the united Germany, because it pleases me no end.

A NEW OPTIC

On June 15, 1989, Kosinski spoke at the Harvard Club to the *WorldPaper* about the tremendous opportunities that existed in Poland since the recent democratic elections, and he outlined the plans he and his corporation PARC had for creating a mercantile bank and for increasing new housing in the country. In 1989, that bank received "License No. 1," the first license to be issued to a foreign bank since 1945; and it opened in January 1991 under the name AmerBank (now DZ Bank Polska).

"Penetrating Poland," the original title given to this talk, is one that I would not have chosen. I would never have used the verb "penetrating." With the kind of fiction I write, there would be no need for that. The question is not so much how to penetrate Poland: I don't think anyone can penetrate it. The question is which optic we should use in examining what is happening now in the very center of central Europe, indeed, in the most pivotal place of all, a place that is at once eminently visible and yet so often overlooked. Even on the extraordinary day on which Poland ceased being a totalitarian country, the *New York Times*'s coverage was dominated by the events in Beijing—despite the fact that most of the people who work at the helm of the *Times* came, one way or another, from the old Polish Commonwealth.

You are probably wondering about the optic that I use. Is it a wide-angle lens? Is it telephoto? Is it a magnifying glass? Quite simply, the optic is

244

Polish, and it is based on my own personal history in wartime Poland. But the true destruction came after the war ended. In Warsaw, that destruction seemed almost atomic: most of Warsaw was gone. Eight million people were displaced, moved arbitrarily to a place that used to be Poland but had since become Germany.

The Poland in which I grew up was marked not only by the actual Holocaust but also by the holocaust of destruction that takes place after any war. Poland was a place of hunger. There was no medication. And, above all, there was no housing. I lived with my family in a ground-floor apartment. Before the war, that apartment was occupied by a single family; after the war, it was occupied by five. Today, there are probably fifteen living in the same house. When I became a student, as an act of rebellion I studied American sociology. Ironically, my first public lectures in Łódź were on American family life. American family life, I discovered, was grounded in a specific territory: a house, or some other place of one's own, not a multifamily apartment.

A few years after I came to the United States, I met an American woman who captured my fantasy just as my ethics captured hers. It was due to her influence that I became a novelist. In the environment of our marriage, I became infatuated with one particular success story, that of her late husband, the American innovator and financier Ernest Weir, who founded the third largest steel company in the United States. He started in the business in 1905 at the age of thirty, almost as late as Conrad when he sat down to write his first novel, by insisting that steel should be thin-plate, not thick. And in a town called Weirton, he began successfully producing his thin-plate steel. I tell you about these experiences because they are the prime American optic that I acquired.

But let us get back to Poland, a country of thirty-eight million people in the center of Europe, a country brought up on the democratic ideals of Thomas Jefferson, a country of inordinately American values such as the right to privacy, communication, and enterprise. As a result of the many partitionings over the years, these rights were often taken away from the Poles, who nevertheless continued to long to be Self-made men—"self" with a capital S. And Poland became a ruined country, ruined by the Germans in the Second World War and later by an equally distorted and unnatural Marxist system, which valued collectivity over the value of life. But with ruin comes possibility, and especially with the extraordinary recent changes in Poland there is again a sense of great possibility.

I am speaking to you now not as a novelist but as the president of PARC, the Polish American Resources Corporation. PARC, by the way, is an acronym that also works in Polish: it means a place where you can self-park your car. It is also a place where you can "park" your account, particularly if you are a member of the twenty-million-strong Polish diaspora. PARC will park your resources in a place that you can trust. If you were to analyze the statistics on economic trends from the Department of Commerce and the information prepared by the American Embassy in Warsaw, you would see a picture of great potential for productivity. But a ruined country cannot recover entirely on its own. It has immediate needs, particularly in housing. The government manages to build only two or three hundred thousand new housing units each year, but Poland needs ten million new units in order to house its people properly.

The Ursus Tractor Factory in Warsaw, the pride of the old Communist system, is as integral to Poland as Wall Street is to New York. In the post-Stalinist period, tractoring was what moved, propelled, in fact dragged the innocent peasants into the horizon of becoming a proletariat. Yet that same enterprise of tractoring is a prime example of the problems of the Communist system. Of the fourteen thousand workers at Ursus, five thousand have no place of their own; they live in hotels sharing rooms, sometimes with as many as six, seven, eight, or nine other workers. And now they are saying to Solidarity, "What are you going to do about this? Are you going to build the necessary housing?" Solidarity, of course, cannot do it alone. Foreign investment is essential.

We at PARC decided to approach the government about opening up immediately to such investment. Our hope was to build a Polish-American financial consortium, a consortium so huge that it would wipe out the remnants of the Marxist inefficiency in Poland. We said to the government and to Solidarity—and we said it in very good Polish—that Poland is a ruined country, but it is not their fault. Nobody is to blame. It is the fault of history, the fault of the Germans being rewarded by the Marshall Plan and the good luck of the Japanese, and the bad luck of Poland, a country that never invaded anyone.

And we said that the one thing that will break the back of what has just been accomplished is the young workers themselves, the men and women who want to have a shelter of their own, to which they are certainly entitled. On television, they see the improved living conditions of the people in Bulgaria, in Albania, and in other unexpected places, yet here in a thousand-year-old country with an extraordinarily experienced free enterprise, a country that produces some of the most successful products sold worldwide, they do not feel that they have the same prospects. Just a digression. For years, Poland has produced the best black-market video-cassette, which the Japanese are buying for seven dollars and reselling for eleven dollars.

In America, housing is an ordinary commodity, but the same is not true for the workers in Poland. And since housing is key, we proposed to take it into our own hands. By having the financial ability to create housing quickly in Poland, by underwriting and building homes for the workers, our corporation could fulfill their most basic and long-neglected needs. Although the government said that they were addressing the issue, clearly they cannot do it on their own; ultimately they won't even try. The workers themselves cannot afford to do it. But we believed that we could create the circumstances by which workers could have the housing they lacked. Yet there would have to be a reward for us, a profit for the corporation, especially since we would be entering what is essentially an area of destruction. In an editorial, *Forbes* magazine noted that "total destruction is the best place to begin," but not everyone would agree.

We proposed to start with "a twenty-year-plan" for the construction of housing in Poland. That, however, required the creation of a bank that operates on dollars and not just złotys. Such a bank did not then exist. The official state bank, PKO [Polish Commercial Bank], is despised by the very people who deposit money in it for their relatives in Poland, and it may soon be out of business. But such a bank is absolutely necessary, since the infusion of dollars is vital to success. As we said to the government, they must understand that they are facing the dreadful reality of being the forgotten country in the center of Europe. Currently, sixty-two million Germans are driving into Poland to buy things that for them, in dollars, are very inexpensive. Let me give you an example. Recently, when my wife and I were in Poland, we hired a taxi for an entire week. The driver worked for twelve hours each day, and he even carried the baggage, since I was too old for that. His services cost us one hundred and twenty-eight dollars. Another example: a Polish construction worker earns in one month what the construction worker who painted our building on Fifty-seventh Street and Sixth Avenue in New York makes in one hour. When I told this to the Minister of Finance, he tried to correct me by saying, "True. Nevertheless, keep in mind that the child of this worker gets a free breakfast and lunch, free education, and free medicine." Yet the fact is that, without the necessary incentive, without a place of their own, workers are not motivated to work. And the underlying fact remains: if you have dollars at your disposal, Polish labor is insanely cheap.

Realizing the pressing need that we had outlined for workers, especially young workers, to have adequate housing, the government agreed to allow us to proceed. Our next step was to meet with the trade union Solidarity. Throughout the period of martial law in Poland, Solidarity had shown extraordinary restraint, as, in many ways, did the government. Without such restraint, the bloodshed could have been enormous. Solidarity must therefore be given credit for creating a highly innovative form of pressure by presence, a pressure that was steady but largely nonviolent. Nothing like it had ever been done.

So we went to the Ursus Tractor Factory, where we spoke to the workers and asked Solidarity to consider becoming an independent economic entity that would partner with us in this joint venture. We knew that the idea we were proposing was quite original, but we needed an original approach in order to achieve commercial success. Free enterprise, we told them, should benefit those who are free and enterprising. After all, many of the nations in the world that are not free envy the freedom that Poles are now experiencing. Even Argentina, I imagine, must envy Poland's economic possibilities. I love Argentina but hate the economy. In the time it takes me to finish a polo game, everything is a hundred percent more expensive than when I began!

Remembering that, during the presidency of Andrew Jackson, the federal government could deposit its funds into banks, I asked if Solidarity would object to allowing the government to keep monies in the bank we were going to create. They said they did not object, as long as it was a free enterprise, a joint venture, in an American bank.

Another original idea that we had involved the employment of existing voluntary labor units. I got the idea when I was being driven around Warsaw—by my hundred-twenty-eight-dollar-a-week driver—and I noticed a group of three hundred uniformed men marching out of a construction site. At first I thought they were prisoners, but the driver explained to me that they were members of a voluntary labor unit. The people in these units, some one hundred and twenty thousand in all throughout Poland, do not want to serve in the army; instead, they volunteer their labor for two years on construction projects, where they learn a new profession. At the time, Poland had ten such divisions of voluntary labor units, which were first created back in 1934.

When we started negotiating our agreement with the Ministry of Finance, I asked specifically if we could draw on this ready work force. I knew that having this particular resource—basically, a future army of one hundred and twenty thousand disciplined and professional builders, and possibly more, if there was a shift in the Warsaw Pact—would ensure American investors in our bank and in our Polish-American consortium that we could indeed move quickly on the construction of housing. The ministry agreed. We then asked Ursus Solidarity if they would object to our using these labor units. They too agreed. This shows just how original it is possible to be in Poland at the moment. And all of this happened because, from my taxi window, I noticed a group of marching men whom I could not immediately identify.

So what we have right now is an effective formula, one that guarantees noninterference by strikers—since workers would not strike against a corporation that builds their homes—or bureaucracy—since the government is already discredited in this area and would not give us any competition.

Moreover, as a country Poland is protected from without. The Soviet Union, which has serious problems of its own, is certainly not going to invade. Investors understand that, and they also appreciate that this project has the full support of the Polish workers, who would benefit most directly from it. Although my critics say that it will not be possible to make money from this kind of construction, I urge them not to judge this enterprise prematurely.

We can design the financial instrument; we can be original. We can construct this bank—construct it in a physical as well as a spiritual sense—and have it open as soon as the beginning of next year. The first merchant financial bank in Poland after the Second World War. That accomplishment alone would be worth all my royalties! That bank could become the prime financial institution in Poland.

I rent an apartment in New York and in New Haven, and I own an apartment in Crans-Montana, Switzerland, a community where there are one hundred and thirty banks. Clearly, Switzerland has no need of my financial innovation. But Poland does. We must bring to that country the best bank that we can design.

But we also must act quickly: our time is awfully limited. The Germans are moving in. And, as you know, the Germans are capable of extraordinary innovation—as well as blunt aggression. In initial discussions, Solidarity asked us why they should deliver to us serviceable land, with water, electricity, and roads already in place, for building when a German company was willing to do those things for them for free. I told them, "Then take their offer. We know that the Germans are expert at demolition. They know how to do it. In fact, they already have the plans of Warsaw, which they took in 1939 with a Zeiss lens from their Stuka bombers." The argument was never raised again. But if we don't act now, Germany or another country will definitely step in.

What is at stake is the creation of ten million housing units that are needed immediately; that is the leverage which we've got. I am convinced that after President [George H. W.] Bush's trip to Poland, a great effort will be made to help Poland and thus to break the back of the Soviet Bloc. After all, Poland is the most powerful country in that bloc: thirty-eight million people, with one language, one value system—and no quarrels on the construction site. Already the Germans are entering Poland to buy the land that they couldn't conquer in 1939.

With Solidarity as one of the main venturers and adventurers, imagine what we could do with a free bank, a bank based on the notion of free enterprise. We could encourage some of the one hundred and thirty thousand people who used to work in Eastern European embassies to buy apartments and invest in Poland. Clearly, many of them might want to own an affordable place on a lake or in the mountains or in Warsaw itself—so close by car, so close by train, so close by plane to the rest of Western Europe. We could form a bridge to the Polish diaspora and give them a direct link to their mother country. Think about the possibilities that such bonds could offer.

BANKING ON HISTORY

In his address to the Philadelphia Stock Exchange 200th Anniversary Symposium in 1990, Kosinski spoke of the importance of investing in other nations and compared the rise of democracy in America in the late eighteenth century to recent events in Poland.

This is really a high point of my almost fictional career, since the advantage of being a novelist is that there are no disadvantages in life: even failure can end up as a successful passage in a novel. Thus, no matter what happens, an author benefits. Parenthetically, it just so happens that Philadelphia plays a very important role in my life as it does in the life of most Poles. I was born in Poland in 1933, which was not, to paraphrase Frank Sinatra, a very good year. That was the year in which Hitler got his Enabling Act, the laws that enabled him to do all that he did. It was probably the worst year ever in European history. I stayed in Poland through the war, left Poland in 1957, and came directly to the United States, where through a set of almost novelistic circumstances I received a Ford Foundation fellowship through the Institute of International Education, and met the woman who was to become my first wife, Mary Hayward Weir. Mary was the widow of Ernest T. Weir of Weirton, West Virginia, who founded the National Steel Company, which became one of the largest steel companies in the United States at a time when the country was made of and built upon steel. I give you this brief introductory note so that you will know that during my marriage, Pittsburgh, Detroit, and the Stock Exchange were clearly essential to my experience.

I just came from Holland, where I spoke at the John Adams Institute. The institute is in the old Amsterdam, where Ambassador John Adams went to seek a loan for a place that nobody wanted to invest in. The Dutch financed the American experiment. And indeed the investment paid off: the fortress of Manhattan became the New Amsterdam and the Dutch are still very much part of our American psyche.

What I am saying is that some investments—when they are made cleverly, when they take into account the size, location, and philosophy of the country—pay off, no matter what. Such investments, however, go beyond real estate. The real investment is in the men and women who care about the land or the work ethic or the future, men and women who want their children to have a better environment and a better government. But not all investments are so progressive. Earlier this century, the French poet, novelist, and critic Paul Valéry, looking from a purely poetic point of view, warned that Europe should be aware of what is happening in Asia, where a dozen gigantic industries in steel, silk, paper, chemicals, and ceramics would soon exist to rival or even surpass Manchester and other centers of production. He predicted that those industries, created by a population which is the most frugal and numerous in the world, would produce goods in staggering quantities and at unbeatable prices. Nobody paid attention to Valéry at the time; he was just another voice. But he was certainly correct. Perhaps he should have opened a bank.

This brings me back to Philadelphia. As you know, there are many places in the world named Philadelphia, some of them in the Middle East. But for me, this is the only Philadelphia, not only because of its natural and human resources, not only because of its associations with historical American persons and events, but also because of its role in Polish history. It was in Philadelphia that the writer Thomas Jefferson—and Jefferson was, without doubt, a writer—conceived probably the shortest but most difficult phrase in human history: "All men are created equal." That declaration was an act like no other in any language. Jefferson prefaced it by remarking that

253

the sentiments of men are known not only by what they receive but by what they reject. These words bear repeating: the sentiments of men are known not only by what they receive but also by what they reject.

The reason that Jefferson was so important to Poland—and Poland to Jefferson—is that after the American Declaration of Independence and the Constitution, Poles—on May 3, 1791—wrote the world's second democratic constitution. Julian Niemcewicz, a leading Polish intellectual who was responsible not only for that Polish constitution but also a great number of other Polish democratic institutions, was regarded as a kind of Polish Jefferson. In 1796, he came with Kościuszko to Philadelphia to pay tribute to the original Jefferson. But, forgetting that man cannot live on liberty alone, Niemcewicz found himself short of funds. "Where to go," he wondered, "how to make a living, in Philadelphia? I wandered like a madman the streets of Philadelphia. How sorry was I that instead of literature I did not possess a technical skill or talent in the arts. Had I had them, how easily I could make a living here. How right was Rousseau when he advised people to teach manual skills to their children; they would not listen. Particularly in Poland such a thought was humiliating. In my own shame and loss and sorrow, I went to pay a visit to Jefferson, whom I had the pleasure to meet in Paris when he was with the American delegation there, and I told him what my predicament was." Jefferson gave Niemcewicz the equivalent of perhaps five hundred dollars at the time. One could say that this was the first major loan that the United States extended to Poland, and it turned out to be an excellent investment.

So Niemcewicz was able to stay on in Philadelphia, where he saw the extraordinary potential of a country made for free enterprise and based on the phrase that "all men are created equal." And when he returned to Poland, he brought those ideas back with him. He also wrote some pretty good novels, including, I might add, the first novel written by a Pole on a Jewish subject. Considering the thousand-year-old history of Jews in Poland, that was quite an achievement.

This brings me to convertibility. I see a direct relationship between "all men are created equal" and the credit card. I was a sociologist by training, so here I speak with the authority of market research. A few years ago, I called a colleague of mine, the president of American Express, to urge him to consider issuing credit cards to Poles. This was around the time that my corporation, PARC—Polish American Resources Corporation—was trying to establish what eventually became AmerBank, the first American bank in Poland, that I helped found. Mind you, Poland was not exactly a postage stamp at the time: it was the seventh largest nation in Europe, larger than Great Britain, larger than Spain, larger than France, with thirty-eight million people who are homogeneous, speak one language, and have no ethnic quarrels. I told my colleague that issuing credit cards in Poland would be easy. I even suggested to him how the card itself might look: a double image of an American eagle and a Polish eagle, possibly with a picture of Kościuszko on it, or a picture of Niemcewicz and Jefferson together.

I told him it would be the most popular credit card in history, because Poles love all things American. They watch American television; they embrace American values. By contrast, can you imagine an international society that worships the German nation? Goethe, yes; Schiller, yes; but not the German nation itself. Is there a society that feels Japanese values to be universal? Don't get me wrong: the Japanese are wonderful people. But American values, including human rights and rights for workers, are truly universal.

So by bringing the credit card to the millions of Poles, Catholic Poles, I knew my colleague could not go wrong. Nothing could be more convertible in Poland than a credit card. But American Express was not interested, so we had to do it on our own.

The way that I and some of my friends at PARC, at AmerBank, and at AmerTrust—a direct investing company and the sister company to Amer-Bank—see it, what Poland can accomplish now is nothing short of remark-able. If the two Germanys could reunite, certainly Poland, with its shared values, could establish a relationship with the United States, a relationship based on the path forged by Niemcewicz and Jefferson. We are, after all, talking about thirty-eight million people, every one of whom has a relative in Detroit who can assist in times of trouble and who could even, if neces-sary, send a check directly to the credit card company. Don't laugh: this is important. Banks ask you for references. For Poles, one reference could be

Detroit and the other the Vatican, home of the Polish pope. The Vatican is itself a pretty old corporation, perhaps even the oldest. You can't ask for better collateral than that!

In any case, what I am saying is this: when I went to Pittsburgh for the first time, my late wife told me how her late husband, Ernest Weir, did something nobody else had done by breaking the Pittsburgh Trust Agreement. He looked to Detroit, not Pittsburgh, for the future of his company as he merged his Weirton Steel Company with Detroit's Michigan Steel to form the National Steel Company. Weirton, the town he founded in West Virginia, emerged as an extraordinary place, a place so successful that none of its steel workers needed to join the United Steel Workers of America. I am in no way promoting the Hyundai plant, which doesn't want to join the United Auto Workers. I am merely saying that Weirton was sufficiently independent, especially through its special partnership with Detroit, to thrive.

When I first saw it, Detroit was a booming city. But it no longer is. Back then, however, Detroit gave everyone an idea and an exceptional product. Henry Ford, no matter what you or I might think about his private philosophy, was a visionary like no other. General Motors, Chrysler: these companies influenced a great number of psyches in terms of how these psyches defined themselves. The first thing that I wanted when I came to this country was a car—that was something quintessential to me. I don't want to drop names but at one time it used to be a Continental Mark II. For the last twenty years it has been the same 1970 Buick, which runs better than any other car and can be repaired by any mechanic. But look at Detroit now. When I mention Detroit, I always recall that it was a Pole, Max Grabowsky, who built the first light utility truck there in 1902.

Poland is a skilled country, among the best-educated in Europe. Its work ethic has been depressed for years by a system that didn't work, even though the people did. But demographically Poland is very young, with many young people in its workforce for years to come. In contrast, by 2025, most of Europe's population will be over sixty-five. I am fifty-seven and I am already fatigued. But, while Poland will be young, a great number of those young Poles will have no place to live. In some small towns now, the wait for an apartment is over thirty years; in big cities, over fifty years. Think what kind of a construction business you could create there. Almost three years ago, in fact, our corporation signed an agreement with the government to build housing. Think about the mobile home industry that could develop there, since a large number of workers have to move from place to place as their plants relocate. What I am saying is look at Poland the way Jefferson would; look at Poland the way, I hate to say it, West Germany looked at East Germany.

Soon Poland will be in a position to make rapid progress in the world economy. Unless we Americans offer assistance to our friends—and spiritually they are our friends—others will step in, proffering worse terms, which Poland might be forced to accept. There will be Germans, and there will be Japanese, and with all due respect they will not come with the phrase "all men are created equal." You can bank on that.

TOTALITARIAN POLEMICS

In an address at the Royal Theatre in Stockholm, Sweden, in 1983, Kosinski spoke about totalitarian polemics and offered several examples from his own experiences as a novelist and as president of the American Center of PEN, the international association of poets, essayists, and novelists.

You may have noticed in the program that the title of my brief presentation is "Totalitarian Polemics: The Theater of the Absurd." And here I am—an actor in a theater again. Last night, *The Ambassadors*, a play by Sławomir Mrozek, a fellow Pole, was performed here. So I think it is appropriate to start with an aspect of totalitarian polemic and the theater of the absurd which took place some years ago in New York.

I was, at the time, connected to the Board of the American PEN Club, the association of writers, translators, and editors, which took action to help some of the persecuted intellectuals in Latin America and Eastern Europe. At the time, the most pressing issue was the imprisonment of several Soviet dissident writers. In its American Anglo-Saxon innocence, the delegation of the American PEN went to the Soviet consulate in New York to plead the fate of the imprisoned Soviet writers.

We were met—very politely—by the Soviet consul, a friendly man. "The issue is one of imprisoned Soviet writers," we said. "Excuse me," the consul said. "What was that again?" One of us said, "This," and handed him

258

the list of the imprisoned writers. The consul took a look at the list and said, "Gentlemen, I don't see any writers on this." And we said, "But, sir, all these men and women are writers." He said, "Are they in prison?" We said, "Yes, that's what brings us here." "If they are in prison," said the consul, "then they can't be Soviet writers." We tried again, saying, "But—they are—they have written and published their work. They are members of the Writers' Union." Guided by Marxist wisdom derived from some sixty-six years of practice and power, the consul patiently said, "A Soviet writer is a person who creates out of the spiritual topography of Marxism-Leninism, one who writes on behalf of the working class, one who acts in accordance with the objective laws of historical and dialectical materialism. That's a writer. Now, a person in prison is, by our definition, a criminal. All Soviet writers are free. Have you come here to defend Soviet criminals?" With a cold smile, he politely ended the discussion.

It was a good case of the absurdity of totalitarian polemic, and a few years later I was reminded of it in an entirely different context. A Soviet journalist was accused by the Soviet authorities of having Zionist connections which, as a Soviet Jew, she failed to declare, so she was asked to leave the USSR. Reluctantly, her husband, who was also a journalist, decided to leave with her. A man in his mid-fifties, he was a specialist in financial writing. However, while she went directly to Israel, he—an avid anti-Zionist—picked the United States as his first stop. But he had no job, spoke no English, and had never been to the United States before. At the time, again in connection with my role at American PEN—and because I spoke Russian—I was asked to assist him. PEN prepared some potential jobs for him, a list which included waiting on tables in a restaurant, parking cars, working in a hotel laundry—all jobs that a man of his age in relatively good health could still do. When he came to my apartment and I spoke to him about the prospects, he recoiled. "A waiter?" he said. "But I was a journalist in Moscow." "Then how about parking cars," I said. "I drove my own car," he said. "I didn't park cars for others." Then I said, "After being a journalist in Moscow, you can certainly learn to park cars in America, even though there isn't as much space for them here." "Look, Comrade Kosinski, you don't understand," he replied. "I am an expert on Wall Street.

259

For twenty-five years, I wrote for Soviet publications about financial developments on Wall Street, about the imperialist fiscal system. Could you possibly get me a job as a journalist on Wall Street?" "What about your English," I asked. "I don't know English," he said. "I could use a translator." "But you wrote about Wall Street?" I asked. "Yes, I had all pertinent documents and sources translated for me. Here, I could write about Wall Street from a different point of view—from the Marxist-Leninist point of view, from the historically objective point of view. I could analyze the inevitable collapse of Wall Street and the capitalist system it represents. Wall Street should know its fate. I have written several books about it." I thought that his books might offer a financial rescue. "Where were they published?" I asked. "In the USSR, Cuba, and Bulgaria," he answered. "Too bad they don't pay royalties . . . " And so, instead of telling Wall Street how moribund it was, he ended up parking cars on Wall Street.

The question is this: how, in a polemic, can we confront our reality when it is interpreted so differently by the Soviet totalitarian state and by our Western democracies, which, without "total philosophy," respond to it only moment by moment?

I noticed that, in one of the conference programs, my earlier non-fiction books about the psychology of collectivity were described as "anti-Communist." Feasibly, they are antitotalitarian, but they are certainly not anti-Communist. Yet, when I arrived here, I was met at the airport by someone who asked me about my anti-Communist philosophy. And I had to say to her, "I cannot be anti-something that doesn't exist and that I do not know. I have never known a Communist state, but I have lived in a Soviet bloc, in a totalitarian bureaucracy." From my perspective, today the USSR is merely a one-party state of totalitarian bureaucracy.

Admittedly, other intellectuals—from Anatole France and Upton Sinclair to George Bernard Shaw and Theodore Dreiser, from e. e. cummings and Richard Wright to Julian Tuwim and Jarosław Iwaszkiewicz, from André Malraux and Edmund Wilson to John Dos Passos and Bertolt Brecht—would disagree with my assessment of the USSR. Anatole France, for example, once said that an intellectual must be resigned to what may come to pass in the accomplishment of justice—even if it is injustice, cruelty, and blood. In *Die Massnahme*, Brecht wrote that the Party is above morality. In his *Terror and Humanism*, Merleau-Ponty justified, from a supposedly Party / Marxist point of view, the need for Soviet concentration camps—and for purging the dissidents—even if this is done by charging them with crimes the Party knows they have not committed!

When I look back on the Western intellectual history of which I am a part, I note that the moral excuse for the Gulag did not come from the Kremlin politburo members or even the professional politicians on the left. Instead, it came from our own ranks—from the Western liberal intellectuals. Sartre, writing about the universe of the Soviet Gulags, noted that "the problem is not one of condemning the entire society because a few people are unhappy. Whatever the present nature of Soviet society . . . the USSR finds itself on the side of those who struggle against exploitation of man by man." At the same time, Sartre admitted that there might have been fifteen million Soviet citizens in Soviet labor camps. Romain Rolland claimed in 1921 that Stalin provided the best guarantee for the rights of men. George Bernard Shaw said that Stalin was one of the best intellectual listeners he had ever met. And Aragon, another supporter of the Communist Party, wrote of the Moscow trials that men such as Bukharin, Radek, Zinoviev, Smirnov, Krestinksy—the very makers of the revolution—were obviously all guilty as charged.

But my issue is not seduction by the revolution. I am not here today to offer my own polemic but rather to celebrate Solidarity, one of the very few mass movements in history which has not devoted itself to revolution, to violence, to terror, to destruction. Solidarity has not created a new ruling party or promoted a new ideology of power and suppression. Solidarity is simply a movement—one of the largest movements of men and women—of human rights. And it is a movement that succeeded where revolutions have failed. Andrei Sinyavsky, who was a "criminal" when the Soviet consul claimed no Soviet writers were imprisoned, said about the outcome of the revolution: "so that prisons should vanish forever, we built new prisons; so that all frontiers should fall, we surround ourselves with Chinese walls; so that work should become a rest and a pleasure, we introduced labor camps; so that not one drop of blood be shed and so that peace will triumph forever, we killed and killed and killed." And then Solzhenitsyn—and you cannot accuse Solzhenitsyn of being very proud of Western democracy; he is, in fact, quite critical of it—in his own, very individual way, wrote about revolution: "A reasonable man cannot be for revolution, because revolution signifies a prolonged and mindless destruction. First of all, revolution, any revolution, does not renew the country but breaks it apart for a very long time. And the more bloody, the more protracted it is, the more the country has to pay for it, the more likely it is to be called a great and a successful revolution." During the Moscow Great Purges so praised by Feuchtwanger, Aragon, and Merleau-Ponty, Akhmatova wrote—in *Requiem*—about a Communist family: "This woman is sick to her bone / This woman is alone / Her husband buried, / Her son in prison / Pray for me." And, as if explaining the tragedy of the Western liberal's love affair with the intellectual myth of "revolution": "The subjugation of *intelligentsia* was accomplished not by terror and bribery—though, God knows, there was plenty of it—but by the word 'Revolution' which none of them would think of ever giving up. It is a word to which whole nations have surrendered, and its force was such that one wonders why our rulers still need prisons and capital punishment. It was simply enough to say, 'Join the Revolution.'"

I can't be impersonal about it. The language of the totalitarian polemic, the Soviet-totalitarian polemic—I have dealt with the American polemic, the polemic by image, in *Being There*—affects me personally, and so I want to be very personal about it. After all, by now half of my life has been shaped by totalitarian polemic. Some seventeen years ago, *The Painted Bird*, my first novel, was published in the United States. It had not yet been published in Poland. To discredit me, however, the Party press in Poland claimed that because my novel had a Library of Congress number on it, it must have been subsidized by the CIA—and written by a ghostwriter, since, they alleged, my own English was so poor—to discredit Polish folk. The Party press argued further that the book was "published by the CIA in Bonn, West Germany, and Tel Aviv"—although, in fact, the German-language edition of *The Painted Bird* was published not in Bonn but in Bern, Switzerland, and the Israeli edition did not appear until ten years later. Now, that too is a totalitarian polemic. I remember that even my mother, who called me from

Warsaw, was quite alarmed by her son's CIA connections. Admittedly, she did not like some of my behavior, but that had nothing to do with the CIA. "Why," she asked, "would your novels have a Library of Congress number, unless you work for the U.S. government—for the CIA?" My mother knew the content of *The Painted Bird*; nevertheless, she still thought that somehow I was a CIA agent, unmasked by the totalitarian polemic.

Another polemic, another absurdity. In August 1982, some sixty members of Solidarity and KOR [Komitet Obrony Robotników / the Workers' Defense Committee] were mistreated by police in the Kwidzyn internment camp—so brutally, in fact, that many required hospitalization, which they did not get. Solidarity categorically protested the mistreatment, and its letter of protest, signed by some of the best-known names in Poland, was eventually published in certain American newspapers. "We condemn this action committed with full premeditation," the letter stated. "We express our solidarity with our colleagues interned in Kwidzyn. We appeal to the moral authorities, to public opinion all over the world for protection of the imprisoned and interned from acts of arbitrariness and brutality."

The official press, which usually presents Solidarity members as lazy gluttons who spend their time in luxurious surroundings, responded by describing the "typical" camp for those interned by the military junta: "Silence, sun, and an atmosphere of vacation-like laziness. Each apartment contains a vestibule, built-in dresser, tiled bathroom with cold and hot water available all day. A higher standard than is available in, for example, the Warsaw Orbis Hotel. Many exotic plants. The café is open from one-thirty to six o'clock; waitresses designated from among the interned are setting tables in the elegant dining room, the kitchen glistening with nickel and white tiles. An uninterrupted stream of packages arrives from abroad for those interned: coffee, tea, hot chocolate, chocolate bars with nuts, salami, ham, shrimp, and other assorted delicacies. The women who arrived here with only their hand toiletries bag leave the centre with full suitcases which they can barely carry to the gate. They are usually awaited there by a reserved taxi." Another example of totalitarian polemic.

A final thought. Like most of us on this panel, I am a child of the war, of the Second World War. I dread war more than anything; war is the end of life—it meant the end of life for most members of my family. And even if I at fifty consider myself old enough not to care about dying, I have lived long enough to know what war is—and learned not to dismiss the threat of it easily. In fact, I would sacrifice anything, anything at all, to avoid war. I would rather be red than dead—and for me, who fears and hates the totalitarian state, that says a lot. Nevertheless, I feel that life is better than no life, that regardless of the violence I myself have undergone, I have no right whatsoever to endorse anything that would lead to violence. I abhor violence, and war is the ultimate form of violence.

It is significant that over the past two days we have discussed Russia and America, the conflict between West and East, but never once directly mentioned the threat of a new world war. No one, in fact, so much as whispered that such a war is even possible. Instead, we have spoken about missiles in Western and Eastern Europe and about the Warsaw Pact and NATO. But why has no one dared to speak of war? Such a possibility is part of the polemic as well—part of the theater of real life. As a child of war, a social scientist, and a novelist of violence, I read various Soviet journals which specialize in modern war and warfare. Those journals clearly articulate—partly as a polemic!—the Soviet military strategy of future war, no longer absurd but rather very deadly. Will it be a nuclear World War Three? A war with nuclear weapons used on a limited scale with some big cities spared? Will it be a superlimited nuclear war, a sort of traditional warfare with small tactical nuclear weapons employed here and there? What is interesting to me is not just the weapons—I fear them regardless of whether they are American or Soviet—but the fact that so much of our business and industry is aimed for war. And I am frightened by the fact that, while neither the U.S. nor Western Europe professes a *total ideology of war*, the Soviet ideology makes them perceive the next war as objectively inevitable. More of the Soviet—totalitarian—polemic.

The Soviet bloc of people's republics led by the Soviet Union even believes that it has a historically objective and moral right to preemptive war. Thus, when you or I enter into a totalitarian polemic, we are—they tell us—subjective; our argument, objectively, is wrong. Objectively, they suggest, even though we may be unaware of it, we are against the working class. And because *they* represent objective reality, we are their enemies. And that is why, in the name of such objective necessity, they suppress Solidarity, which they call an organ of the CIA. Solidarity, they allege, might start a war!

In my polemic, all I lay claim to is *chance existence*. All I claim to know is life from *moment to moment*. And all I know about life is that I learn it as I go about it—and I go about it as if it was a novel without much plot. Totalitarian polemicists would claim to know what even I don't—that is, for what historically objective reason I have exceeded my historically allocated "decadent" time. And it is the role of the totalitarian polemicist to ensure that I won't exceed it further. It is their philosophy of a "preemptive" strike that makes them so absurd—but also so dangerous. War, after all, is another form of polemic.

On Sex

Sex is the key force. It is at the center of experience. It permeates every aspect of our being. Anything truly sexual is by its nature positive and fulfilling. It brings about a sense of being alive.

The only thing I am really fascinated by is seeing places where people can be themselves, which means I go to the exchange bars, swinging places, places where people dance without wearing any clothing. . . . I am absolutely fascinated by human proximity, proximity which is not based on hostility. To my generation, sex was the only positive force in society. It is the only force responsible for life, for you, for me, for them. Every other force I have seen was basically negative. Military, ideology, bureaucracy, state—these were forces that were responsible for destroying all of us.

CLUB SEX

In "Kosinski's Passions" (originally published in *BIGnews*), one of the final interviews Kosinski gave, he spoke of the role of sex in his writing and in his life and discussed his fascination with New York's sex clubs.

It is not sex by itself that interests me, but its particular role in the American consciousness and, at the same time, in my own life. A novelist has a specific poetic license which also applies to his own life. This was particularly true when, as a sociologist, I wrote about family life in the United States.

Sex interests me as a part of life, not as an isolated instrument of pleasure. This is why I am fascinated by sexual motivation and its forms as reflected in writing, film, photography, vaudeville. One trait which differentiated New York from European cities was the incredible freedom and ease, not found elsewhere, in which life, including sexual life, could be carried on, on many levels. This need was satisfied by the existence of a large variety of sex clubs in the 1970s, which were open every day from the afternoon until the early morning. Total anonymity was the rule in these places. For someone such as I, interested in sex, this was important, and New York was a rich source of experiences and associations, some of which later resonated in my prose.

Now, in the late 1980s, the character of sexual behavior has changed. AIDS has decimated spontaneous behavior. In the city center of New

York, there used to be several dozen places where one could go to view "live sex"—exhibitions as incredible as the things seen in the paintings by Bosch. I don't have to add that this included full copulation. For me as a photographer, sociologist, and writer, this was a golden vein of subject matter. It excited my imagination, aided my writing. At the same time, my interest in Buddhist philosophy served to underline the importance of sex as intellectual inspiration, not just as a source of mental enjoyment. I often described in television interviews what went on in the sex clubs. I wrote about it with irony, but "extra-realistically," because as a writer I do not advance anything except the idea of creativity. There were long fragments in *Cockpit, Blind Date,* and *Pinball.*

Whether [at the sex clubs] I confined myself to looking is a question that may be asked of my books, not of myself. After all, there are many types of participation. One can observe so intensely that one becomes part of the action, but without actually being an active participant. This is part of the freedom found in these clubs. One can be at the center or at the edges, in total anonymity, without consequences, catching the essence of sexual life in a group form, one not often seen by writers.

Now, I do not have the opportunity to witness such variety, including the "live" exhibitions that had such a stimulating effect on my imagination. My interests are few, but those that I do have run deep. For example, I do not own things: I prefer to rent them rather than to possess them. But I do collect human relationships, very much the way others collect fine art. At the clubs, there was the democracy of sexual ethics—ethics without misunderstandings and faux pas. I always brought a woman with me, because it was required. A man would not be admitted alone. This was to maintain a balance so there would be no conflict. I had several female friends, who were in a sense companions—journalists, actresses, painters, sculptors—and who, for one reason or another, were interested in this life. These were intelligent persons, used to the street life, because one had to know how to behave in these places and respond to the different kinds of situations. One could not just suddenly spit at someone. One could not be shocked or surprised by what one saw. Since I always took someone with me, together we wandered from place to place, observing and conversing. Then we would tactfully go elsewhere.

The clubs were highly specialized. Starting with the nudist clubs, they ranged from the orgiastic clubs to those where the guests wore costumes of leather, rubber, latex, silk, and so forth, and where the conversation was limited to intimate topics. There were touch clubs, with highly sensual dances and partner swapping—clubs which served as the take-off points for further adventures. Some clubs had small private rooms; others had orgy rooms for several hundred people, dining rooms, gymnasiums. There were also clubs which did not require an equilibrium between men and women; a number were exclusively for men or for women. In some clubs, transsexuals or hermaphrodites dominated; others catered to transvestites, the so-called cross dressers.

Thanks to these trips, which took place after the end of the normal day, I met some of the most fascinating people in New York. For example, one day a couple happened to sit next to me, and it turned out that the man was the president of one of the largest banks in the United States. Since he recognized me, he invited me to their home, where I saw things that Bosch would prefer not to have seen. They looked like a couple of quiet, peaceful people, yet the visit to their home gave me a case of goose flesh.

In these gatherings, pure sex played the least important role. For me, the sexual atmosphere was the most important. I am inspired by human sexuality, the thing that makes people sensitive to life. The act itself is mechanical and holds little interest for me. I must also add that each of these clubs had a restaurant, and the price of admission included a disco, gym, swimming pool, video arcade, billiards, et cetera.

PACKAGED PASSION

Kosinski was fascinated by popular culture, especially by American attitudes toward sex and sexuality as demonstrated in popular magazines. He spoke often—on the *Tonight Show* with Johnny Carson and elsewhere—about such attitudes, and he drew on them, often parodically, as subjects for his own fiction and for essays such as "Packaged Passion," which was written soon after the publication of his fourth novel, *The Devil Tree*. It was first published in the *American Scholar* in the spring of 1973.

At a time when magazine readership in this country has decreased so drastically that such national institutions as *Look* and *Life* have had to cease publication, at least one group of magazines has increased in number and in circulation, saturating the popular magazine field with accounts of *True Romance, Modern Romances, Intimate Romances, Real Romances, Your Romances, My Romance, Secret Romances, Daring Romances, Personal Romances, Revealing Romances, Real Love, True Love, Modern Love, True Life Confessions, Confidential Confessions, Real Confessions, True Confessions, Thrilling Confessions, Daring Confessions, Actual Confessions, Romantic Confessions, Exciting Confessions, Intimate Story, True Story, Bronze Thrills, Secrets, Confession Secrets,* to name just a few of them. Despite stiff competition from Hollywood movie and crime / detective magazines, home-and-skill-improvement periodicals, men's magazines, and countless pornography

272

tabloids, these romance / love / confession publications have successfully created and glutted the fantasy market during the last three decades,
providing textual and pictorial illustrations of everything from so-called
uninhibited sex to gracious living and loving.

One of the secrets of these magazines' commercial success is their
availability. Unlike pornography, which is expensive (from $3 to $15 per
magazine) and must be sought in special shops, and the semi-pornographic
magazines for "swinging guys and sinning gals" ($.75 to $1.50), these
confession magazines are inexpensive (their prices usually vary from $.35
to $.75) and can be found at legitimate, almost unavoidable, dealers—
supermarkets, drugstores, and newsstands throughout American cities
and suburbs.

Collectively, millions of copies are sold every month. To indicate their
popularity, we take one publication—*True Story*—as a typical representative of the confession genre. According to the 1972 "Simmons Audience
Data on Adult Female Readers," *True Story*'s total distribution per issue is
4,193,000, the median age of its readers is 33.1, and there are 2.46 readers
per copy, giving *True Story* a reach of over 10 million.

The 4.2 million female readers of *True Story* have a median household income
of $8,000 per year; approximately 1,685,000 or 40 percent are employed, of
which 30 percent are employed full-time.

Of the 4.2 million female readers of *True Story* 1,231,000 are between
the ages of 18–24; 2,305,000 are between the ages of 18–34; 3,199,000 are
between the ages of 18–49. In the over-18 age group, 3,364,000 or 80.2 percent
are heads of households; 2,784,000 or 64.4 percent are married; and 2,139,000
or 51 percent are mothers.

Of the 4.2 million female readers of *True Story,* 2,581,000 or 62 percent are
in households with one or more children under 18; 1,334,000 or 32 percent
are in households with one or two children under 18; and 1,246,000 or 30
percent are in households with three or more children under 18.

Of the 4.2 million female readers of *True Story,* 2,337,000 or 56 percent live
in metropolitan areas, of which 1,214,000 or 29 percent live in metropolitan
central city areas.

Because of their vast readership, the confession magazines must be considered a major source of popular entertainment, deserving attention in terms of the social and national myths they simultaneously foster and sustain.

According to the magazines' editors, all published articles are authentic, unsolicited, "true-life dramas" selected from manuscripts submitted by readers; the photographs are supposedly of "real-life" situations. The stories remain anonymous, the magazines claim, and the names of persons and places are fictitious simply to protect the authors' privacy. Unlike the cinema star gossip magazines, the editors insist that their material originates not with clever journalists or Hollywood superspies equipped with mini-recorders and infrared cameras, but with ordinary Americans who have written about their life experiences out of a pure and decent impulse to share them with millions of other ordinary Americans. Implicit in this claim is the notion of mutual dependence: the author needs someone to listen to his or her plight, and the reader ostensibly benefits by learning how certain predicaments were handled.

But behind a superficial appeal to the reader's sense of voyeuristic adventure is a more insidious appeal to his sense of safety, indeed of non-adventure. In contrast both to the sensational Hollywood magazine which concerns itself with the unreachable—the film and television star—and to the pornographic magazine—which examines the exaggerated actions of anonymous male and female bodies—these confession magazines insist on familiarity and objectivity. By emphasizing that they are the confessions of ordinary Americans, the stories suggest that they are revealing no more than the average social and human condition, in a bid to establish the reader's sympathy with the protagonists. At the same time, since these protagonists are involved in obvious aberrations from the stated norms of social behavior, the audience is allowed to feel a certain superiority over the unfortunate protagonists: the female reader is comforted by the discovery that, although her life may seem unrewarding, she has managed to avoid the disasters of nymphomania or frigidity that other ordinary women encounter. As average as the male reader feels in terms of his income, taxes, mortgages, and emotional capacity, he emerges closer to the stated norm of prescribed social conduct in comparison to the "other" men who "confess" to various acts of lust or depravity. Ultimately, the reader is deceived into thinking that he has achieved relative moral stardom within his uneventful private domain.

As might be expected, the magazines do not attempt to present anything but what they define as the most conventional relationship between the sexes. One predominant pattern emerges in every magazine: man is the agent of rationality, torn between societal responsibilities to his profession and to his family, while occasionally victimized by the demands of his own sexual instincts. Woman, on the other hand, is the agent of passion, completely at the mercy of an insatiable, instinctive sexual urge; she is continually astounded by her own capacity for wildness, and incapable of either assessing or controlling it. A cursory look at the content of six or seven magazines indicates this distinction between the male and female protagonists.

Although all the stories function within a rather rigid code of propriety and of elementary moral standards ("I had a clean house but a dirty mind"), those supposedly written by women either celebrate the transgression of social taboos ("A straightforward report on 'How to talk dirty in bed and love it!'"), or emphasize the impossibility of avoiding sin ("Frigid with my husband—wild and wanton with the guy next door"). The male point of view, on the other hand, produces stories implying a certain amount of moral character and judgment: "She drowned her sorrow in sex: while I made war, my girl made out"; "My mother raised me in a brothel: now, she came back to ruin my life."

Meanwhile the female confessors continually sacrifice all moral or social concern to physical satisfaction: "Decency, honor, love—they mean nothing when faced with that wicked urge of my body"; "Fun is all that counts—so what if I was a lousy mother"; "I traded morals for money."

Thus, the magazines establish a stereotype of human relationship that has remained unchanged in spite of new trends in popular culture. Political and racial polarization, the war in Vietnam, the homosexual and women's liberation movements have been incorporated into the articles but have in no sense altered the magazines' assumptions, or had any impact as *ideas* on their basic formula: the reduction of situations to a vindication of male dominance. Beyond the matter of pure availability, it is this "simplification factor" that accounts for the magazines' continuing success; by appealing to men as conventional social protectors and providers, and to women as the ideal bedroom animal, the editors have created a model so basic, so crude, that it denies the complexities of modern existence and pretends to offer an easy alternative to a confusing reality.

Despite the magazines' claim that these are authentic stories, the most superficial analysis indicates that they have all been written according to a standard formula and edited to the point of predictability. Traumatic events seem to be invented, not for their dramatic impact but as an excuse for verbal exaggeration; and since the inflated expression is attached to such a limited range of situations and emotions, the language becomes repetitive and bombastic. The result is a disproportion between the event and the reaction to it—no matter what the circumstances, hysteria is the usual response in story after story. The peculiar details that might distinguish one author from another are subordinated to a familiar emotional monotone.

Almost without exception, the accounts are written in the first person, reminiscent of confessions or diaries. Experience as narrated is "autobiographical," focused backward, to illuminate the author's past. But unlike real autobiography, which may work like fiction to extend the reader's imagination beyond the event as recalled by the author, and unlike other forms of fiction, which generally allow the reader to consider himself and his own experiences in relation to the narrative, these magazines offer nonevocative reading. The reader is insulated; the narrated event—confined to someone else's "real" past—is already "over." Moreover, the classic resolution of most of these stories shows its protagonist suddenly speaking as an objective observer, denouncing the experience he has just narrated both because it did not achieve anything practical, and because it may have involved or led to immoral behavior. In a curious mode of self-abstraction, he discredits the adventure without admitting even the basic educational value of that adventure. Experience leads to no enlightenment about the world or the self, which might be applied to future experience; the narrator judges his situation as if nothing had happened, as he would have judged it before his last escapade. The story no longer needs to be decoded by the reader; while the author admits to his failure as a protagonist of a meaningful experience, the reader is encouraged to feel additional pity and superiority.

But the reader's final disengagement has been prepared for all along. All the stories depend on situational stimuli that call for responses from a preexistent, almost Pavlovian emotional grammar. As in soap opera and melodrama, the characters remain basically happy or miserable, basically good or bad, and only the strongest feelings—the favorite being pity—are allowed to surface. Time is telescoped so that moments of intense fear and relief or joy and suffering are juxtaposed, but the motives behind these emotions are never shown. The reader is never required to be involved beyond his simplest feelings and perceptions. The dramatic situation is encoded in order to reinforce in the audience a sense of predictability, of normalcy. Like TV's *All in the Family*, which condenses bigotry to fit into thirty minutes so that an average bigot can easily feel that his attitudes are ordinary or even moderate in comparison to Archie Bunker's, and like common TV serials, no matter how varied and traumatic the protagonists' experiences are, the stories always end with a palliative vision; some measure of order and balance is always restored. The reader returns to the emotional kindergarten while his psyche slips back into trouble-free sleep.

Without exception, the romance magazines carry a substantial number of advertisements ranging from cigarettes, detergents, cosmetics, and kitchen accessories to products designed to remove unwanted hair, to relieve pain, to lengthen nails, to slim the thighs or increase the bust. Even though these ads and statistics indicate that women are the major target—from the middle-aged housewife to her teenaged daughter—the booksellers insist that the magazines are read by men almost as often as by women. A more pertinent explanation may be found, however, in the fact that in these stories the image of women and men feeds conventional fantasies of sexual and social domination. Primarily, woman is an animal whose needs and interests are purely physical.

SHARON: I guess I'm into sensuality because what gets me wilder in bed than ten tigers in heat is oral sex. By that I don't mean just fellatio and cunnilingus. They're the most important part of it. But there's lots more. I love to go over

277

every tiny inch of a man's body, kissing, licking, sucking—just go on and on with it. . . . But before I could reach my goal, his hands were pushing me away. I looked up in surprise, to see an expression of disgust printed on every feature of his face. "Pete. What's wrong?" I asked, a chill running through me. . . .

PETE: "Sharon, I can't believe you meant that. A girl like you—a sweet, nice girl. It's filthy—I've always thought so, I'd never ask a woman to do that to me—at least not one I respected."

For the first time that night I discovered how wild and uninhibited a woman could be. Sharon was like a female animal, totally without restraint or shame. Then, when the passionate fires subsided, she purred like a kitten, stroking my chest, wanting to talk about what we'd done. . . . It was insane, I admitted. But Sharon could make a man do insane things.

Because women are continually looking for sexual stimulation and satisfaction, men are defined in terms of their sexual potential.

". . . your husband is alive, but he was injured in action earlier today and—"
"How bad?"
"Quite bad. He received a spinal injury. He is paralyzed from the waist down."
"He's paralyzed," I cried. "Oh, Lord, why? Why did it have to happen?"
"It's not the worst thing in the world," Tracy said slowly.
I stared at her in shock. "How can you say such a thing? Don't you understand what that means, Tracy? He—he's no longer a man!"

Even time is measured by sexual clockwork: "I know now—many orgasms later . . . " Woman's ultimate craving for sex thus allows her to ignore physical violence and fear, and elicit pleasure even from rape.

He slapped his hand across my face, and a little line of blood trickled down my nose.
I stumbled to the door, but his body was in front of it, and he began pulling off his trousers.

"I'll scream!" I threatened.

I couldn't scream. Or maybe I didn't scream because I didn't want to.

When he pushed me down on the bed, I felt the insistent tide of pleasure wash over me in spite of the blood that seeped into my mouth.

"You want it. You want it so badly you'd gladly get raped to get it," he said.

He went on and on, pounding that truth into me, and I couldn't feel pain—only the pleasure that wouldn't go away, the pleasure that ultimately shut out his words and caused my body to respond to the rhythm of his.

He looked down at me, triumphant. I told him I hated him, but I hated only myself.

This interpretation of woman as animalistic is the source of a very important "reverse flattery" designed to keep her happy with her unthinking state: she is praised for being instinctive, closer to the earth, and continually in touch with her savage roots and primitive urges.

Allison was a child, but her body and instincts were those of a woman. Although consciously Allison was innocent, subconsciously she was trying out a woman's ways on Dale.

With a wild laugh he yanked at my filmy nightgown, tearing it from neck to hem. Then he sprawled beside me, his lips on mine in a savage, bruising kiss. I twisted, pounded his chest with my fists and tried to kick, but it was useless. Slowly the fight went out of me and strangely the fear seeped away, too. My heart was almost beating to pieces and not because of the exertion. Something savage and eager surged through me as if my inner self had been unchained at last.

That night I found out the true meaning of sex and learned what it was to be a real woman—and to have a real man! Art's selfish haste and Luke's former gentleness hadn't prepared me for this primitive, magnificent mating.

This attitude toward women leads not only to a deification of sex as woman's major obsession and prerogative. It also implies that there is an optimum feminine sexuality that can be achieved, and a standard of "perfect

sex" between a woman and man that is the sole basis of happy existence. If not achieved, the resulting sexual imperfection can wreck marriages and ruin lives.

We'd had long conversations and discussions about every aspect of our lives and pasts, and especially about our failed marriages. We were both candid and honest, admitting that sex problems had caused the break-ups. We'd read and heard before and after our divorces that if a marriage had a strong sex basis it could survive anything. And we were both living proof of the trust of that conclusion, we said to each other many times.

I knew our wedding night was thrilling to Bruce. To him, it was everything he thought it should be, but to me, it was a shattering failure. In the days and nights that followed, Bruce wanted me more and more—and although I gave myself to him willingly, each time hoping I could be fulfilled by him, his lovemaking never satisfied me.

Woman's most familiar and reliable role in the majority of stories is predictably that of the idiot child. She is never seriously involved with current issues, and is expected to remain indifferent to the ideas presented by social events and movements such as women's liberation. A woman who thinks is as suspect as one who becomes sexually overdemanding: "God knows I still loved Mitzy, even though I couldn't understand the way she'd been acting lately—wearing hot pants, reading books, talking about sex . . . "

As kewpie doll, woman cannot have a profession, since competition with men in a man's world would directly reduce her viability as a woman. A job is either a temporary means for financial security while husband shopping ("I needed money more than morals. I worked for a rent-a-lover service"), a form of access to eligible males, or—given a husband—another form of entertainment.

One day I could be scared I'd lose Joe; the other I'd be restless looking for some kind of I-didn't-know-what-excitement.

It was boring sitting around the house all day and Joe didn't want me to work. He told me to "find something to do" if I was bored. Just about all that

interested me was going to the beauty parlor and shopping for clothes or trying
out new ways of wearing makeup.

**If a woman is energetic or needy enough to get out of the house, her choice
of job will be determined by sexual factors.**

MALE: Is it the variety of men or the variety of acts that turns you on the most?

JANET: Oh, the acts, definitely. No question. As I've said, I dig making it with
different guys. Frankly, that's why I got a job as a stewardess. I knew that if I was
working in any kind of office and started sleeping with this guy and then that
one, my life would get too complicated.

**In this increasingly repressive universe where sex is the central theme,
there is only one desirable social role: the wife. Marriage is assumed to be
all women's primary goal because it offers instant, legitimate social status;
thus any suggestion of thought on a woman's part has to do with her entrap-
ment schemes.**

It was all part of my plan to latch onto a man. I was tired of waiting for Mr.
Right to enter my life. I was ready to settle on Mr. Anybody who would take me.

Problem number one. What did I want? I wanted a man. He had to be somebody with a good job and position in the community. Looks didn't matter as
long as he wasn't absolutely homely. Feelings too were out of the question.
Perhaps in time I could learn to love him . . . as long as I could respect him
that was enough.

Next problem: how to get him? Well, what would such a man expect of a
wife? A comfortable home, of course, and good meals. I wasn't a bad cook, but
why not become sensational? There were a million cook books in the library. I
would start with French Cooking. I had plenty of time to practice now on Dad.

**Generally, there is a strict division between premarital sex and the kind
of physical relationship acceptable in a marriage, a distinction that sets up**

281

further important sexual categories and antagonisms: "I'd had enough sex. As much as I had loved Ross's love—maybe almost as much as I'd loved Ross—I regretted deeply that I had given him the love that should have been saved for another man, my husband."

Although marriage is a social necessity for women, it is not always an ultimate good. No matter how great her carnal appetite before the wedding, it is assumed that marriage inevitably leads to sexual boredom, to a reversal of woman's primal nature. In most cases, however, this reversal is accepted as a natural consequence of monogamy. When the tamed wife periodically renews her image as sex kitten, she goes to premarital lengths not for her own pleasure but to renew her husband's "orgasmic" energy: "Almost before I knew what was happening, Ken had the black lace panties off me. I didn't have the satisfaction of the slow build-up for our lovemaking that I dreamed about. But black lace panties turn men on—fast."

But sexual incompatibility and boredom are only secondary, predictable problems; a woman's relative "failure" in the world and her disillusionment with marriage is as often due to financial, as to sexual, inadequacy.

> So, if there were stars in my eyes when I married Larry, I had a reason. Everything was magic; things had to go right for us and work out just perfect. When he took the job at the gas station, I didn't mind living on a mechanic's salary. I guess I expected him to own the station in no time.
>
> But it didn't work out that way. Larry's appealing shyness and modesty about how terrific he was carried over into the job area, too. He was too easygoing to be pushy, the way you have to when you want to get ahead, and he was perfectly happy to go on "making do" on a mechanic's salary forever.

A good marriage is thus a solvent marriage; domestic comfort and security still reign supreme, and a good shopping spree can compensate for any emotional misunderstandings.

> I lay snuggly against Ken's warm back and stared at the ceiling. The romance that was lacking in my marriage was mostly my fault. . . .

I will buy myself some new clothes, I vowed. I'll also buy the velvet sofa and redecorate my whole house. I drifted into a peaceful sleep, thanking God I was lucky enough to have a husband like Ken.

Aside from wife—and occasionally mother—there are various minor roles woman can play. She can be a sexual therapist, for example, for whom attraction is replaced by pity, and who consequently treats man with contempt.

Seconds later he gave a cry and collapsed in a sweating, happy mass against my breast.

"How was that, Nita?" he asked cheerfully after a minute. "Pretty great, huh?"

"Is that all?" My voice was shaking a little. . . .

I began to feel slightly detached, and once I even counted silently to myself (one-one-thousand, two-one-thousand) to see how long it took him from the moment of penetration to the moment of climax. On that particular occasion he was especially brisk; by my reckoning it had taken only ten seconds.

I knew that if I said no, he would feel that it was because he was crippled; so because of my pity, I said yes to him. I said yes to a dingy room in that small town's only hotel. And I said yes to a brief hour of lovemaking that had no love in it at all.

After it was over I felt as though I had completed an act of penance— penance for not giving myself to Fred. . . . What I had done had been an act of therapy, an act of kindness. I didn't feel soiled by it, but I knew that I would never do it again, either.

In general, however, these "kinky" roles are rare, both because they demand extraordinary women and because they contradict the usual positive vision of the male. Normally, the man is a multidimensional animal, possessed of a mind as well as a body.

. . . because there are differences between orgasm in men and women. . . . A woman can benefit from learning the basic facts about male orgasm. This includes learning what goes on in a man's mind as well as his body. . . .

To begin with, you should know that the most important sex organ a man has is his mind. Pleasure in sex is inseparable from the man's emotional reactions. A man who thinks he is loved and desired actually feels more pleasure than a man who is uncertain about his partner's affections.

Because he is endowed with powers of reflection, man can realize his problems and solve them. Unlike woman, who is never engaged in a learning process, a man occasionally recognizes his potential for (although never full achievement of) self-knowledge. It is interesting to note that whereas a woman is never defined in professional terms, the man's failures are almost justified by the fact of his taxing social role as the typical American businessman in such stories as "Too Young to Be an Old Man": "I was an all-work-and-no-play husband. I guess I was the typical American businessman: tense, ambitious, paranoid, overweight. The difference was that I had a perfect wife, but I tried to mold her in the image of myself."

Finally, a man quite often represents conventional morality in opposition to a mother who represents indecency, even depravity: "I caught V.D. from my own mother!" "My mother the campus tramp. She got 'A' for Affair . . . All my life I'd known tramps, but I married the first decent girl I met. Now, I had to protect her from the first tramp I'd ever known—my mother."

In general, the physical presentation of the magazines is slick, their photographs posed by professional models, the covers glossy and in bright colors. An exception must be made, however, for the several magazines aimed at the black audience, which are printed on lower-grade paper, and whose graphic layout is cruder and less professional. These magazines use black models in photographic illustrations and ads and refer to the black experience in their stories. They are identical to the "white" magazines in terms of advertising, but their situations are even simpler, their characters' reactions even more naive. The black heroine offers the most exaggerated example of woman controlled by sexual instinct. Although no women in these magazines—black or white—are allowed any serious thoughts, some are granted consciousness, and are aware of their passions. The black woman's sensuality, on the other hand, appears as a restless pursuit of a pleasure she cannot even name; her white counterpart at least engages in conversation, but the black woman is given no identifying characteristics beyond the physical. While the white woman has at least developed certain idiosyncratic—although unsophisticated—tastes and preferences, the black heroine remains undefined, always at the mercy of sudden, anonymous sexual encounters, during which she is even incapable of differentiating between her white and black lovers. While the Caucasian woman may give up waiting for "Mr. Right," she at least acknowledges the categories and is usually given some small measure of choice. The black woman willingly accepts whatever man picks her up, registering only the most impersonal details. Nothing of personal interaction between her and her men is even remotely suggested.

I hadn't gotten far when a big, white car pulled up to the curb. The man reached over and lowered the window. "Want to go for a ride?" he called.

I kept walking and he drove along slowly. "Mighty dangerous for a girl to be out all alone."

Then he came to a stop. "Come on, sweetheart. I won't hurt you. I'm just as lonely as you are."

I glanced at his face and he looked lonely. I wondered if his wife was dead or out drunk somewhere.

"Come on, kid," he said again. This time his voice sounded serious.

I got into the car and the man pulled away from the curb. It was totally dark and I couldn't make out his face. He said we needed a drink and drove straight to the motel where he said he was staying. I guess he was afraid to take me anywhere else because I might change my mind.

We went into a lovely room that had a big double bed with an orange bedspread and brown carpet. There was just a corner lamp burning. The man removed his hat and there were lines around his eyes. My stomach churned. What had I done?

He came around with the drinks and I gladly drank mine, although it was my first. I just wanted to forget. Then he had my blouse off and was pushing me to the bed. I tried to push him off, but the drink had dulled me so I couldn't. I don't remember his lovemaking, but I do remember him calling a cab for me.

Once in my own room, I remembered very well what I'd just done. I found a small Bible and promised myself never would I do such a thing again. I'd try to talk to somebody and I'd try to find out what was wrong with me. I thought it might be physical because of all the beatings I'd had.

Although it is easy to expose the fantasies of these publications and to renounce them as unrealistic and biased, it is impossible to ignore their enormous popular support. When, on two occasions, I presented collective reviews of these magazines on the *Tonight Show,* the response to my remarks was astonishing. The countless letters sent both to the network and to me revealed that the majority of readers considered the magazines accurate in their reflection of "real events" and accepted the stories uncritically, as vivid slices of contemporary life.

It would appear, therefore, that the vast numbers of people reflected in the Simmons survey not only read but also believe what they read in the confession magazines. Considering the readership statistics, this fact leads to several important conclusions. To begin with, one could say that there is a demand for bad art, an art chosen to remove the reader from his own condition, and by doing so to abstract him from the human condition in general. Ironically, since the reader continually isolates himself from others by reading stories that demand nothing of him and never extend him beyond the most prosaic emotions, he becomes a victim, impoverished by his own unexpanded, underdeveloped self. Although it may be impossible to generalize about the spiritual and mental makeup of 4.2 million women, it is safe to say that the majority of readers probably do not privately oppose the magazines' social, racial, and sexual hierarchies. This support indicates, among other things, a fundamental mental and spiritual passivity. As they resign themselves to the imaginative vacuum of the stories, the readers admit to a double bankruptcy: if in their vicarious lives they settle for the fraud implicit in these magazines, one can only speculate on the experience component of their actual lives. Although it may be assumed that man's natural instinct is to avoid experience, to prevent the possible failure and consequent knowledge of the self as an ultimate loser, it is significant that in a society that is continually tending toward the individual's isolation, there is so little awareness of this trend. In fact, there seems to be an increasing desire on the part of mass audiences to reinforce social divisions and barriers, and to ensure individual isolation. As the primary exponents of this sterile self-protection, the confession magazines cannot be dismissed as just another stream of popular trash, as the epitome of preferred bad art. They reveal a significant popular need for yet another soporific: a literature that can defuse the imagination, dismiss emotion, and ultimately leave the reader disarmed, unable to face his very self or to cope with the unknown—his own existence.

KEEPING A MAN

Kosinski's take on American sexual attitudes was both humorous and insightful. These remarks were excerpted from his presentation at Franklin and Marshall College in 1988, but he repeated some of the same anecdotes in other talks as well.

A recent magazine article that I read offers advice on "How to Catch—and Keep—Any Man You Want." The proposition was interesting to me for several reasons. First, because I write about things like this in my fiction. And second because, from a certain point of view, when I was first married in 1962, my late wife was very well-to-do and therefore feasibly I could be considered a kept man. Moreover, by that time, I was already kept by the United States, a country which wasn't mine. In our household, I could pay for certain expenses, but as the writer of just two books then, both of them nonfiction, my pay was rather limited. My late wife, on the other hand, was a widow who had inherited a substantial estate which ranked her among the top taxpayers in the United States. In fact, I figured out that I would have to write for some three hundred years just to pay her taxes.

"How to Catch—and Keep—Any Man You Want"—an interesting proposition psychologically, since I already know that I am kept by history. I cannot escape it. I can run away from you, but not from myself, and certainly not from being a Polish Jew. That's why I am still here.

But the focus of the article to which I referred is not psychological but practical. It said that "for most women the time finally comes when all the freedom and fun and affairs aren't enough anymore and they long for that closeness that can only come from a loving relationship with one man. They wish for a settled life and home they can call their own." So "every man who crosses their path is measured as a possible life partner." And the question becomes how to catch Mr. Right. The notion is a little unsettling to me, because—as a Jew—when I hear the phrase "catch a man," I think immediately of arrest.

According to the article, however, in America, you catch a man by sending him a greeting card. "There is one to match every mood, and they are as close as your local gift shop. Sometimes a carefully chosen greeting card can say more to a man than hours of halting conversation, especially if you're the shy type." The cards come "in all shapes, sizes, and styles—cute, corny, romantic, sexy, even downright dirty—and they show you care." If that fails, "Cook him dinner." As you can tell, dinners don't do that much for me. But apparently the folk saying that "'The way to a man's heart is through his stomach' is often true. Even liberated men appreciate a woman who can cook well." And so forth.

Then there is breakfast in bed. "If he was the world's best lover last night, what better way to reward him than by serving a tempting tray of victuals to restore his virility?" "Go to the beach" and rub suntan oil on each other. According to the article, "For two mutually attracted people, lying together on a blanket on the beach can be a form of foreplay." Or "Pack a picnic." "Write a poem—it doesn't have to rhyme." Create a "courtship album."

An even better suggestion: "Take it off." Surprise him with a striptease some night. Start with exotic drinks and work up to his secret sex fantasy. "Did you know that the urge for sex originates in the head?" Only Americans would ask a question like that. Europeans have known it for a thousand years. Where else does it originate?

"Act it out, sexy showers, bubble baths, sweet music, erotic magazines, naughty nighties." Oh, yes: "Rent a motel room." And, if you are already lovers, "don't be afraid to give him oral pleasure." Now I distinctly remember when I arrived in the United States, to me, oral pleasure meant Haggadah.

What else is there? I mean the rest is a pleasure, no doubt about it. But true oral pleasure comes from storytelling. You are now experiencing—at least I pray that you are experiencing—such oral pleasure. I don't want to be too intellectual about it, but to play on words, as the Hasidic Jew has always done, I am giving you my head. This is the supreme act of oral pleasure, and therefore you laugh and have a good time. So when a fellow student at Columbia University advised me to "take her out, because she loves oral pleasure," I asked myself what kind of story I should tell her. Should it be about the Second World War? That would traumatize her instantly. Or should it be something different, a story that would drive her crazy as she wondered how it would end and that would induce her to come home with me? But clearly that is not the case in America. "Don't make him ask for it," the article recommends. Perhaps this is why my good friends, as much as I love them, never learned to tell a truly good story.

"Learn about his job." Can you imagine: all this stuff so far, after all the Bloody Marys in bed, and you still don't know what the man does for a living? The article goes on to suggest entertaining his family. "If things are starting to get serious, it's a good idea to establish cordial relations with your man's relatives. Be charming and polite and gracious, and give them lots of reasons to like you." The trouble is, I don't have any family to meet. It is not because they are not the greatest people in the world. Quite likely, they were. But they are no longer alive. So I would have to say, "Honey, I don't have any relatives." And that might evoke the following response: "No relatives? Well, where are they?" And I would say, "They no longer are." And then she would say, "Wait, what happened?" To be honest and friendly and sufficiently candid, I would say, "They died." And if she was very American, and as candid as the greeting cards that suit every occasion, she would say, "What do you mean they all died? All of them?" And I would say "Yes, all. All but two; and now they are dead as well, which means I have no relatives." And she would say, "Did they all die at once? In a bus? In a car? A plane?" And I would say, "Yes, in a plane—a plane called history. They died—because they were there." Being there. There was no other reason.

But do I spoil a date by telling her all of my history? I doubt it. That would not be the kind of "head" that the author of the article had in mind.

PRO-CREATION

With interviewer Barry Gray in 1982, Kosinski spoke about the power of the sexual force and noted the important link between sexuality and spirituality.

Society came to us, to my wartime generation, as a destructive force, as a force that would separate us from those we loved and those who loved us, from our parents and from our families. The State came to us as bureaucracy, as the war machine, as Nazi or Stalinist propaganda. Human contact was always dangerous, always unpredictable; very often, it resulted in death, in denouncement, in being crippled. The only force, therefore, that my generation would trust was a force that would spring from within—spirituality of existence, which means the life force, sexuality. Sex is an instinct; it's a force which is procreative. I am a creator of my own life; hence, I have to be pro the procreative force. To us, to my generation, to those good Jews brought up on the best of what's in Judaic religion, sex was a rewarding and life-giving force.

After the war, my father kept reminding me, "Don't ever feel guilty about it. We do not believe in the 'original sin.' There is nothing to be ashamed of. If you trust sex, you will never go wrong. If you trust bureaucracy, army, ideology, you will die." And so, to my generation, once again—and I have retained the attitude—sexuality is God given. I look at it as a life force, regardless of what shape it takes, as long as it does not harm anyone,

291

as long as it does not lead to any form of abuse. And it shouldn't. If it does, then it is bureaucracy. If it does, then it is something else, because sexuality as perceived from within is always pure—it is a force that brings us closer and is finally responsible for life. And any form that leads toward courtship, fantasy, adornment is therefore positive because it contributes both to life and to our feeling of being alive. And that is the most important feeling one should have. The way to worship God is from within. When you feel alive and you feel good about it, you pay the best tribute you can to whoever is responsible for the life that you feel.

When I came to the United States, I noticed that the Protestant society is generally open, except for that occasional censoring finger which makes the expression of sexuality threatening and dangerous and occasionally results in punitive attitudes. You asked me before about my fiction. One reason that I am not well reviewed, that I am censored, is because my characters express themselves sexually. *Pinball* is a very sexual novel. I like to think I am a very sexual being. I react to people sexually. I am one of those who stares at people. I am one of those who goes anywhere, including sex clubs, to discover something about human sexuality. As a novelist and as a man, I look upon sexuality as what is best in our life, and I look at the rest in life with far greater suspicion.

Sex is a gift from God. And precisely because it's a force responsible for life, it has to be godlike. This also applies to my religious belief. I believe in the gift of God. In other words, I am not so much preoccupied with the giver as with the gift. I am here not to ponder who the maker is. I am here to ponder how to make the best of the gift. That is the only way I can be creative, the only way that I can be procreative. And that is the only way in which, in fact, I can worship what is godlike in me—my own spirituality. Anything else is deflecting. Anything else becomes academic, becomes scholarly, becomes theology. I am not a theologian. I am a human being worshipping the act of my own existence.

On Television

In the little world of television, all is solved within its magic thirty minutes. In spite of commercials, the wounded hero either rises or quickly dies, lovers marry or divorce, villains kill or are killed. Addicts are cured, justice usually wins, and war ends. All problems are solved again this week, as they were the last, and will be next week.

By its nature, visual art puts you in the position of a spectator. Things are preset for you. You can merely look, but you cannot retract, you cannot redo. It's all done for you. Only fiction, in fact, refashions you from within.

When you are watching television, you are in control of the images. It's an actress up on the screen who is experiencing everything. It's passive. But literature does the opposite. You have to see yourself in what you read.

COMMENT

In a draft of his remarks for *Comment* (on New York's WNBC-TV in 1971), Kosinski pondered the legacy of television, specifically its tremendous impact on the intellectual and political lives of today's students, and related it to his own experience as a professor of prose.

During the last four years, I have taught at Wesleyan, Princeton, and Yale University, and I have often lectured at other schools throughout the country. I am appalled by what I think emerges as the dominant trait of students today—their short attention span, their inability to concentrate on anything for more than half an hour.

I feel it was television which turned them into spectators since, by comparison with the world of TV, their own lives appeared slow and uneventful. When they first believed that what they saw on TV was real, they overreacted, only to feel cheated when the next program demanded a new emotion. Later, they simply felt manipulated by whatever drama they witnessed. By now, they have become hostile—and so they either refuse to watch TV altogether or they dissect the medium and throw out all that upsets them.

It was from the daily log of TV that they accepted the world as single-faceted and simple, never complex. After all, if the world was accessible to TV cameras, it could not possibly be otherwise. It was digestible, emotionlessly marching in front of them. From TV's comic cartoons, they first deduced that death is not final, since their hero, no matter how dead, would rise again. It was TV that taught them that pain need not be experienced but could be avoided; hence they remained at the mercy of the commercials for pain relievers. It was TV that first convinced them that drugs were to be trusted and that, with their help, there was no suffering, no need to be tense or unhappy.

As a professor of prose, I am constantly reminded of television's legacy. The students don't describe; they announce, as if an ever present screen orchestrated their meaning for everyone. In hundreds of essays, none of them approached the realities of killing, illness, passion. All this was dismissed by shorthand: a victim "suffers" or "feels bad"; a lover "throbs innocence"; the recipient "sweats sweetness."

During their scholarly and leisure pursuits, students switch from subject to subject with exactly the same intensity and staying power as if they were changing TV channels. Fifteen minutes is all a teacher can hope for, assuming the classroom is freezing and the students' chairs are very uncomfortable. Whether discussing Vietnam or a lunch menu or a film, they seem incapable of reflecting. Even though their stomachs are full, like exotic fish in the Amazon, they swallow indiscriminately, quickly ejecting all as waste.

Reading, however, is solitary; it requires effort and imagination to translate a symbol into one's own private reality. Hence, the young seldom venture beyond required reading texts. Or, worse, they limit themselves to condensed aids. And so, at the campuses, the novel is not dead but its readers are dying fast.

The students never seem to be alone for more than a few hours. To them, solitude means feeling lonely; when awake, if they ever are, they join the group. Others provide a stage for being turned on, since the students can no more turn themselves on than the TV set can. This act requires assistance, and moviemakers, music pushers, encounter-group merchants, fashion promoters—and television—are here to keep the young plugged in.

Another myth of this greening of America is that the young are using drugs to create mystic experiences and self-discovery. A drug, whether "soft" or "hard," is the crudest "do-it-yourself identity kit" remedy. Using it, many young people miss their identity in the same way so many of their elders, who were engaged in the so-called sexual revolution, missed the meaning of love in the guise of being free.

Rock is another safely collective rite. At best, they can claim it is a shared situation: they listen to music in a group. Deadening sound effectively rules out every exchange and permits each of them to escape direct contact with the others. They barely retain the memory of the lyrics and the beat.

The students' political revolution has been no more than another football trip. There are the momentary heroes, the cheerleaders, the spectators, a bit of virility and of machismo. Yet, in the last ten years, the white young rebels of this country have not sustained an ideology, formed an effective group or party. Politics, after all, is for them another channel to turn to and be turned by.

Those of you who feel that what I have just said is valid, make no mistake: to the young who watch me, now is nothing but a billboard temporarily occupied by a public health message of sorts. They are ready for the next program.

Why, therefore, you ask, do I still teach at the university? Because, as with TV, there is always a chance for a better program, for a different generation, or—at least—for a few profound "specials."

AGAINST COLLECTIVIZATION

In his address to the National Council of the Teachers of English in Louisville, Kentucky, in March 1987, Kosinski applauded the teachers for their role in fighting television and other collectivizing forces in modern society and for attempting to help students discover their selves through language, literature, and analytical thought.

We have come here today to pay tribute to you because, in today's America, you represent a true missionary force. In our atomized, disjointed, technological society, with so little attention paid to the individual and his inner life, men and women need more than ever the strength to carry them through the daily pressures. This strength must come from early exposure to one's own life at its most real—to the very essence of *who one is* and *what one becomes.*

Who are we? And what have we become? A sample of random answers. The average working adult American spends approximately one-third of his life sleeping. Of his one hundred and thirteen waking hours per week, he spends about thirty-eight hours working and twenty-five hours eating, dressing, and commuting to and from work. That leaves fifty hours per week for leisure.

Of this, an average American adult watches television twelve hundred hours per year. In addition to other activities—such as listening to the radio, socializing, travel, athletics, reading magazines—he typically spends ten hours a year watching movies, two hours going to the theater and concerts, and five hours reading books. The average American television set is on for six hours a day; the average family watches it for five hours a day. A youngster, especially if he is from a low-income family, grows up under its influence. For every book an average college student reads, he sees twenty films on and off his TV set.

We know about the financial crisis of our libraries yet, at the same time, the business community spends one and a half billion dollars every year on thirty-second television commercial spots. The United States Office of Education's "Right to Read" estimates that forty to fifty percent of the pupils in larger cities have serious reading problems, and that about twenty million Americans over the age of sixteen are unable to comprehend job applications and simple questionnaires. In New England alone, the setting of some of our best schools and colleges, there are over two hundred thousand functional illiterates who cannot complete an elementary driver's license, Medicaid form, or bank loan application. Meanwhile, in the last twenty-five years, suicide among the young has risen to become the second leading cause of death in that age group. The leading cause is accidental death. Many suicides are often listed in this murky category. A prominent politician's poll shows that of the people who voted for him, only fifty-four percent did so because they knew and agreed with his views. Yet eighty-four percent voted for him because he "appeared to be sincere and honest on television."

No wonder that the Gallup Poll on readership in America established that fifty-eight percent of our countrymen never read—never finished—a hardcover or paperback book other than the Bible or a textbook.

This, ladies and gentlemen, is the basic climate in which you conduct your mission. Students accept television's distorted views of life as real. When something disturbs them, they simply tune out and try to change the channel. With their short attention spans, they have become spectators rather than participants in life.

Moreover, modern society, in its increasing collectivization, offers every conceivable escape from the realization of the self. Participation in collective rites such as mass spectator sports and rock and pop festivals is a stage in the loss of the self, which has assiduously been rubbed off from earliest childhood by the collective conformist eraser. What the collective offers is the hypnotic notion that just as others are and always will be, so one is and will continue to be—that one cannot fail because only individuals, setting standards for themselves, fail. The collective, at worst, only underachieves. As if betraying a profound guilt, the collective jargon sometimes tries to rescue a single face from the blur of the crowd. The phrase "doing one's own thing" is really no more than a mockery uttered by people whose "own thing" is to be a part of an amorphous supergang.

The entrapments of collectivism are overwhelming: TV and radio, which permeate our privacy and destroy the aloneness out of which it becomes possible to learn to build a self; drugs, which smash the mirror of personal identity; the virtual disappearance of creative self-employment and of professions and opportunities which ask for the use of the self; the terrifying featurelessness of the modern physical environment; the debilitation of the arts; the great gray educational machine; the devaluing and disparaging of the imagination; the "own things" of the eroded self.

The search for inner strength by Americans—and especially young Americans—is mainly conducted through language and literature, which have the ability to trigger the imagination, that oldest trait which is typically human. However, if it is true that "industrial man's natural instinct is to fear any new experience, to abhor failure and avoid facing one's self," then it is also true that, above all, it is in your classrooms that this trend is counteracted. It is the teacher of English, of literature, who every day, steadfastly and often in desperation, carries that protracted fight against the diffusing of the imagination, against the dismissal of the emotion, against the individual's isolation, against the sterile self-protection, against the popular trash, against the soporific bad art. That's why it is finally the teacher of English who, day after day, refuses to leave his students emotionally and intellectually disarmed, who forces them to face their very selves and to cope with the unknown and with their own existence. Because of these rescue missions that take place every week in their classrooms, the teachers of English are this country's major missionary force. We admire you for what you do for us and for our children. We are grateful to you for it. We need you.

TELEVISION AS PROPAGANDIST

Kosinski, as he explained to Michael Spring in an interview for *Literary Cavalcade* in 1977, believed that television induced passivity and transformed its viewers, especially young viewers, from active participants in life into spectators who are unable to serve as protagonists even in their own dramas.

Film and literature should not be ranked: one is no better than the other, any more than painting is better than music. Film and literature are two independent forms of art, each one demanding a particular involvement.

The moving picture—film, television, et cetera—affects from *without*: the concrete, prerecorded images depend on the spectator's willingness to become a witness to what is portrayed on the screen. Literary experience affects from *within*, starting with the general—language—and depends on the reader's effort and ability to evoke concrete characters, situations, memories, and feelings.

The central role reserved for television in the life of an American family is the perfect symbol for our preoccupation with the visual and the notion that life centers around being distracted. The distraction comes to us in the form of popular TV shows, and television, by its nature, renders the viewer passive: physically, by immobilizing him in front of the source of distraction; intellectually, by offering the distraction that is predictably preannounced, demanding no effort, posing no challenge, and promising no surprises. In current American life, television manages to turn most Americans, particularly the young, into passive onlookers. When not systematically counteracted, the TV viewing habit increases life's deadly routines: it stills emotion, restricts the drive toward other people, deadens free play of the imagination. It slowly turns human beings into spectators, each one a passive recipient of life rather than an active, eventful protagonist of his own drama. And drama it will—it must—be. The book of life was, after all, written by a first-rate dramatic novelist.

Television has become the major conveyor of the values of our popular culture, its most effective, never-ceasing propagandist. The current popular culture is the product of, let's say, the last fifty years. It reflects primarily the outlook and aspirations of the postwar American middle class. One could summarize its major tenets as optimistic and sentimental—with a life of easy rewards as the ideal for the satisfied consumer. It takes a "Master-Charge" attitude toward life: it promises a high credit rating in life's every encounter and an easy acceptance by the society and one's peers. It offers no imaginative stratagems for dealing with life as it comes by, moment after moment—with life's unavoidable events: crisis, failure, accident, sickness, old age, death. It stresses consumption, not awareness, simple acquisition of goods, not necessary awareness.

Because of false sentimentality and fraudulent optimism, the popular culture is unable to generate art that is authentically concerned with the real aspects of life—with the unpredictable, indeed with failure of any kind. Television, reduced to the situations that are obvious, that are almost all gestural, that are action and plot-oriented, is not able to confront any ambiguity as an integral part of life, to portray anything complex and idiosyncratic and existing beyond the crudest black-and-white division of "good/bad," "right/wrong," "success/failure," "healthy/sick," "love/hate," "sad/happy," "rich/poor."

If the helpless soldier has always been the cannon fodder of the military state, the passive individual is the computer fodder of the superindustrialist state. Metaphorically speaking, in the classroom of life, neither one can stand up to raise his hand to define, to deny, or to affirm his place in life.

This TV-induced passivity of the individual, this easy acceptance of things as they are, is steadily and directly feeding the political, moral, and economic miasma of our environment: decreasing support of the schools, colleges, and universities; unlivable cities; the absence of sufficient public transportation; the dehumanizing work routine of the working man and woman; minimal care for the ill, for the maladjusted and the aged; the decreasing awareness of their plight; the blatant commercial exploitation of the naive and helpless customer; political corruption; growing penetration of business by the underworld; et cetera.

As routine, passivity, and isolation increase in our society, school is about the only remaining institution that has as its sole purpose to help tomorrow's adults become thinking individuals, strong enough to evaluate, judge, and counteract these deadening forces. The classroom experience in general and the reading experience in particular are two of the few demanding mental activities left in our society. A moving picture is not a sentence, a word not a picture. What sets them apart is the demand made on the recipient. The word activates from within; the image acts upon from without. Thus the impact of the popular culture, particularly of its visual components—video, film, et cetera—is felt particularly in the domain of reading—it effectively suppresses the ability to read and to evoke, to generate a spontaneous free play of inner images, or to verbalize this inner play of thoughts and associations.

Today, teaching novels is not just teaching literature; it is teaching ways to cope with reality, ways that are emotional, intellectual, historical, imaginative, pragmatic, sad or funny or neither. Students often assume they read books because they should "learn" literature. I think they must be asked to read books not for the sake of, let's say, English 101, but as ways of self-definition, to generate their own unique emotional, spiritual, imaginative ways of coping with life, which no film or speed-reading course or "how-to" manual can, on its own, in a long-range way, teach them. Being sufficiently mentally and emotionally equipped to cope with one's life is a process that, in itself, is not visible. Its subconscious "crystallization" takes time: the more one reads, the more one thinks and absorbs and imagines. And the more mature one's mental process will be.

Today's high school students need the lesson. They have coming a lot of surprises. The real world in which they will live has hardly anything in common with the neatly slotted world of *Police Story, Starsky and Hutch,* and *Charlie's Angels.* Already at the outset, the popular culture stereotypes are against them: in the real world, to be a normal woman, one must learn to be satisfied with being merely an ordinary female, neither a "police woman" nor "bionic." To be a man, one must be a mere male, neither a "six million dollar man" nor "Baretta."

The students of today will have to face, each in his or her own individual way, the narrowing of life's material rewards, the high price for the decades of rampant consumerism. Most of them, quite likely, will be affected by the forthcoming energy shortages that might skyrocket the prices, by the inflation, by the shrinking value of the U.S. dollar at home—catching up with what has been happening to it for years abroad—rapid deterioration of urban and suburban neighborhoods, growing no-man's-lands of the ghettos, the sluggish economy punctuated by high unemployment, decreasing standards of societal efficiency, of individual services, of corporate, state, and federal reliability, et cetera.

The question now is whether the young men and women who grow up today are emotionally and professionally prepared to face the fact that, quite likely, most of their middle-class expectations are simply not going to be fulfilled. Are they emotionally ready for what in their parents' eyes might become a life of failure and conflict and disappointment? Do they have enough inner strength—as opposed to the out-and-out hysteria of such popular culture heroes as Clint Eastwood, Charles Bronson, and others— to survive the unemployment lines, low credit ratings, the possible lack of a car or a fancy house, decrepit neighborhoods with no "good schools" for their own children?

Will they be ready for the ambiguity of the rapidly changing sexual mores and customs that might make them ill at ease or even fragment their lives, their families, and their relationships? Does *Star Wars, Close*

Encounters of the Third Kind, Saturday Night Fever, Magnum Force, or *Semi-Tough* prepare one in any way for one's own private encounters? Would the naive, simple, and crude lyrics of most of our pop rock really suffice when one is asked by a business superior to state one's position in a business matter? To write a meaningful business memo? To defend oneself when unjustly accused? To unmask a fraud? To be articulate when one's place in life might depend on stating one's case?

VIETNAM IN THE NEW VISUAL ERA

In this excerpt from an interview in August 1971, Kosinski discussed the way that television shapes people's reality—a topic he examined so perceptively in his third novel, *Being There* (1971), and in other works.

In the past, before the visual era, in the literary era, the notion of reality as opposed to the notion of art was very simple. When you went to the movies, you were not going to see reality; you were going to see art or actors. No movie claimed, "I am life." But now, for the first time in history, there is a medium—television—that is neither reality nor art.

Television never says, "I am a program." So it is very ambiguous. It takes the place of reality for many of us, and even more for the children who are growing up in front of it. Many people, in fact, did not believe that the moon shot actually took place; they thought the whole thing was staged in the studio. That is because, in the universe of television, there is no difference between what is real and what is unreal. Everything on the TV screen is, to some degree, both of these things.

The war in Vietnam, for example, is all too real. But when it is broadcast on television, especially when it is reduced to a half-hour program, it loses much of its intensity and its reality. I think ideally that those who want to prolong the war should show even more such programs, since the very fact that the war is on television grounds it in the unreal universe.

Only because of television, in fact, could this war have lasted eight years. It became a fixture, a daily program, built into our lives the same way every other program is built into our lives.

If one wanted to increase apprehension about the war, it would be far more effective to say, "And now, for Vietnam," and to show a blank screen for a half hour. Then every viewer would have to substitute his own private horror for what he could not see, and he could not possibly survive that confrontation with what he would imagine was actually taking place in Vietnam while the screen was blank. The most tragic thing about the war in Vietnam was that it was programmed on television.

On Acting

Acting is something very opposite from what I like to do. A novelist is entirely on his own. What I do is mine. It is my psyche, my spirit, my vanity, my conviction. In a movie, nothing is yours. It is all the director and the crew. A movie is an entirely different being.

I was greatly surprised . . . by my reaction to being in Reds—to being directed, to seeing myself on the screen. . . . I was absolutely horrified, put off by myself [in the movie]. If I ever came into conflict with my own physicality, that was it, then, the moment. It made me cringe. I literally had difficulty watching myself, the emotions I generated . . . emotions that had been dormant in me, emotions I'd rather not have.

I realized that I should be braver than I have been so far. If Warren [Beatty] takes so many risks as he goes along, then why shouldn't I, as a novelist, take even more? So I learned from Warren Beatty—and I shall be grateful to him for this as long as I live—this bravery, and a sort of steady, adamant, almost poetic determination to do what you want to do on your [own] terms.

ACADEMY OF MOTION PICTURE

ARTS AND SCIENCES

In 1982, Jerzy Kosinski was invited by the Academy of Motion Picture Arts and Sciences to present the awards for Best Original Screenplay and Best Adapted Screenplay. He was introduced by host Johnny Carson, who noted that, in the previous year, several writers—including Norman Mailer, Fay Kanin, and Jerzy Kosinski—had "put on makeup," and consequently "all are now eligible for consideration as Best Writer in a Supporting Role." Kosinski's remarks that evening were brief but very warmly received.

My experience as an actor has taught me the importance of a writer. We who act owe so much to those who write. The Bible tells us that in the beginning was the word. When the universe was in complete disorder, Moses was called to the mountain. A warning bolt of lightning, an overture of thunder, the skies parted, and a mighty hand reached down to give Moses the stone tablets. In a way, that was the first script. Some critics thought it was overproduced for just ten lines—but, by following it, mankind restored order out of chaos. If succeeding generations had stuck to that magnificent, original, and noble script instead of ad-libbing around it so much, today this would be a better world to live in.

ACTING VS. WRITING

In his interview with Mike Cerre in 1982, Kosinski contrasted the roles of actor and novelist and spoke of his experiences in *Reds.*

MIKE CERRE: The latest chapter in Kosinski's life reads the writer-turned-actor. Was it tougher playing with Warren Beatty in *Reds* or being . . .

JERZY KOSINSKI: Being here. This is the toughest. That's life.

MC: Compare getting out of Poland and playing that role in *Reds.*

JK: There's no comparison. Playing *Reds* was fun—the childhood action I never had. The only childhood I have now is being an actor in roles. It was very, very inspiring, very funny and creative, and very challenging. But I was disappointed by seeing myself in the film in the final cut.

MC: A lot of critics thought you did a terrific job.

JK: Yes, but as I was making it, I imagined myself as Gregory Peck. I didn't want to watch any of the rushes. Everyone thought I was very modest, but I was very vain. I was imagining myself as Gregory Peck. Then I finally went to see the film. I was no Gregory Peck. I promptly left for the Dominican Republic for two months.

MC: You're supposed to be a shy, unassuming author stuck at the typewriter.

JK: Are you kidding? You have seen the clips [from *Reds*]. I would have loved to be handsome and powerful. Too bad Warren Beatty was in the film.

MC: If *Pinball* were to be made as a film, it seems that you could play either of the two characters: the older musician who is looking to find new spirit or the younger musician who is a mystery, who will not come out of hiding.

JK: Whom would I play? I would play the author Jerzy Kosinski, who wrote the book. He is not in the story. I will not act anymore. Once is enough. I learned a great deal about myself. Basically, the experience was useful for *Pinball*. I wrote part of it while I was on the film set. I did it more as a novice than as an actor. I am not an actor.

MC: But they say that you get most of your work from the people that you meet. It's not accidental. You go out and find strange places, characters, and events. People in New York told me that you know all the subterranean haunts in New York and probably seven of the major cities of the world. When you come to San Francisco, what kind of trouble will you get into?

JK: No comment.

MC: One of our columnists, Herb Caen, said that we have a very inbred society here in San Francisco. You probably have invitations to dinner tonight and to hobnob with all the elite of San Francisco. But where do you find your activity and energy in this town?

JK: I won't tell you.

MC: I can't get anything out of you.

JK: Maybe later. Remember: I hide. *Pinball* is, in a way, about San Francisco. I am plugging a book here. That's what I am here for. To a degree, what I find in San Francisco is the human climate. It's an easy town. I can be myself. I can have fun. It's a city which, I think, censors you less than any other city in America.

MC: You cast one of your characters here.

JK: At the time, no one had read my book or seen my chest [on the cover of the *New York Times Magazine*]. San Francisco and the Bay Area were very good to me. I always had readers here. I come here twice a year to get reassured, to get encouraged.

MC: But still no comment on what you do when you get here?

JK: Primarily, I come here to have contact with a larger group of people, with a community, because that's what sends me back to the typewriter.

MC: As an émigré from Poland, do you ever feel left out or lost now that you're in another country, another language, another philosophy, another type of people?

JK: No, half my life was spent in Poland, and there are parts of me which respond to American situations as if they took place in Eastern Europe. For instance, the cover story about me in the *New York Times*—I got so frightened by it that I promptly left for San Francisco. Still, I like it. Obviously, I seek exposure. That's part of my life. But the other part of me is terrified by it. I think it has to be a disaster. It's like seeing yourself in a [Communist] party newspaper. The next thing you know, they ravage you. They purge you. They do something terrible to your family.

MC: Don't worry, Jerzy. Keep your shirt on. You won't get arrested in this town.

BECOMING ZINOVIEV

In a conversation with the film critic Gene Shalit in early 1982, Kosinski discussed his role as Zinoviev in *Reds*.

GENE SHALIT: Had you always wanted to be an actor or did Warren Beatty have to drag you, kicking and screaming, onto the set?

JERZY KOSINSKI: I didn't, because as a novelist, I can do what I want to do, and I can do it on my own terms. But I am glad Warren offered me a role. I loved the adventure. And while I did not like myself in *Reds*, I loved the movie. I think it is a very profound, fine film. I had quarrels with my own image of myself but I guess that's unavoidable.

GS: That's unavoidable, but the people who have seen the movie absolutely have all praised your work. Nobody—except a sick person—has a great opinion of himself. The first time a child hears himself on a tape recording, he doesn't believe that's his own voice.

JK: Yes, but I love myself as a novelist.

GS: We'll let the public judge. You play a bad guy in the film, right?

JK: Yes, a committed bureaucrat.

GS: In the Communist Party.

315

JK: The adversary of John Reed.

GS: And John Reed is Warren Beatty.

JK: Right.

GS: The confrontation scene between the two of you is very powerful. What is your memory of making that scene?

JK: It's really Warren. Let me tell you this. As an actor, I really believe that you depend entirely on the people you act against and act with. What you don't realize when you see this scene is that I was being directed very cleverly.

Warren is an incredible director, and he manipulated me. For instance, he surrounded me with extras who happened to be Soviet immigrants living in Spain, where the scene was shot. They made me so uncomfortable. I had to speak Russian with them. I didn't like them. They didn't like me. They thought I was a rotten actor. They never heard of me. They didn't like my books. Didn't like my accent. They didn't like the way I portrayed Zinoviev. In their midst, I became Zinoviev. And here was John Reed, the sweet, naive American—Warren Beatty—bothering me when I had problems with his people, who hated my guts. The hostility I developed toward Warren as John Reed was very authentic. Whenever Warren came dressed as Reed, I would say to myself, "What does he know?"

What I am saying is that if you play against a great actor like Warren Beatty; if you are directed by a great director, who happens also to be Warren Beatty; if you have someone who is a great screenplay writer—in this case Warren Beatty—who lets you write some of your own lines; if you have a great producer like Warren Beatty—you cannot fail. Anybody could have done the scene as well as I. Well, maybe not exactly as well, but . . .

And that's the secret of acting. And that's why I wanted to go back to my novel with what I had learned on the film set. I went back to *Pinball*, where I could cast anybody I wanted and could be the master of my own work.

GS: So while the film was being made, you were writing your novel *Pinball*? And you still had time to be that good on-screen?

JK: I was better in *Pinball*.

ABOUT BEATTY AND *REDS*

In one of his conversations with Barry Gray in 1982, Kosinski recalled how he first met Warren Beatty, how the casting of Zinoviev came about, and how he believes that his writing benefited from assuming the role.

I met Warren Beatty in 1968 in Los Angeles. He was very kind. Very wise too. Of course, everyone had heard of Warren Beatty; no one had heard of Jerzy Kosinski. He came carrying *Steps*, my second novel, and told me he loved it. The first question he asked me was, "You studied in Eastern Europe, Mr. Kosinski. Have you ever heard of John Reed?" I said, "Yes, of course," and then we talked about it, in the house of Roman Polanski, I think. That was a year before the tragedy that ruined Roman's life, when Sharon Tate and all our friends were killed in his house [by Charles Manson and the "Manson Family"]. Warren tried to cast me as an actor in another movie. It was not *Bonnie and Clyde*, it was some other movie. But I turned it down.

When Beatty was working on *Reds*, he felt that, because of my background, I should play Zinoviev, that I should somehow contribute the bureaucrat in me. "The man who invented four bureaucrats surely could play one," he said. "You studied in the Soviet Union and Poland. You would know how to portray a man who is both committed and detached at the same time." What's more, I shared with Zinoviev a similar background. Zinoviev came from Poland before he joined the Soviets. And when you

317

look at the photographs of Zinoviev, the similarity is really striking—although he was slightly heavier than I. So Warren felt I should play Zinoviev because no Hollywood actor could convey the detached commitment so typical of Communist leaders and because Zinoviev was an important historical figure. I turned it down initially because I didn't see any reason for me to become an actor. I feel that being an actor takes you away from yourself. My whole life has been based on being close to myself. Then Warren countered by saying, "You may not need it as an actor, but you need it as a novelist. It's a new experience. It is something that you have not done. You are writing *Pinball*. Maybe acting can contribute to something in *Pinball*. How do you know it won't?" It was a convincing argument. So there I went to Spain to become part of the crew of Warren Beatty and Diane Keaton and all that, to play a character whom I actually find unpleasant, a character I would never have become in life. In a way, as an actor, in my first and probably my last performance, I portrayed the very opposite of myself. Zinoviev and Jerzy Kosinski have nothing in common other than *Reds* by Warren Beatty.

I admire Warren profoundly. He is an incredibly intellectual, well-read, and educated man who pretends he is a movie star. I think it is a very Byzantine performance. He is a genius. He is certainly one of the most perceptive men I have met. I have never heard Warren offer a judgment which was not very well founded. Almost without exception, when I asked him about something in his own work that I felt should be done differently, he had a very convincing reason why he had done it the way he did, which means he is a very conscious artist. I like him a great, great deal, and I am very grateful to him. As a novelist, I think I benefited from seeing how he works and how *Reds* was made. I suddenly discovered the freedom and power I have as a novelist. Look, I can do so much on a printed page. Here is Warren, a brilliant man who needs a studio, thousands of extras, millions and millions of dollars. So, by implication, I have discovered myself as a novelist. And I have accepted myself to a far greater extent thanks to being an actor. Now, I know that I should go back to my typewriter because this is really what I want to do.

On Popular Culture

I'm a wunderkind misbehaving in the living room. I'm invited to be nice, but I come to tell bad stories, and not only do I tell bad stories, but I say I've been to the places where they take place.

The creative self withers when turned into a public property. A writer who loses his head over his public will end by being publicly beheaded.

BLOWING YOUR COVER

In an interview with Sue Simmons and Liz Smith in 1982, Kosinski speculated about visibility, fame, and the unpredictability of everyday life.

LIZ SMITH: In your writing, in your life, in your work, so much of what you do is observing and role playing. Being invisible in the world. What happens to a man when he—I want the camera to get in close [*to the magazine she is holding*]—when he appears half-naked on the cover of the *New York Times Magazine*?

JERZY KOSINSKI: I was tricked, frankly. This was not one of the photographs that was supposed to appear in the *Times*. On the way home, the woman from the *Times* said, "How about another picture?" And I said, "Go ahead." Obviously we don't know that much about the *New York Times* these days, do we?

LS: That's right. The *New York Times* is surprising us every day. But doesn't that sort of blow your cover?

JK: No, what it does is to polarize you. You have to decide what it is that you want to do. I'm a novelist. I like to speak about my books, about the philosophy that I think is important in them. And so you are a public figure, whether you like it or not—unless you write under a pen name. And those

321

are the choices faced in *Pinball*. Since I am not a very popular novelist, I have to defend certain points of view.

SUE SIMMONS: I think at this point we ought to describe *Pinball*. What it says on the outside of the book is fascinating, so we can imagine what the inside is like. Tell us a little about the plot.

JK: *Pinball* is basically about a rock star who resolves the issue of his visibility by making his music known and his heart known—but not his identity.

SS: And he's bigger than Elvis Presley and bigger than any superstar we've ever known.

JK: Yes. And we don't know who he is. We've never seen him. But we know his music. And we think that maybe the music company—his record company—arranged this as a hype. We don't know if they really want him to be visible. Maybe he's crippled. Maybe he has no personality that might lend itself to this kind of visibility. So *Pinball* is about the predicament you and I face: could we possibly do what we do without being seen? Now, Goddard, the character in *Pinball*, does. But there is someone who doesn't like that and who goes after him in order to unmask him. And that's basically the suspense of *Pinball*. There is a penalty that is involved. The penalty is visibility. Someone can find you and kill you. No way out.

LS: Partly, *Pinball* is a book about fame and its penalties.

JK: *Pinball* is about what all of us have to ponder today. How much do we want to commit ourselves publicly to what we do?

SS: They say that in a lot of your novels there is mayhem. Explicit sex. Violence. Espionage.

JK: I love it. Suspicious sex?

SS: Explicit sex. And a little controversial sex, I might add. In this country, incest is controversial.

JK: I came from a background in which I saw life easily destroyed by government, by bureaucracy, by the army, by technology. To us, sex was the only procreative force there was, the only authentic force, the only unharming force. I still see it that way. And I am going to see it that way, no matter what. It is the only warm, affectionate instinct that survives.

LS: Tell me, Jerzy. A while ago, you said that your novels are not popular. I was stunned by that. *The Painted Bird* is a classic. Do you mean that your novels are not popular with the critics?

JK: No, no. I have a small but devoted readership. But I may make up for that now, after *Reds*. Frankly, it is very sad that now I get stopped by people on the streets who have seen seventeen minutes of me on-screen, and they say, "Mr. Kosinski, you were great in *Reds*." And then I say, "After seventeen years of novel writing, you should see how great I am in my novels." It's unfortunate, in a way.

SS: The whole thing—whether you win an Oscar nomination for your first film role, no matter how many books you have written—all of this doesn't impress me as much as the fact that when you arrived in this country in your early twenties, you did not speak English. Yet you ended up teaching English, at Yale and elsewhere.

JK: So many immigrants come to this country and have to make their way up. This was easy.

SS: Maybe for you.

JK: It's easy for those of us who had no way back. In a way, that is a common predicament.

LS: Are you, in a way, living on borrowed time? When I think about your life . . . You were a child of the Holocaust. Barbara Gelb [in her *New York Times* profile of Kosinski] described you as being in pieces, as holding hands with death, as a child. And you barely escaped being at the house the night that Manson's gang killed Sharon Tate. And you play polo like a crazy person.

JK: And I get photographed, half naked, by the *New York Times*. Now, that is taking risks.

323

LS: Are you another victim, like the writer Jack Henry Abbott happened to kill?

JK: I honestly think that none of us knows what is going to happen. You might as well define yourself in terms of the moment. This moment is the life I have right now. Why should I worry?

SURVIVING

In a brief interview with reporter James Brady in 1982, Kosinski spoke about being a novelist, an actor, a sportsman, and a survivor.

JAMES BRADY: What do you hear these days from your controversial friend Roman Polanski? Are you in contact with him?

JERZY KOSINSKI: Yes. Roman lives a very creative life; he's an actor. He's free in France to do whatever he wants. I have a feeling that what happened here was quite terrible, and—I have to say it again, this is my own speculation—I think Polanski was set up.

JB: By the girl? By the mother? By the state?

JK: A setup is a setup. "By circumstances and surroundings"—that's the phrase from the penal code of California. When you deal with minors, that's all that matters: circumstances and surroundings. The minor doesn't testify. A certain appetite for younger people is not a crime in France, and I am absolutely convinced that there was no crime in what Roman was after in California.

JB: Warren Beatty didn't win the big prize the other night, the Oscar for best film, for *Reds*. What was his reaction?

JK: Given the amount of effort and time and money that went into the film, I think Warren was quite likely upset that *Reds* did not win the best movie of the year. But I think that's a sign that *Reds* was a good film. The movie was clearly adversarial. A movie about an American Communist, a movie about a spiritual figure, a movie about a writer who went looking for something that he could not find at home—why should such a movie be rewarded by the rather conservative community of Hollywood?

JB: Your new novel *Pinball* has gotten mixed reviews. I think it's fair to say.

JK: Bad reviews.

JB: There have been some good ones. You are criticized . . .

JK: Tell me about the good ones.

JB: I'm going to pull them out of my pocket. Some critics say that you do too much of this, too much of that, that you are almost a dilettante, that you waste your time. What's your reaction to that?

JK: Are they reviewing my life or my book?

JB: They're reviewing your book, but they're reflecting on your life.

JK: They sound a bit like the Soviet censors—reviewing your life. Maybe that's the whole point. Maybe they should review *Pinball*.

JB: Some of the critics describe the sex in *Pinball* and other of your books as kinky, sadistic. You're accused of treating women as sex objects.

JK: I think the reason some critics think I'm unfair to women is that women in my novels are just as mean, just as professional, just as driven, just as obsessed as men. They are no better, but they are no worse. They are dramatically equal.

JB: There's so much legend about you. How do you differentiate the legend from the fact? For example, one story is that you occasionally don disguises and wander around New York's seedy neighborhoods late at night, that

Mike Wallace once said to you, "Jerzy, you are going to get yourself killed!"
What is the truth?

JK: Seedy neighborhoods happen to be found in Detroit, Chicago, or Los
Angeles. Western industrial cities are seedy neighborhoods. Disguises cost
three dollars to buy. We use them in theaters. We use them psychologically,
in many ways, as well. What I do once in a while is what I do best: hide a bit.
Kids play the game of hide-and-seek. I had no childhood to play such games.
I was hiding during the war, like hundreds of thousands of other kids.

JB: You're always called a "survivor." I think you refer to yourself this way.
You wandered around as a child, the backwash of a terrible, terrible war.
How much of that lives with you every day of your life? Or does it come
back only when you think about it?

JK: Let me qualify it. As horrible as it sounds to an American, these were
typical experiences for hundreds of thousands of children. Hence, we never
looked at it in terms of anything heroic or anything unusual. I still don't. It
was another form of hide-and-seek, except that I was hidden and no one
found me, that's all.

JB: But if you lost the game you were dead!

JK: So were millions of others.

JB: You were mute for five or six years as a result of your experiences.
Then, in your mid-teens, your voice came back in a skiing accident. What
was that first rush of words like?

JK: The trauma began with the speech. During my period of muteness, I
was relatively at peace with myself, since I didn't feel I had to confront the
world on its terms. Language establishes a barrier. You have to respond
the way this encounter takes place. Without language, I was at peace. The
minute I got my speech back, I had to see myself again as a meaningful link
between my private life, my inner self, and society. Society happened to
be the Communist society. The Communists came after all of us and after

me, demanding answers, commitments, pledges. A mute person doesn't pledge anything.

JB: Do you consider that today you are emotionally scarred because of what happened then?

JK: I like to think that because of what I experienced I am emotionally sensitive. I react to certain situations, perhaps, with a greater degree of trauma, and I don't like bureaucracy. I fear totalitarian systems of any kind, left or right. I'm not competitive. That's, perhaps, the main facet that sets me apart from most of my fellow Americans.

JB: But you're a passionate polo player. You play to win, don't you?

JK: No, never for points. I'm not even rated. I don't believe that we are here to compete against each other. War is a competition at its worst. I repeat: we are here to coexist with each other, not necessarily to like each other. Everything in my fiction reflects that philosophy. Coexistence, that's the best. Indifference is acceptable only as long as we don't upset each other or harm each other.

JB: So war is never justified?

JK: No. Never.

JB: That from a man who's been there.

FLOATING LOTUS

In an address at Timothy Dwight College, Yale University, in December 1986, Kosinski explained how, by redirecting his breathing and focusing his energies, he achieved the "floating lotus" state of Yoga and mastered his long-standing fear of water.

I was tempted by my own vanity to deliver this address at the Yale swimming pool. Then it occurred to me what might happen if I drowned. In my fictional imagination, I already saw the headlines: "Polish Fakir Dies at Yale." But that's not all. I also realized the horror of the bad publicity that would likely result. Dramatically, a great idea for a brief, brief play perhaps, but not good press for the university.

After that initial vision of disaster, I decided that I probably would not have drowned—although drowning is feasible in any place. But I am here tonight as a novelist, as a storyteller, and indeed if I have anything to demonstrate, then clearly it is the downfall of the novelist within. As a novelist and a storyteller, I should be able to describe, never to show. But just in case I fail, I brought photographs.

I mentioned to a man at a bar in New York that I am now for the most part firmly grounded at Yale. When the man asked what I would be speaking about today, I said, "About a water act which I do from time to time. But my presentation is really a conversation, hardly a lecture. It is basically the sharing of an experience." He looked at me strangely. After I showed him the invitation, he said, "Cocktails, Irish coffee, brandy and liqueurs—with an introduction like this, you can tell your audience anything." Nevertheless, whatever I say here today, I say as a storyteller. That means that quite likely this could be fiction. In fact, it definitely will be fiction. Indeed, it already is fiction; it is part of my next novel. I tell you this not merely to plug the next novel [*The Hermit of 69th Street*], which won't be out for another year, but merely to warn you that this event is already part of a fictional process.

The phrase "floating lotus" needs no explanation; we all know what it means. I am probably no more Oriental than anybody in this room, quite likely much less than our distinguished host [Robert Ferris Thompson, Master of Timothy Dwight College]. My romance with Yoga is highly literary, which means it began as something academic rather than practical. Yet the notion of the lotus is appealing to anyone who feels that somehow there is more to us, that there is some additional buoyancy to us, some spiritual sense to us that is not directly perceivable, that indeed there is some subtle body inside of the meager physical structure. The Oriental notion is that the subtle body does things for us that our physical body, our moral or amoral body, cannot do. It is a nice notion to have.

The teachings of Buddha include some very moving narratives about a lesser lotus and a bigger lotus, a more buoyant lotus and a sinking lotus. I started reading about Yoga through non-Yogic and non-Oriental sources. My initial source was Stoic philosophy, which made me think how nice it would be to have a buoyant relationship with the world—nonswimming, noncompeting, nondirectional, just being there.

The second source is more difficult to recall exactly, but it came from growing up in Poland, where the Hasidic philosophy was quite dynamic. Many notions in the Hasidic philosophy correspond, more or less, to certain notions of Buddhism. Most of us who grew up after the war tried to disengage ourselves from the political process by looking at phenomena which were nonpolitical and which in fact offered a rather passive stance—passive vis-à-vis the state, which was always active. The state would act upon you even when you did not want to act against it or when you did not want to respond at all. The Yogic posture, therefore, would have been the only defense—and no offense—vis-à-vis the state, the martial, directionally oriented competitive police state.

The third source of my preoccupation—one which began before I became a novelist—was a philosopher of Romanian origin whose name you might or might not know: Mircea Eliade, a professor of religion at the University of Chicago. Eliade, who wrote in French and in English, was an émigré who did not see himself as an émigré, and I shared a certain kinship with him. At the time, I saw myself in a passive sense, not as one who proposes but as one who merely analyzes. This was a very attractive stance to someone who came from another country and moved to the United States at the age of twenty-four. Since Eliade offered me an attractive example to follow, I began reading his books. From these sources, I moved toward the reading of the Yogic texts. Other than that, my contact with the old aspect of Oriental philosophy, as I said, has—until I sat down to write my first novel—been very academic.

The notion of a passive stance vis-à-vis society is a classic Judaic narrative stance. A man can do no better than to tell a story which is fictional. By doing so, he spreads no rumor, he offends no one, he guards himself against ever naming reality. A Hasidic painter is not supposed to paint a face or flesh; once you do that, you reach something tangible—tangible, meaning a trap. If you want to be buoyant spiritually, stay away from reality; reach into yourself. By sheer and lucky coincidence, I noticed that this is, for me, the twentieth anniversary of that particular philosophical stance. When I published my first novel *The Painted Bird*, I tried to make it as abstract as I could: no locality, no names, indeed no biography of the author at the end of the first edition or the paperback edition. Nevertheless, despite my abstract stand, somewhere I failed, since the book was dragged into my life and my life into the book. Attempts were made to turn my fiction into autobiography, and my autobiography into fiction.

And then, firmly armed with the Yogic attitude, I sat down to write my second novel, *Steps*, which I completed twenty years ago—in November 1966—and which was published two years later. So this is indeed an anniversary. As the motto for the book, I chose a quote from the *Bhagavad Gita*, which is the source of Yoga: "For the uncontrolled there is no wisdom, nor for the uncontrolled is there the power of concentration; and for him without concentration there is no peace. And for the unpeaceful, how can there be happiness?" *Steps* itself opened with the Yogic notion of traveling south, meaning the country of the interior, of oneself, and it ended with the notion of buoyancy in water, as the protagonist of the novel dives down and looks up to the surface—not from the surface down but from the bottom up. That was more or less the way I looked at myself at the time.

Steps had some Tantric undertones—Tantric, in this case, meaning an aspect of Yogic thinking that I tried to harness via codified behavior. As I designed it in 1966, *Steps* was a novel that did not name but tried to insinuate. Despite my gentle insinuations, however, I offended a great number of critics. Some objected to the notions of menstruation, for example, that came in and out as phrases—and as Tantric elements—in the novel. In fact, I noticed that many of my foreign translators "corrected" me. Instead of the classic Tantric phrase in the novel "I want to make love to you when you menstruate," the German translator wrote "I would like to be intimate with you on one of your days." So, essentially, just as I failed in the abstraction in my first novel, I failed in the Tantric designs in my second.

Then, in my third novel, *Being There,* I decided to get out from the dimension in which things can be grounded in life. *Being There* had a character who ultimately is buoyant. Chauncey Gardiner is an ideal Stoic and Buddhist, who is lost or found in the American milieu. In the beginning of the novel, I said that when he looked at television, "he was buoyed up by a force he did not know and could not name." He did not know the force but I did. Yet I wasn't buoyant, and he was. At the end of the novel, he dissolves into nowhere; we do not know what actually happens to him. However, at the end of the movie, to make the notion of buoyancy more direct, Chauncey Gardiner walks across the lake. His umbrella sinks; he does not.

That is how far I had gone at the time—into the whole notion of physical and spiritual buoyancy. But then I asked myself if it was possible that I was flirting with something that could have an even more important impact on my actual life, not merely on the philosophical one, not merely on the fictional one. What more, I wondered, could one possibly do with physical breathing? Was I a fraud borrowing ideas from a very valid philosophy without knowing more about it?

That is a dangerous notion for a novelist, but not for a sportsman. In the two sports which I have always liked—skiing and horseback riding—breathing is extremely essential. The older I got, the more aware I became that the issue is not the building up of the body; in fact, there was no body to build. What matters is the actual breathing. The flesh ages one way or another; so do the bones. Yet the lungs maintain their oxygen supply and capacity. When my father wanted to reprimand me, he looked at me and said, "No oxygen." There was something to that. My father, a mixture of a Stoic and a Talmudic scholar, clearly had something in mind when he kept saying "oxygen," meaning the breath of life.

A minor digression. When I arrived here tonight to talk about my experiences in the water, I ran into—of all people—the Secretary of the Navy. This would be comparable to someone who was lecturing about confession running into the pope.

Now, skiing and horseback riding made me recall my father's dictum. Polo, a kind of horseback riding, is a demanding sport. Most people don't realize that polo is as tough on the heart and on the breathing as marathon running. Those who don't understand polo assume that, once you are on the horse which carries you out on the field, there is nothing to worry about. But you have to slow down the horse, which is twelve hundred pounds of muscle trained to run at a flat-out gallop. Moreover, you change horses every two to three minutes. So every two to three minutes you have a new horse who doesn't want to be slowed down. That is where the rider's oxygen is desperately needed.

And so I started to look at Yoga again, merely in terms of breathing. Forget Chauncey Gardiner for a moment, forget menstruation. Is there anything practical that one could learn from Yoga? Is there indeed an internal force that one could harness to make one less tired, particularly when one ages as quickly as this one does? And once you age in sport, you begin to see clearly the inability to cope with the demands that the sport you love makes upon you. You simply fail in your own eyes. It is not that you cannot ski or ride horses with people half your age; it is that you yourself feel that you are falling way below the standard that you should be able to maintain. Back, therefore, to Yoga, from an entirely different point of view—the point of view of a Westerner who is trying to borrow from another culture and who has a very valid preoccupation with breathing, with getting oxygen to the brain.

I was born in Łódź, the second largest city in Poland. About ten years after I left Poland, I realized that the name "Łódź" actually means boat. But, in one of the ironies of Polish existence, there is no water in Łódź. Indeed, there is no river, not even a lake. Yet Łódź, sometimes called "the Polish Manchester," is named after a boat. Probably no one in Poland thinks about it. But I did.

Water was the one element in my life I couldn't cope with philosophically and physically. Not only because there was no water in Łódź—that would be an easy excuse. I was frightened of water. Water was not just a fictional device—that is, a device in my fiction—but also a real one—that is, the device that cuts off the breath. No more oxygen to the brain.

My negative attitude was augmented by the fact that, as a child, I had three or four unpleasant experiences that involved water. At one point, water closed over me and I almost drowned. To this very day, I wash my hair under a faucet and not under a shower because I don't like my breathing passages to be cut off. This tells you something about the degree of estrangement in my relationship with water. And yet Chauncey Gardiner, a totally fictional device, is a floating personality—designed by a man who cannot bear any notion of water.

About four years ago I was in California, a state where people swim a lot and where there are pools everywhere. The rebellion against the canyons is the sea, and the rebellion against the dryness and the constant heat is the pool. In California, I was probably humiliated more often than in any other place and reminded of my uneasy relationship with water. Whenever someone would suggest going for a swim, I would respond, "Go ahead, and I will just go inside." Or else I would sit at the edge of the pool, or I would get into the shallow end, because I could not dive. Diving was a terror like no other.

In 1982 a close friend of mine—a good swimmer—befriended a woman whom he since married. That woman used to be the junior swimming champion of Southern California. Despite my reluctance, they suggested taking a cruise together, along the most pleasant waters imaginable—beginning in Italy and moving along the Corsican coast—and in the largest boat available for hire. Nevertheless, the cruise proved to be a disaster.

Every day, all of the other people on board would dive directly into the sea. That was a horrific idea to me. My one attempt to dive using the gear of one of the bodyguards ended almost catastrophically. Apparently, I collected too much air in the scuba diving suit, which was too large for me. Too much air in the legs and not enough in my head, so I almost drowned in the suit. Don't laugh: it's a frightful situation. The suit that should allow you to float forces you instead to drown. If there is a fictional device worse than that, I cannot think of it.

Therefore, the trip ended on a bad note for me. It was a reminder that water and I were not meant to be friends. Yet water is essential. Water is the womb. And in both the Judaic and Christian ethos, water is an important and symbolic element. And here I was using water fictionally, even though I was a fraud in terms of my actual relationship to it. I was introducing water into all my novels: in *The Painted Bird* the marshes threaten the Boy; in *Steps* there is nonstop water; and, of course, water is central to *Being There*. And then in *The Devil Tree*, my fourth novel, water is punitive. It is used by one of my protagonists to destroy two of his enemies. He leaves them on a sandbar, and when the high tide comes they drown. That is how I used my enemy, since water and I were not friends.

After the trip along the Corsican coast, my friends announced that they wanted to do something special to celebrate my fiftieth birthday. "Where would you like to go?" they asked. I looked into myself, and the answer was Thailand. I had never been to Thailand, a Buddhist country—pure Buddhist, not Hindu, with no Japanese influence. Thailand—an open, passive, floating country, a Venice of the East, built entirely on water. So we went to Thailand.

And now the actual story begins. Being on water, Bangkok threatened me far more than Venice did. Had I fallen into the canals in Venice, at least I could have communicated with those who might have saved me. But in Bangkok, where no one understood me, I could drown and nobody would even know. As much as I love the Thai people—and, hypothetically, their philosophy—clearly we could not communicate. So I dreaded the boats, the narrow little kayaks that could overturn at any time, and the murky water, which was far worse than the abstract marshes I had described in *The Painted Bird*.

One morning, intending to stick to solid ground, I left my companions —my wife Kiki and my California friends—at the hotel and went out with my camera to take some photographs of the local temples. Now, before I tell you what actually happened, let me briefly digress and say that Hatha Yoga, a fifteenth-century document, is, in a way, the bible of breathing, postures, being free with yourself, and developing your inner sense of self. In Hatha Yoga, the abstract highest point one could possibly achieve would be a floating lotus. Hatha Yoga says: "When the inside of the body is filled to its utmost with air, the body floats on the deepest water like the leaf of a lotus." Abstraction to the nth degree. Floating like a lotus? Certainly a very abstract notion.

Bangkok again. I go down to the pagoda adjacent to the hotel swimming pool, where I prepare to photograph the pool. There is nothing else to shoot at this particular time, except the empty pool which reflects the shape of the temple. Just then I realize that someone is about to spoil my shot. A corpulent little fellow is entering the pool. I assume that once he gets in, he will ripple the surface, ruin the reflection, and spoil my picture. I am about to lock my camera and walk away, but I say to myself that maybe I should consider photographing him instead. I forgot to mention that he is a monk, with a bald head, the kind of person you don't readily meet at Yale University. As he steps into the deep end, I notice that there are no ripples in the pool. How can that be? He must be swimming or at least treading water, making some motion. But I look again and see a pristine surface, not a single ripple moving through the pool. Seven feet of water; four feet of man. Obviously, I misjudged the pool or I misjudged the man. But I take another look and there he is, standing in the deep end without touching the bottom. No movement, no ripple.

I watched him for about five minutes before asking, "Excuse me, do you speak English? I can't help noticing that you don't do anything and

336

yet you don't drown. What's the trick?" And then the voice of the Orient replied, "My dear sir, I do not do anything. There is no trick. You see for yourself: I do nothing." I said, "But when I do nothing, I drown." And he said, "To drown is to do something. I do nothing."

Then I said to the monk, "When I get into the pool, I have to start swimming. Otherwise I will drown." And he said, "Don't do anything to the water. Let the water do things to you." My next question was, "Is there a place that I could learn this? To learn how to stay in water, totally free, totally abandoned?" Free speech, without any movement whatsoever—imagine that. Kosinski as a lotus, finally. A dream like no other. And he said to me, "Yes, indeed, there is such a place. Only you yourself can do it."

"The water and I"—I replied truthfully—"have not been friends." Then he said, "May I remind you that two-thirds of the human body is water and two-thirds of nature is water? To have a negative relationship with two-thirds of yourself may not be the wisest stance in life." I asked, "Where can I learn?" He said, "Any water would do." And then, after excusing himself so that he could meditate, he allowed himself to be carried off by the current of the pool. He did nothing to carry himself off. It was the inner movement of the water in the pool. And he floated away.

Thus began what you might say is the social drama. I didn't take his photograph; I had invaded his privacy enough. Instead I went upstairs to my hotel room to confront my three Western friends—the woman with whom, by then, I had lived for nineteen years and my hosts, the same couple with whom we had traveled along the Corsican coast. "Look," I said, "I just spoke with a man in the pool who didn't move at all. His head was way above the water. The water did not touch his shoulders. He remained in this vertical position, with his legs slightly horizontal, standing at attention without really being at attention at all. He was just himself, and yet he did not drown."

Our hostess—let's call her Barbara—said to me, "Jerzy, I was a swimming champion. I know the water. That man might have done what you say for a minute or so, but no more than that." I said, "No, no. We talked for about fifteen minutes." My host—let's call him Ted—agreed. "Jerzy, it is unlikely that the man could float like that on his own. Did he have a flotation device?" A semiprofessional diver, Ted dives better than most professionals do. "Flotation devices," he continued, "are very popular in California. Lots of people float in the pool as a countergravity exercise. The swimmer wears a vest which allows him to be free in the pool, without feeling gravity. That way, he can move his legs, arms, hands, and so forth." I said, "No, he did not wear a vest. He had no flotation devices, as far as I could see." Finally, my wife Kiki said, "Jerzy, this is a brilliant idea for a novel, but I wouldn't press the point. Drop it." But I said, "I saw it. I was there. We spoke."

And so, after we left Bangkok, I undertook a classic case of intellectual adventure—a notion, an old notion, which a capable intellectual defines as something that is both a continuity stemming from his or her life and a novelty sufficiently separated from the past to indicate that it is indeed something different, that it is a dramatically different entity, truly an adventure. One doesn't have to be a novelist to know what it is. Yet here I was, disbelieved by the three people closest to me, about a physical act I had witnessed and then described in very plain terms.

After our friends returned to California, Kiki and I headed to Switzerland. For sixteen years, we have gone to one particular place—for fictional purposes, let's call it ValPina—which is a modern Swiss resort, as practical and pragmatic as a Swiss resort can be. There, people engage in many sports—skiing, golf, swimming, climbing, bridge, and backgammon; the last two require perhaps less oxygen than the others. There is a fitness center on every corner, a swimming pool in every hotel. Just to indicate my familiarity with the resort and the resort's familiarity with me, I should tell you that the granddaughter of the mayor is my godchild.

Having come to this resort straight from Bangkok, I embarked on the notion that by then there was nothing in Hatha Yoga that I didn't know except the lotus, which, at least, I had observed. Therefore, there was no reason why I, Jerzy Kosinski, born in Łódź, meaning a boat, could not feasibly one day achieve the lotus as well. I started by changing my routine. As everyone at the resort knew after sixteen years, I had never been in a swimming pool. So I went to the pool. And, of course, I immediately started to sink and almost drown. Most of my friends assumed that I was embarking on a very peculiar—possibly ethnic—notion of a suicide by chlorine.

Over the next few weeks, I sank and almost drowned in every pool in ValPina—and there were twenty-eight of them. I sank and almost drowned in a very ungraceful fashion: by vomiting, because I was a bad drowner. No one, after all, is a good drowner. But imagine someone who refuses to wash his hair under a shower voluntarily being in this particular situation. Kiki refused to comment. Even the local doctor told me that what I was attempting could not be done: there was no way a man could float without movement for more than sixty or seventy seconds, not even a man with my dimensions, as lean and as boneless as a good Polish ham. It was an abstraction, the doctor told me, and he brought some documents with him to prove his case.

Meanwhile, I kept practicing everything I knew about controlled breathing and concentration. I focused on what was happening inside me. When I was tired, was my breathing the same as when I was strong? When I got up to an altitude of eleven thousand feet, was my breathing the same as it was at five thousand feet? But even as I examined the changes in my body's responses, I kept sinking and almost drowning. The result was that I was banned: three or four swimming pools refused to let me in. But I was determined to continue. I had seen it done and therefore knew that it could be done.

Tired of my experiments, my close friends launched a massive propaganda attempt, bombarding me with materials claiming that such floating was impossible. But I kept trying. I knew that if I were to remove from myself all the reflexes that prompted me to act against water and against myself as I had known myself to be until then, I would become a different entity. I even went without sleep to break down the physical barriers, spending three nights in a disco—a place I basically despise—and three days skiing. Afterward, I barely knew where I was anymore, but I could still feel my breathing and knew my lungs were still functioning.

Across the street from where I lived was a hotel appropriately and ironically called Hôtel de L'Étrier, the hotel of the rider, and I have been riding most of my life. It was there that I decided finally to float or kill myself in the attempt. Tired as I was, I thought I might ultimately drown without ever knowing it. I went straight to the pool, saying to myself, "Just breathe normally. Think of breathing, nothing else. Keep the oxygen supply going. The rest is not important." At the deep end—the most threatening end—of the pool, I submerged myself slowly and just let go. No resistance. No notion of myself. No notion of anyone or anything around me.

And in about three or four seconds I realized that I was floating. A lotus opened up. A thousand petals kept me afloat. I wasn't drowning. I was aware of myself, but I was not drowning. Where was the water? I wondered. I didn't feel it in my mouth; I didn't feel it in my nose. That meant the position worked.

I woke myself up sufficiently to call out to the bartender, who was inside the hotel, "*Monsieur, s'il vous plaît.*" I wanted him to see it. After all, he was the first one to tell me I was going to kill myself. Now he would be the first one to see that I had not. I will never forget his expression. He said, "*Oh, mon dieu!*" Then he called to a woman in the kitchen, "*Marie Thérèse, Marie Thérèse!*" Marie Thérèse came out, and he said, "This is the man who almost drowned every time he climbed into the pool. Look at him now!"

So there we have it. The adventure was over. The buoyancy was discovered, and from then on it became great fun. Essentially what happened is this: I reversed the whole pattern of my life. Imagine yourself having a nose like mine and then suddenly, without plastic surgery, having a very short nose. Imagine yourself being dark and gloomy and suddenly waking up happier, perhaps even blond and blue-eyed. The change was extraordinary. Afterward, I went home and slept for about sixteen hours. On the following day, I said to Kiki, "I knew that once you have it, you have it. It is within us." To drop names again: Secretary Lehman, the Secretary of the Navy, was here before all of you arrived. When he looked at my album of photographs, he said to me, "Would you be willing to show this position to my sailors?" I said, "Yes, sir!" I couldn't wait. Kosinski could show the Naval Academy how to float. It would be good for Kosinski and clearly good for the Naval Academy as well. This is what is called vanity, and vanity is a very buoyant force.

In fact, if I were to weight this force, I would say that it is perhaps one of the most buoyant forces we know. I had never tapped it before. But I tapped it in Switzerland. And once I did, I realized not only that I can remain buoyant in the water without any movement but also that I can assume any position I want. Technically I could get into the pool right now and show you—though I spared you the cold trip to the cold pool. I would have climbed into the pool at the deep end, but without a microphone—the danger of electrocution, of course, the Polish fakir electrocuted at Yale; it's a horror story now. And I would have remained standing in the deep end with the water never rising above my shoulders. Then I could have locked one lung—it, too, can be done—and I would have moved to a totally flat position on top of the water, with my head staying absolutely vertical and my feet as flat as possible. Anyone can do this if he goes through the necessary motions.

The question now is why, other than vanity, continue doing it. One good reason is that being suspended in the peaceful element of water is eminently relaxing—peaceful beyond belief. There is no need to do anything: floating is thoroughly passive. Yet the steady supply of oxygen to the brain is not unlike concentration. An intellectual, a worker, anyone who concentrates on anything develops exactly this kind of relationship between himself and his lungs. Concentration means an additional supply of oxygen; without oxygen, there would be no concentration. It's a greater effort of the brain, yet no different than the effort of any muscle. It is a matter of summoning up the resources right here in the chest, no matter how meager the chest.

Floating, in fact, is merely the transfer of concentration to the physical realm. Parenthetically, there is a name in Yoga for the mastery of this particular stage: Kabbalah. To quote: "On the completion of Kabbalah, the mind should be given rest." Indeed, the mind is being given rest: one is as peaceful as possible. And in this position in the water, vertical or horizontal, you can fall asleep as peacefully as if you were in your own bed. You fall asleep instantly without drowning. Consider that for your waterbed.

One assumes that getting into the water means making waves. That is because, in terms of philosophical implications, making waves is what Western man is all about. But when I canceled out the Western man in myself, I wiped out an anxious Kosinski—the Kosinski afraid of drowning, the Kosinski who worried that the minute the water rose above his chin he was in trouble. I didn't think anymore. I merely breathed—a reflex, no need to counter it or support it; a body by itself, with no brain to censor it, no brain to give it directions. Looking at the physiology of the body, I realized that the brain, not the body, was the main enemy of buoyancy. The brain kept saying it cannot be done. When the head goes up, the feet go down. But that is not true. The brain kept saying be afraid of water. The brain kept saying you have never floated before; why should you float now, at the age of fifty?

The lesson for the self is obvious and well worth pursuing. So I like to think of this as an intellectual exercise, not just a physical one. That is the only reason that I allow myself and you to be exposed to it. But there is also a moral to it. The moral—as my father had said—involves the issue of oxygen, of inner breathing. The only way to convey this inner thought process to you is in a very novelistic fashion. But once I share this story with you, you yourself have to take it up or down from there.

On *Being There*

Being There portrays a condition very important. That is, a man without self, a man with no notion of himself, and how such a man is used by society for various purposes. Being There, standing in the center of the six novels, addresses itself to the condition that the remaining five novels actually elaborate.

Americans are masters at avoiding confrontation. Passivity is the national phenomenon.

CASTING PETER SELLERS

In the question-and-answer session following a lecture at the Smithsonian Institution in 1988, Kosinski explained how Peter Sellers won the role of Chance and discussed the challenges of adapting his novel *Being There* to film.

I wrote the screenplay for the film version of *Being There*. But I was discreetly involved with the project for many years before that. Peter Sellers was a friend of mine. He loved the role and always wanted to play it. But I felt that if I ever decided to turn *Being There* into a film, Sellers was not the right person for the lead. I felt the role should go to an unknown. When I finally decided to make the movie—and to start looking for an unknown actor—friends advised me not to be so rigid. So I went to Peter Sellers and shared my concerns. I told him that he was too great of an actor to play Chauncey Gardiner. People in the audience would know that he was Peter Sellers and would never sufficiently suspend their disbelief. Therefore, the movie could never be convincing.

In a very deferential fashion, Sellers said to me, "Jerzy, if you want to hire an unknown forty-year-old actor, quite likely he won't be very good. Otherwise, why would he still be unknown at that age? An unknown actor will only make the movie unknown. Do you want that?" And then he said, "What is more, an unknown actor will try to build up the character. But he has to strip him down." I asked him how he thought he could do that. And he said, "By being so elaborate in other roles, I can strip myself down to nakedness. That is what everyone will see." Then he went on to show me.

Suddenly I realized that he knew more about my character than I did, and I made a one-hundred-eighty-degree turn, one of the very infrequent U-turns in my life, in which I decided—in fact, I was convinced—that only Peter Sellers could strip himself of any falsity, of any deliberate acting. Then I said, "What if the director directs you out of this innocent movement? What if the director stabs you with his finger and says, 'No, no, I want you to be different. I want you to show that you like EE [the wealthy wife of financier Benjamin Rand, played by Shirley MacLaine].'" Actually, the only thing Chance "likes" is to watch. He has no drive, no attraction to EE. To him, she is just another person. He does not want her—in any way. The notion of having anything, in fact, is alien to him. Sellers said, "I think I've got a director who will respect that purity: Hal Ashby. He will know that in this case to overdirect is to kill the character."

And so, having spent six years telling everyone, "Peter Sellers? No way!" I came out of the meeting telling my wife that it's Peter Sellers or nobody else. When she asked what changed my mind, I said, "I saw him. He *was* Chauncey Gardiner." He was a man without a false move. He was a man I had never seen before, because when I write I do not see my characters physically at all. After that, I knew that my role was to stay away and simply let Sellers become the character. Interestingly, at one point, when I was in Washington, D.C., where some of *Being There* was being filmed, a reporter from the *Washington Post* came to interview Sellers and me. I had to answer all of the reporter's questions, because Sellers did not want to step out of the role. He was pure. He did not want, even for a minute, to lose the character —who, it seems, was ultimately very much like Sellers himself. Perhaps Peter Sellers had always *been* Chauncey Gardiner, and roles like Inspector Clouseau in the *Pink Panther* films and Dr. Strangelove were only masks that he had put on his face to hide his pure Chauncey Gardiner–like innocence.

CHANCE ENCOUNTERS

In an undated interview (ca. 1979) with a foreign correspondent from Ticino, Switzerland, Kosinski spoke about his notions of chance—and of Chance—in the film and novel versions of *Being There.*

INTERVIEWER: The film *Being There.* Is it a fairy tale? Or is it an allegory?

JERZY KOSINSKI: I like to think that *Being There* is both a story and an allegory, a literary allegory. But I also like to think that it is very firmly based in social fact. So for me *Being There* is a sort of imaginative projection in which the situation is obviously literary but at the same time perfectly plausible and feasible.

INT: In the book, whose foreign title is *Chance*, to whom are you referring?

JK: Again, I like to think that the story of Chance could refer to any one of us and to the role of chance in our individual lives. We are the result of chance—in other words, each individual is subjected to conditions that cannot be foreseen. We may try to anticipate them, but we really cannot. Basically each one of us is unique: each individual is a very special creation from a very special private garden and with a private chance, so to speak. Philosophically, in my own life, I reject the notion of determinism. And so, in the film *Being There*, what I tried to portray is a character who was born by chance—that is why his name is Chance—and whose life, in fact, is entirely at the mercy of situations he cannot foresee, both in his garden and eventually outside of the garden as well. In this way, he is no different from you or me.

But, of course, I am also aware that many people don't like the idea that our lives are governed by chance. They believe instead that there is a kind of determinism, that our lives are somehow predetermined—by religion, by certain beliefs in a spiritual being, by Marxist determinism, or, as is very often the case in the United States, by the belief in astrology. They object to the notion that individual life is indeed the result of chance.

INT: Yet you yourself believe in chance?

JK: Yes, I believe in chance. But I believe much more in myself. If my life is not determined by the Communist Party, or by astrology, or by the position of the stars, then I have to determine what my life is based on, at any given moment of living. So then I have to see myself as a very special dramatic event which, of course, at any given moment can be canceled out by chance. Because of this—because life can end at any moment, because I might be expelled from my private garden—I have to take enormous care, spiritually, of my individual importance and pay much less attention to those who tell me that I am not important, that as an individual I am one of millions and millions whose lives are governed by abstract laws of historical materialism, or by this or that. In such a way, therefore, both in my private life and as a novelist, I am very strongly antideterministic.

INT: Your character Chance reminds me of Voltaire's Candide. What is the difference between the two, Chance and Candide?

JK: I cannot think of a greater difference. In fact, I don't think they have anything in common. Candide was in a state of conscious search. He embarked on a search for happiness. He was a merchant, a man of worldly experience which was imposed on him by events, and so Candide was capable of rational judgment. He was, for instance, very upset by the wickedness of man. Basically Candide was a rational eighteenth-century character, no different, in fact, from any other contemporary intellectual.

Chance in *Being There* is the very opposite. He is not a man of exposure. He is not a man of the world. He never ventures outside. He is in no way involved in any kind of search for happiness or for anything else because he does not know what search is and he doesn't know what happiness is. Unlike Candide, Chance has no sex drive. He is basically a very modern character: the world comes to him only through technology, only through television. Unlike Candide, who was active, Chance is enormously passive; he personifies passivity. One could also say that Candide was not a saintly character, and Chance feasibly is our saint. He is innocent. He has lived in his Shangri-la and only by accident is expelled from it.

Some theologians in the United States made an interesting point about Chance, calling him—in my book and in the film—the only saint we have today because he knows the world. But like a true saint he is not contaminated by it. He is not tempted by wealth. He is not tempted by riches. He is not tempted by the flesh or by sex. He is indeed truly innocent, perhaps the only innocent man we have. That is why, at the end of the film, I wanted to indicate this innocence by having Chance walk on the water. And that, I think, is the difference between Voltaire's Candide and Jerzy Kosinski's Chance.

INT: Who could Chance be today?

JK: I think anybody could be Chance. Frankly, to a degree, I think we are all Chances. By now, most of us are exposed to looking passively at the world through television. So that is one thing we already have in common with him. Any child growing up in front of television will eventually, to a degree, resemble Chance and the portrayal of Chance by Peter Sellers in the film. In other words, these people will have a great deal of passivity, a limited sexual drive, and a very limited vocabulary.

At the same time, many of our public figures—whether in Italy or Germany or the Soviet Union or the United States—are to a degree, to a large degree, like Chance because we know them only by image. We know them only by how they come to us through the public media, which is basically visual. Their main projection is the projection of image, not of character—a projection of charm, of looks, of *bella figura*, if you want, but not of ideas, not of anything which is complex. They come to us extremely naively. To a degree, every president, like every child, resembles Chance from *Being There*.

INT: Why did you choose the garden and the television as metaphors?

JK: Because they represent the basic dimension of our lives. As you probably know, I live and write in the United States, and basically *Being There* is about the United States. Americans devote much of their time to watching television. In fact, watching television is the third most common activity, after sleep and work. So television became a very natural metaphor for an activity everybody knows and everyone is engaged in. I didn't have to describe it at length in the novel. We are no longer at the mercy of society but primarily at the mercy of a very arbitrary filter—television—through which society comes to us.

On the other hand, we are made of flesh. We are subjected to life and death. Therefore, whether we like it or not, we are part of the natural world. Regardless of how long we watch television, even if we watch it twenty-four hours a day, we will not become immortal. So the garden is the only natural environment we still know and have. A tree growing on the street is the last reminder that things might die and so might we. The buildings do not tell you this; the highways do not tell you this. They seem to be immortal; they will always be there. But the garden is what we are: this is our natural world. We are all individual gardens. So I reduced Chance to these two dimensions in a very natural way. Although he had never been outside the garden, which could have been in Rome, or Lugano, or Geneva, or Paris, or New York, or Chicago, he did not suffer from removal from the world because the world came to him through television. That is why I thought that he had to be both connected and detached. That is why he is what he is. That is why he has no anxiety. Because he is not part of the superficial world, he is not driven to the world: he doesn't want to become rich, he doesn't want to become famous, he doesn't want anything. He simply wants to be as he has been, in his garden, separated from the rest of the world, which comes to him as channels, as images as arbitrary as rain or sunshine. And that is why he is a peaceful man—because he still has his garden. Someone said to me that he is probably the only man in modern cinema who suffers no anxiety, who suffers no anguish, who has never been to a doctor. And society, I repeat, does not disturb him because it comes to him only through television.

Now, I may also have wanted to make another point, that maybe, maybe television is for us an escape from society. The reason we watch so much television—whether it is in Switzerland, or Italy, or France, or Germany, or Japan, or the United States, or Poland—is not only because television is there but also because it keeps us from going out into a society which we do not like, which threatens us, which brings disorder and anxiety into our lives. And by watching television, possibly we remain in the private garden of our lives. And that is why I used both images.

INT: Man has entirely subverted his relationship with nature. Do you think this relationship is broken forever?

JK: The relationship is obviously broken. In terms of our daily life, especially through technology, we have lost contact with the natural world. But, far more important, we have lost contact with our spiritual nature and with the nature of our spirituality, with our inner private garden. As I said, that's why I don't like the notion of deterministic philosophy, why I object to the notion of psychoanalysis, of Marxism, of astrology. All these devices tell us, "Don't worry about your private inner garden. You are part of a much larger process over which you have no control. So give yourself over to society. Be at the mercy of societal forces, whether the force is capitalist society with capitalist markets or a communist society with a Communist Party. Let the society tell you what you should be and what you should do." The relationship with our inner sanctum, with our inner spirit, is natural, but it is broken. A man who drives his Fiat or Mercedes or Ford to the mountains is not really having contact with nature. He is part of industrial society, which has already destroyed most of nature.

Yet this is not the nature which interests me. What interests me is the inner nature, the nature of our inner life. And I am afraid that television, by penetrating so much of our life and by turning us into passive observers, shelters us from society and removes us from that inner life. But this, of course, is not the fault of television; the fault is ours.

INT: Do you believe that someone like Chance could enter the room where all the buttons and switches are located, push those buttons, and change the destiny of the entire world?

JK: Obviously, yes, to a degree Chance is conditioned by a mediated relationship with reality. He is, in a sense, a very modern technocrat. From such a point of view, he could also be an ideal bureaucrat, which means he could be an ideal figure for a totalitarian or corporate state. He certainly could: he would not be aware of the human consequences of such a switch.

INT: It seems that from Woodrow Wilson on—with some exceptions, of course—the president has been a person full of spirit. The film *Being There* is infantile in this respect. Is this just chance or is it inevitable?

JK: Any head of state today, by the nature of the job, has to be full of spirit because the job is too complex, too enormous, to allow any kind of Renaissance man to deal with it. I think the president is a remnant of the old king, the tribal chief who was supposed to be aware of what was happening around him. Today, though, the president is a figurehead. He is basically an image given to things which are too complex for us to understand, so it is just as well that he comes across as full of spirit. I think both President Carter and President-elect Reagan are probably very complex men. But we will never know them as complex because they are given to us as elementary images, simply to justify the need for the tribal chief. So instead of wondering about the government, instead of trying to understand the mechanics of complexity, we just watch a man who comes across as simple and nonambiguous as Chance. He gives imprimatur to our belief that things may be as simple as we would like them to be.

INT: To what is the pure man condemned? Are candor and innocence punished? When reading your book, one could think they are.

JK: I don't think that my books punish innocence. I think it is the Second World War that punishes innocence. I think it is the potential Third World War that punishes innocence. I think poverty punishes innocence. I think the seven hours of daily television that people watch punishes innocence. I don't think I have invented the punishment of innocence. What I am trying to do in my novels is to say that the only innocence worth having in this world, and the only innocence that makes sense, should be the innocence of one's own spirit, to preserve one's own innocence against being corrupted by the vicious social systems, by oppression, by the war, by various forms of totalitarian ideas or totalitarian taboos, whether in a capitalist society or a communist society.

The Painted Bird, Steps, and *Being There,* as well as my other books, make the opposite point: that the only innocence worth having is the inner innocence of spirit. The rest is not innocence but becomes a target for society to go after and destroy. I know. I was once an innocent child during the Second World War. I know the price for the punishment of innocence. And so, when I emerged from the Second World War, I was no different from the contemporary children of the ghetto or the countless children of Latin America who come to the world innocent. And what do they find there? Not Kosinski novels to punish them. No, they find a very oppressive social system. The only way for them to survive is to realize how unique they are inside and to defend themselves outside. That is basically what my books are all about: the sense of one's own inner innocence.

INT: Are you a moralist or only a witness?

JK: I think I am both. By nature of being a novelist, I am a witness to what I know. Then I leave the judgment in my novels to the reader. By doing so, by confronting the reader, I force him or her to pronounce a moral judgment upon the events portrayed in my fiction. And in such a way, as a novelist, I am both a witness and—I like to think—a moralist.

INT: The American Jesuits have said that you are their Dante. Do you accept this statement?

353

JK: I think what they meant by that statement is that, in my fiction, I confront certain aspects of contemporary hell. It is not that Kosinski is Dante but that there are Dante-esque elements in my fiction. Not many novelists confront the reader directly with what is unpleasant, what is threatening, what is hellish in our existence. Only in this sense was I defined as using, as utilizing, certain Dante-esque elements: the portrayal of the threat to one's spirit, the portrayal of contemporary hell, which is war, bureaucracy, passivity, all the forces that destroy the sacred spirit in man.

INT: You have stated that *Being There* is the most diabolic of your books. Why?

JK: Because the character Chance is beyond self-definition. He can no more and no longer define himself. He is entirely at the mercy of the environment. He is therefore a total victim. And even though the movie is a satire and we laugh at it, he is basically the most tragic of all my characters because he can no longer defend his innocence or his spirit. Quite frankly, he might not even know that he still has this spirit. That is why, of all my seven novels, this one is in a way the most hopeless.

INT: What are the features of a millionaire?

JK: You would have to ask a millionaire. What I know comes through indirect exposure to the American rich, through my marriage and my late wife, who died ten years ago. I think the American rich are quite different from the European rich. The American rich see themselves as being much more functional, following the Protestant ethic of work. I wrote one novel about it, *The Devil Tree*. What I think about the American rich is probably best portrayed in *Being There*, especially in the film.

INT: How did America appear to you upon your arrival?

JK: The United States appeared to me as a typical advanced industrial state with a surprisingly great degree of individual freedom. At the same time, I realized that the inner conflict of American society had been quite camouflaged by the very large middle class. In the United States, I was far less aware of the conflict between the poor and the rich, between those who have and those who have not—possibly because the war in Vietnam camouflaged it a bit, possibly because the United States never developed strong opposition parties. The two-party system we have here is not really that of great opposition. This is basically the view of the United States that I still have—except that I think the country is changing. It is going to be far more polarized in the future, possibly resembling European polarization.

INT: In your opinion, in Western countries, which values prevail in society?

JK: I think the values that prevail are those of the middle class—the values of cumulative wealth, of collecting goods, of buying gadgets. But these values are doomed to failure. They do not enrich the spirit. They do not make the individual freer. Instead, they make him a prisoner of his own house, of the credit system, of inflation, of the credit card. In such a way, they detract from his spirituality. Most people eventually realize that they have to confront themselves directly in terms of their spiritual life, in terms of their sexuality, in terms of their inner drive, and not in terms of the kind of car they drive or the kind of apartment they live in. Also, I think the crisis of these values is reflected in the fact that they are useless for millions and millions of people who are poor, for millions and millions of people in the Third World. I think we are witnessing the shrinking not only of the middle class in the West but also of the middle-class values.

INT: As we move toward the year 2000, what do you foresee?

JK: I see the future as being enormously controlled—in the West, by a corporate capitalist state which controls individuals, energy, and which monitors one's professions and activities. There are too many of us, while energy, of course, is scarce. And it will become even more scarce. Computers allow the control. In fact, they enforce social control even better than the totalitarian state can. Similarly, I think control in the Communist countries will increase, not decrease. It will also become more computerized. There will be fewer places for the dissident spirit, both in the East and in the West. That is how I see the future: as more of a marching column.

INT: My last question. How did you like the film Being There?

JK: I liked the film a lot because it followed my screenplay. I had a great deal of control while the film was being made. All the dramatic choices were mine. So I think the film conveyed the essence of my book. I was also very pleased that the film gave Peter Sellers the opportunity for what is probably his biggest ovation ever. After all, he waited ten years to play that role, and he died soon afterward. So I am extremely pleased both by the fact that Peter Sellers could play the role he loved so much and by the success of the film in the United States and in other countries. Therefore, in general, I am delighted with Chance and *Being There*.

THE IMPACT OF *BEING THERE*

When Kosinski was asked by an interviewer if *Being There* was in any way a warning to Americans who are obsessed by television, he responded that such a reading misconstrued his intent.

I do not read it that way at all. I see it as a story of a man who managed to retain a great degree of inner innocence precisely because he did not let himself, or because chance did not let him, be part of the world outside. In some Latin countries, the novel was called *Out of the Garden,* quite a perceptive title. Chance remained locked, so to speak, in the garden, a natural dimension. He grew up in his natural time, as a spiritual being—one could say almost an American Buddhist—not affected by the terrors of real life, or affected by them only when he was forced to leave the house. But then he manages quite well. He remains peaceful and sufficiently buoyant to practically walk through water, if not necessarily on it.

Although every conversation Chance has is related to the garden, his words are misconstrued and interpreted as a deep understanding of politics, of world events, of everything. In fact, that is not so unusual. Misconstruing is part of our lives. In my view, some of the things that have been said about my novels misconstrue them, but I may be entirely wrong and the critics may be right. Yet it is also feasible that it is the other way around. Who is to decide? That is the real freedom: nobody has to make such a decision.

There is no need to decide. In other words, we are free to interpret any way we want. For me, that is an essential freedom. Chauncey Gardiner in *Being There* can carry his private garden within and let others misconstrue what he is saying. So what? What great damage can come from that, if someone misconstrues what I have written? Is what I have written so important that it cannot be misconstrued? Not at all. It is fiction, and therefore it must be misconstrued.

But the misconstruing of it should have no bearing on my life. I should not be arrested by a police officer who misconstrued the meaning of my novel; I should not be prevented from writing my other novels any way I want. Spiritual expression should be literally lifted above all other considerations. That is the only chance we have to remain individually sane and sound, and to remain individuals leading creative lives. Otherwise, we become like robots. We might turn into Chauncey Gardiner without the benefit of his spirituality, of his pureness, of his innocence.

On Violence

My books are profoundly moral because they generate moral judgment. I leave it up to the reader as the reader, in life, is left to himself. One is on a blind date with life. We can't know what we're going to be confronted with. And I portray the violence objectively. The point is not to be seduced by it, the way one is seduced by popular sentimental stuff which turns a Robin Hood, an essentially cruel figure, into something glamorous. The point is to resent it and by resenting it to learn what one resents in life. By imagining it, there's the possibility of becoming stronger.

I don't prejudge my characters or the events. The reader decides: Was the violence invited? Was the violence justified? Was the violence inflicted gratuitously? . . . Tragedy and brutality bring man closer to life.

MRS. ROSENBERG AND

THE PAINTED BIRD

In this excerpt from an address that Kosinski gave to a luncheon sponsored by the International Forum of Jewish Holocaust Survivors at the Waldorf-Astoria Hotel in New York City in 1982, he related a fascinating anecdote that illustrated the way that one reader perceived the depiction of brutality and violence in his first novel.

Eighteen years ago, just after the publication of *The Painted Bird*, I was invited to address a Jewish audience in Connecticut. The rabbi who invited me wanted me to discuss the issue of survival, the same issue that we are confronting here today. At first, I wondered how one could possibly make sense of oneself in the complex world of World War Two, an event that happened a long time ago but is still very much a part of our lives. I was eager to go to Connecticut, and so I went—or was driven. I arrived to confront a group of nice, healthy Jewish men and women. They looked so Jewish, in fact, that I could not help but reflect on the fact that had they lived in Poland during World War Two, probably none of them would have survived. It was, to a degree, a friendly talk. Some of the people in the audience had family members who died the way my family did, so I felt an especially warm bond with them.

In fact, I felt that I was very much a part of their group until the chair of the Hospitality Committee—let's call her Mrs. Rosenberg—approached me. "Mr. Kosinski," she said, "thank you very much for coming." Then she continued. "You are perfectly polite, nice and well dressed, although a bit too thin." Then she paused and said, "May I ask you a question?" I said yes, that is what I am here for. And she said, "Why did you write this terrible book?" I thought—I hoped—she meant one of the Novak books. She said, "The Novak books? No, *The Painted Bird.*" Then I hoped that she meant that the book was terrible from a literary point of view; that kind of criticism would have been all right. So I said, "What do you mean—terrible?" She said, "Why would you write about these terrible things?" I asked her what it was about the actual novel that bothered her so much. She said, "The gouging out of the eyes, the drunken peasant who gouges out the eyes of the other peasant. Why would you write about such things?" Then I had to control what was probably an authentic delight. I remember asking her, "Nothing else in the book bothered you?" "The rape of the Jewish woman," she said, "but mostly the eyes." I tried to get her to recall the trains going to the gas chambers on the margins of the pages of *The Painted Bird.* "There are trains carrying Jews," I said, "people like you and me, like everyone there in the room." She said, "Well, gas chambers . . . fine, we understand them. And the trains, we know about them too. But the gouging out of the eyes—that was terrible. An absolute horror."

That is also the reason why I am here today. Maybe it is not an accident that now, eighteen years later, I am being confronted for the second time about the issue of survival. I see myself growing angry again, something a speaker is not supposed to do—at least not in Connecticut. As I told the congregation in Connecticut, I had talked to some of those who had escaped from the trains which were heading to the gas chambers by pulling themselves out of the windows. One of them, my close friend [Dr. Stefan Skotnicki], is now a renowned cardiothoracic surgeon in Holland. And I was told—and I have seen the evidence—of children who had their eyes gouged out, sometimes by the elbows of their fellow Jews, in the trains bound for the camps. The congregation was very upset to hear this.

And I told them that art—any art, be it sculpture or drama or a novel or film—should be open-ended, that its purpose should be to create a sense of tension, a sense of drama, and not just, according to the old Aristotelian notion, to purge the spectator or the reader. I told them that art should be dramatic because it has to convey a sense of reality. If the sense of reality is not dramatic, it will pass by unnoticed, as the trains in my novel did for Mrs. Rosenberg. For her, the trains were so much at the margins of the novel that she did not notice them at all, even though she understood what they stood for. And she understood the gas chamber, too, even though by then the gas chamber was just another symbol—not threatening at all. No gas chamber could find her, so far away in Connecticut. Still, I felt that I had failed Mrs. Rosenberg, and that was painful to me.

The Painted Bird was a novel; that was how I wrote it. But, although I hate to admit it, perhaps it should have been stronger. Perhaps it should have been written the way that Emanuel Ringelbloom, author of a book about Polish Jews during World War Two, had written his autobiographical account of the ghetto. Perhaps The Painted Bird should have been written on the harshest terms that I knew and that I saw. But it wasn't, in part because—I repeat—it was a novel, not an autobiographical document. Since my autobiography is not so different from yours, why should I write mine when you have not written yours? But even though I was writing a novel, why wasn't I more direct, more powerful? Was I creating a shock absorber for my late wife? Anyhow, I never liked the novel. That's why I wrote the next one, and the next, and the next.

A large number of the Jewish critics who initially reviewed The Painted Bird felt that the experiences I described were too brutal. I did not agree. I felt the novel was not brutal enough. Someone else observed that The Painted Bird worked as a novel, but then he wondered how it could possibly have failed, given the experience I was writing about. Meaning: give a Jewish child a war like the Second World War and he will write a novel about it. I often wish now that I had not written that novel altogether.

When my Swiss-German publishers published The Painted Bird, they appended an apology to it, noting that the events in the book might be too brutal for some. Even as recently as last week, when I was in California promoting my latest novel, I was confronted by a radio interviewer about an incident described in *The Painted Bird*, when the nameless boy is thrown into a pit of human excrement. The interviewer said, "You have written about something quite awful. You have written about a child thrown into a manure pit." For that interviewer in Beverly Hills, the notion of being thrown into a manure pit in Eastern Europe was a vision of hell.

Of three and a half million Polish Jews, only five thousand children survived the war. Of fifty thousand Jewish children from Czechoslovakia, only twenty-eight survived. I am, therefore, part of a very small society, a society of five thousand and twenty-eight. How much should I tell those who are not a part of that society? Should I be as blunt and as direct as I can be, because that is what I think? Or should I camouflage my language—and be polite and well dressed and funny? Should I be absolutely brutal and traumatize you so that you can begin to feel some of our pain? On whose terms should we—those of us who survived the war—speak to those who are merely here to hear us? How do we define the terms? Should we compromise and create the illusion that somehow the experience can be conveyed on your terms, not ours?

THE ESSENCE OF VIOLENCE

In discussing his newly published novel *Blind Date* with Tom Brokaw in 1977, Kosinski explored the nature of violence in fiction and in film, and he explained how his use of violence was not merely gratuitous but rather integral to the philosophy of his novels.

TOM BROKAW: Jerzy Kosinski is a man absolutely fluent in English; it is the language in which he writes. Yet he was born and raised for much of his life in Poland, war-torn Poland. [*To Kosinski:*] You've just received commendations from English teachers in America for writing for adolescents.

JERZY KOSINSKI: Yes, for contributions to adolescent literature.

TB: And yet you write—there is always, I think, in your work an underlying theme of violence. Maybe it is not explicit, but it is there nonetheless.

JK: I think it's explicit.

TB: In many passages it is. But even when it is not explicit, it is implicit.

JK: The point is that violence is part of our lives. We take it for granted almost. It is ambiguous. It doesn't always come to us like Clint Eastwood in *Magnum Force*. It comes in dozens of ways. Unlike the visual media, the novel can utilize violence differently. In my novels, I make the reader aware

365

of violence on his or her terms. In fact, fiction makes us more able to deal with violence: to know it, to recognize it, to reject it.

TB: Don't you think that because you were born and raised in what was, in effect, war-torn Poland and because you lived during a very bloody time in international politics, it affected your own life and writing? You're more sensitive to violence. You're more aware of it.

JK: All right, I'm more aware of it from the necessity of knowing it. I feel it, but I'm not a violent man. That's why I keep writing about violent events. I think it's a very important distinction.

TB: Are you desensitized by all the exposure that you've had to violence over the years?

JK: No, I think it's the opposite. I look for it. I know it, and I can avoid it. I have lived for twenty years in violent New York, Los Angeles. I didn't have one single unpleasant encounter. Now, I do a lot of traveling. I do a lot of walking at night. I don't hide. Not one unpleasant encounter. Why? Because I know how to avoid them.

TB: Do you think that this society in which we live is becoming more violent?

JK: No, no more than any other industrialized society. I think some of us are less able to recognize it. Again, I repeat, we look for a major event. But violence doesn't come in obvious forms. If it did, we could avoid it.

TB: One of the things that you write about in this book [*Blind Date*] is about a rape. Rape is never gentle. It's a violent act in any event.

JK: It's one of the events in the life of George Levanter, the protagonist of my book.

TB: Right.

JK: Here is an example from my generation after the war. A rape was a very common experience in Poland, the Soviet Union, central Europe. We had been raped by war so an act of individual rape was mild. I hate to say it, but most of us at school specialized in one form of rape or another because, in contrast to what our parents did with bombers, gas, concentration camps, and so forth, it was a game. It was a sport. We were neutralized to this particular form of violence by a far greater violence, the staggering violence of the war itself.

TB: Do you feel great shame?

JK: No, but now I appreciate the violence. I know it now. I know it quite well, and part of this is in *Blind Date*. That's a way of settling it, saying I know it, I have gone through it. Look very carefully at the violence. It's very complex. It's not just a mere attack. It's not something that takes half an hour on television. No, it's something far more complicated. Again, I think a novel can portray the complexity and make the reader—man or woman—aware of potential violence far better than any other medium.

TB: What is your reaction when you see what is often described as senseless violence, the violence we have on television or in films these days?

JK: I don't think it cheapens violence. What it does perhaps is neutralize it, and it creates a false impression that violence is quick and easy to recognize. It isn't. It really isn't. It's just as complex as love, as complex as any other form of behavior; and because it is complex it has to be written about.

TB: Your life has been intertwined in one fashion or another with more dramatic forms of violence. You had expected to be at the Tate mansion [home of Sharon Tate, wife of Kosinski's friend and fellow Pole Roman Polanski] the night of the Manson murders, and there is a passage in this book written from the point of view of the victims.

JK: The point of view of Wojciech [Frykowski] and Gibby [Folger], both very close friends, who were there. Wojciech was invited by me to the United States; I brought him here. The reason I have the passage in the novel is not for the sake of the bizarre, not for the sake of violence. But think how many books and programs have been made about the killer, Manson, as the center. Do you know of any one from the point of view of the victim?

367

That's violence too, violence committed by us to them. And so, by bringing them out in *Blind Date*—people I have known intimately, two of my best friends, Wojciech and Gibby, who died there, and Sharon—I feel it is an important reminder to the reader that violence very often comes at random. It was not a destined pattern here. That is part of the philosophy of the novel, and that is how you have to define yourself.

LIFE AS BLIND DATE

Life, Kosinski told interviewer Ron Nowicki in the *San Francisco Review of Books* in 1978, is a series of moments, or "blind dates." But every encounter, no matter how violent or unsettling, offers imaginative possibilities.

RON NOWICKI: Are your novels about specific morals in Western culture?

JERZY KOSINSKI: Well, the "task" of my novels is to give the reader a jolt which could lead to a recognition, to a judgment, a new attitude toward his mental environment, most of which is, of course, the moral ballast of our Western culture. But I try to make my novels as unobtrusive as possible—they are not "about"; rather they are "concerned with" the modern character. Their language is direct and easy. The reader is to be moved from Western culture's waiting room to his own private examination room, so to speak. Once he is there, ideally, he should be made aware of what he should have known all along: he is mortal, he is vulnerable, he is not protected—yet he survives. It should be a joyful feeling, the awareness of being alive—still in a *cockpit*, still a protagonist of his unique *blind date*.

RN: Reviewing your latest novel *Blind Date* in the *New York Times,* Anatole Broyard wrote that you "seem to have lost faith not only in morality but in art as well." How do you as an artist respond to that?

JK: By quoting Arnost Lustig, the eminent novelist, essayist, and literary critic, who, reviewing *Blind Date*, wrote that "Deep below Kosinski's stories there is an important meaning and a sincere message about the frightful world we are living in. His questions are the old, but never satisfactorily answered questions: What is man? What is our life really about? What to do in this world where one must be indifferent to avoid one shock after the other?"

RN: Broyard claims that you're a "poet of morbidity." True or false?

JK: And Lustig claims that "Accumulating stories of different, sometimes ambiguous meaning, giving to himself as well as to the reader the same chance for interpretation, Kosinski traces the truth in the deepest corners of our outdoor and indoor lives, of our outer appearance and our inner reality."

RN: Anatole Broyard also says that "There is a considerable portion of sexual activity in *Blind Date*, and most of it can be understood as a search for something other than pleasure." Is that the way you intended it to be interpreted?

JK: That "something other" was, apparently, easier to discover reading *Blind Date* in Washington, D.C., than in New York. Arnost Lustig has found it. He writes: "Sex is for Kosinski not only a mysterious, never fully discovered part of our lives, but also motive, action, and impact at the same time. For Kosinski, people discover in sex their courage as well as their fears, their 'normalities' and 'abnormalities,' because—perhaps long before the beginning—in every male is an embryo of a female, and the other way around. Sex is the most reliable open door to the human soul, says Kosinski; through sex a person can most reliably reveal his image to himself, as well as to others." That's it. I've nothing to add.

RN: Given what you have said, your last novel implies life as being a series of chance encounters, blind dates. Do you consider yourself an existentialist?

JK: Not at all. But I do subscribe to the scientific concept of "chance and necessity" as expounded by Jacques Monod, the Nobel Prize–winning French biologist—and one of the characters who appear in *Blind Date*. In any case, right now our conversation is an incident, a blind date of sorts. Your presence and mine, the language, the mood, the emotions all fill the narrative space of this particular moment, defined by you and me as "the interview." Any other aspect of our life is subordinate to what we are doing right now. Implicitly, this moment involves many other aspects of our lives—a larger fabric of existence—but it is still a self-contained dramatic unit. That particular kind of immediate drama and our place in it is what interests me most, in my life as well as in my fiction.

RN: At the Book and Author Luncheon here in San Francisco, you said—and I'm paraphrasing you—that we should accept the various phases of our life as necessary, that is, we should not feel that we have been singled out if we encounter failure, illness, accident, disaster, even death. Given that attitude, what do you feel is the role of religion in Western society?

JK: Any religion offers a moral model, a spiritual design. So does literature, art, philosophy. Our collective awareness is a form of a collective religion, reflected in our language and means of communication. To "particularize" it, one must substitute what is "real" in one's life for what is "unreal" in the popular culture, that most obvious, ever present, and most accessible form of collective awareness. The substitute generates new *individual* awareness that starts with the notion of temporality: my life may run out at any moment. I suppose such constant knowledge is creative only if one is emotionally and philosophically—or religiously—geared to such a recognition and its consequences, a highly conscious existence responsible for every act and for every moment. If one is not, the task of one's awareness is to constantly jolt oneself to make one's familiar and therefore often unexamined reality suddenly unfamiliar and demanding examination. Our lives are often "unseen"; habit dulls them, and the imagination doesn't perceive them as unusual, as dramatic, or as modifiable. Instead, it perceives them merely as "being there." The purpose of any imaginative encounter from poetry to photography, from fiction to drama and film, indeed to religion, is to hint at the various possibilities of change—emotional, physical, political, spiritual—to instigate a change of will, an awareness of the power of the individual to change one's life.

371

RN: In *Blind Date*, you reconstructed the exact manner in which Sharon Tate-Polanski [Roman Polanski's wife] and her friends were slaughtered. Why did you feel it necessary to inject that scene into the story of George Levanter, the central character of *Blind Date*?

JK: In my novel *Steps*, published only months before the Tate-Polanski tragedy, I wrote: "Many of us could easily visualize ourselves in the act of killing, but few could project ourselves into the act of being killed in any manner. We did our best to understand the murder: the murderer was a part of our lives; not so the victim."

Since *Blind Date* incorporates in the life of its central characters many "real" personages that have been at various times and in various manners central to our lives—Jacques Monod, Lindbergh, Svetlana Peters, Stalin's daughter, and many others—I re-created the final Helter Skelter blind date at the Tate-Polanski home on that fateful night. As a well-known public event, philosophically as well as morally and historically, it belongs in *Blind Date*, a novel concerned with chance and necessity, reality, plausibility—and our perceptions of our own private destiny.

RN: Still, the victims were your intimate friends: Sharon Tate, wife of Roman Polanski; Wojciech Frykowski, your boyhood friend with whom you and Polanski went to school and whom you brought at your own expense and responsibility to the States; Abigail ("Gibby") Folger, your former student turned friend whom you introduced to Frykowski on a blind date, then advised and assisted in taking Wojciech away from New York to her home in California. You cabled from Paris your arrival at the Tate-Polanski home several hours before it was invaded by the Manson gang. But a chance unloading of your luggage in New York delayed you by a day—and probably saved your life that night. Wasn't this private motivation the real reason for the inclusion of this "public event" in your last novel?

JK: No more, no less than the inclusion of any other dramatic incident or character that, for whatever reason, I have come to know firsthand. By its nature, fiction—as art—rises above the world of realities and stays within the realm of perception. Clearly, my concern for the victim has been one of the leitmotifs of all my novels, my fiction's true killing ground, so to speak.

RN: Speaking of *Steps*, there's a passage in the novel that intrigued me: "I walked through the districts where they lived surrounded by fetor and disease. They had nothing to possess or to be proud of. . . . I envied those who lived here and seemed so free, having nothing to regret and nothing to look forward to." This strikes me as being a rather bland point of view. How do you apply that to your own life? Like Levanter in *Blind Date*, you were once married to one of the richest women in this country, who died in 1968, and lived a decade as a member of a rather glittering international circle.

JK: The purpose of life is, for me, the same as that of art: to evoke a state of being aware as opposed to merely being mortgaged; to pause to feel and to think, and to articulate that moment. The freer one is from various cultural self-mirroring devices as well as from societal artifacts that entrap, the more time and energy one generates for such a pause. In that moment of feeling fused with articulation, one's very life expands. You can buy and sell and rent everything else but that moment. I didn't learn this from my rich wife whom, curiously, I met on a blind date, not knowing who she was. I learned this when I was seven, during World War Two, as a child of war, at war with everyone around. I felt as strongly then as I do now.

RN: Some reviewers have said in general that in writing about destructive and negative acts, sex, vengeance, and violence, you tend to mirror the American society, if not Western culture. Others claim that one of the reasons for the commercial success of your novels is the public's prurient desire for prurient arousal. Do you think that either the critics or the public has missed the point of your writing? What is it to you?

JK: I think the instructive power of the "destructive" protagonist in fiction might be greater than that of a sentimental *Love Story*-type of character. A "negative" character shows us at least one optimistic aspect of nature: the power of the individual. In this sense, didactically, Iago might be dramatically a more powerful character than Othello. Iago embodies a greater

373

degree of energy and an enormous creative, rational potential—even if misdirected—that can be used to effect changes in one's immediate "personal" as well as institutional sphere.

The fiction of Dostoyevsky, for instance, even though enormously receptive to the individual's psychic and societal suffering, tends to retain him as a passive, permanent sufferer, a hopeless victim of his total jeopardy. My fiction is structured to portray the self in a state of recoil against the all-pervasive, all-powerful, ever-present forces—state, other people, language, sexual mores, et cetera—that render man's existence dependent upon *arbitrarily* imposed notions of life and destiny.

RN: What do you think a reader achieves by seeing a mirror in which someone like him is portrayed as a violent person? What do you intend the readers to perceive from what your characters tell and show about violence?

JK: By engaging my reader, on the one hand, in the concrete, visible acts of cunning, violence, assault, and disguise—as opposed to the diluted, camouflaged violence of our total environment—my fiction is, on the other, purging his emotions, enraging him, polarizing his anger, his moral climate, turning him against such acts—and often against the author as well. In a word, generating a uniquely private moral judgment, the novel *confronts* the reader arbitrarily and is designed to involve and to manipulate him. As my fiction does not impose on the reader any easily detectable, predigested notions of "how to" read it or react to it, it also doesn't soften the impact of the ethical collision. From its start, it aims to generate rage and judgment, to evoke affirmation of the reader's unique moral stand. This is for me the supremely didactic role of literature.

RN: What about women and homosexuals in your novels?

JK: Measured on the scale of dramatic properties—perhaps the best scale to use in fiction—they are equal partners to men and heterosexuals, with "equal time" morally, philosophically, and emotionally. If some of my protagonists in some instances do exercise a state of dominance or sexual submission, they are, equally, men and women, hetero, homo, trans, and bisexual. And if the quality—but not the drama—of the male-inspired acts differs, it is merely to reflect the historically different role of men in the sexual as well as economic and military combat zone.

RN: Your protagonists always seem to be moving, or fleeing, or on the run. Do you think that your description of your characters as always moving and fleeing is a reflection of your own life?

JK: Possibly, since from the age of six I've always been a "portable man." Most of my characters are picaros, the type of characters who are constantly in a stage of becoming, who tend to live their lives rather than merely to ponder their condition, and who champion their selfhood. On a recent visit to West Germany, I was discussing various aspects of American life and letters. One German novelist argued that "self" is an imperialist idea. In his view, each of us should be defined entirely in terms of the community. I assured him that his wish had already been fulfilled in a large part of mankind, led by the Soviet Union and China.

But even here, in the States, the popular culture dismisses such a quest. It has taught man to turn away from himself, to believe that his fate is sealed. The small man who "makes it" into the middle class assumes that, because he has made it, life will take care of itself while he watches it the way he watches TV. He has lost the ability to say "no" to the consumer society, to realize that he shouldn't have bought the house or the big car or the boat that holds him in debt. In relying on a "MasterCharge" attitude to life, he becomes neither master nor in charge of his own existence.

My characters are all agents in the service of counteracting the emotional suppression. They are desperate to turn a commonplace of daily routine into a dramatic arena, to transform mere experience into adventure. If they succeed, my novel might detonate a fragment of reality which has lost for us its detonating power. The explosive force is still there; a reader can see himself as a protagonist of his own story, a hero in charge of his life and his soul who accepts the inevitable deformities—physical and psychological—as a normal part of life. After all, each of us is deformed; nobody is "perfectly average." Sickness, social conditions, employment, accidents deform us; age destroys us. And all this occurs on a blind date that might end at any time.

RN: A reviewer of *Blind Date* in the *Atlantic* wondered whether, given "the sterility of your vision that leaves little room for compassion or warmth," your "effort" is worthwhile. Do you wonder too?

JK: I do, and such denouncements, while not discouraging to me, do not make my effort any easier. But I also know that they spring from our popular culture which, while promoting the "healthy" consumer and the growth of his spending habits, must discredit as "meaningless" all forces that counteract it, including imaginative fiction.

And so "the denouncers"—they're not really critics, are they?—rush, on the publication date or sooner, to categorize such fiction as "morbid" and "monstrous" because, to them, it is dealing with the "bleak" side of life. One's life, apparently, like a motor car, has its "sides." They label it as "brutal," as "cheap thrills" that "strain" the reader's "credulity," "appalling," and "too simple by half." Desperate in protecting their sentimental super-market of pseudo-art, of spurious avant-garde, they ban from it as "moral conundrums" any authentically concerned probe of the pains and failings and dangers and joys of life—and of our vision of it. Insecure and empty in their own pursuits of the banal and expected, opposed to any individually motivated rather than culturally safe imaginative interplay of fantasy and societal fact, they promptly relegate any such play to a *"mondo-weirdo,"* a sidewalk-show of human curiosa and deformities. And by doing so, they pronounce a verdict on their own estrangement from the human condition.

SIGNATURE EVENTS

In this excerpt from an interview in March 1982, Kosinski discussed the nature of violence during wartime and in postwar society, especially in contemporary American life.

INTERVIEWER: Your book *The Painted Bird* describes unspeakable brutalities on the parts of the peasants among whom you lived when you were a boy.

JERZY KOSINSKI: Not true.

INT: For me, those brutalities were unspeakable.

JK: For you, yes.

INT: I mean gouging out one's eyes.

JK: By a drunken peasant. Have you been downtown in this city, or uptown, or in midtown at four o'clock in the morning? There is nothing that happened to me during the five and a half years of the war that you don't see in any large urban community today. And yet I survived the war in spite of the trauma that my presence could have created for those who harbored me. Of course they were brutal, but they were brutal to each other. Of course they raped each other, and occasionally visitors too. Of course I was beaten up, but what was the other choice? The train to a gas chamber—was this a civilized choice? You object to the eye being gouged out. Is the gas chamber better?

In *The Painted Bird*, what horrifies is a specific incident, because that is what I meant to do: to horrify you by one minor incident, a drunken peasant gouging out the eyes of another peasant who seduced his wife. Meanwhile, the trains are rolling through the villages, and through the pages of *The Painted Bird*. The trains full of innocent people, traveling straight to the gas chamber—that is the horror that we accept.

INT: I would like to get to how you write. Your books have a way of coming back to me, two or three days later, in the mind. Do you think about that? What is your style? Do you rewrite a lot?

JK: I rewrite a lot, but I am not certain that I am as conscious of the impact of my writing as I would like to be. Of course, I would like to create an impact on the reader. Of course, I want to involve you. Why do you think I sit down to write? To tell my own story to myself? I already know it. What I want to do is in some way to map it, to make a topography of it for myself but through someone else. In fact, I aim at this encounter. Hypothetically, I don't see you; in a way, I don't see you now. Not really. But I have an image of you. This is what I want to do.

Now, I try to be as cunning as I can be. I say to myself, "That's too much. Let's remove it." Of course, I could make it easier for you. I could say in *The Painted Bird* that while one peasant gouged out the eyes of the other, the trains were rolling. But I am not going to do that. Had I done it in the earlier draft, I quite likely removed it.

INT: As a youngster, you saw all of this brutality?

JK: As a grown man as well, as recently as last week. In fact, I see it every day.

INT: If ever there was a candidate for an American psychiatric session . . . Had you been a youngster in America and gone through this, we would have put you into—

JK: You would not. You wouldn't know how.

INT: Given what your books are about, how would a reader know that you like life? Your books are really filled with violence, with pessimism.

JK: That is how you read them. I don't. That is how I write.

INT: They are full of rape, of murder. There is an incredible amount of violence.

JK: And also a great deal of compassion—of being drawn to life, of protecting it, of defending oneself against bureaucracy, oppression, arbitrary imposition of someone else's will. Men and women in my novels are dramatically even. If men are oppressive, so are the women. If men are sexually driven, so are the women. There is, I like to think, a great deal of balance. What's more, I know that is the case.

INT: Do you see your novels ultimately as instructive?

JK: To a large degree, as hypothetically instructive. A novel is an open platform. It doesn't teach anything. It doesn't propose anything. It's a bit like a painting, really. There is a gallery. Here is my painting. If you want to see it, come in. Whatever you will see in the painting is right. I don't argue with your view of my painting. As a reader, I just read it differently. But you are free to project, to re-create in your mind anything that you want. There is no way to stop this process. That is why, I think, the value of drama is not that it should be instructive, but that it should trigger a sense of yourself. If you as a reader feel that you are threatened by my novels, fine. Defend yourself against them. You may need this kind of an emotional summoning up of energy in some other places. So if they are instructive, they are instructive in some very remote emotional way. They merely challenge certain notions that I, as a writer, or you, as a reader, might have. That is all.

INT: The other side of Mr. Kosinski. You are a polo player. You ski. You are a photographer. There is a whole other side. When do you have time to do all that?

JK: Many writers are more prolific than I am. They have families; they have children; they have relatives. And they write reviews; they teach; they do a great deal of things I do not. True, I organize my time as well as I can. Sports are very much part of my being. They always have been.

INT: Did I read somewhere that you sleep in four-hour-shift segments?

JK: In two shifts. It's not a very big deal. I merely divide my sleep time into four hours in the morning, four hours in the afternoon. I will go to sleep after this program, for four hours. I will wake up in the evening to my normal life, if you want to call it that. Quite likely, I'll go out. Then I will come back, go to sleep around three or four o'clock in the morning, and wake up at eight.

INT: You make it sound so normal.

JK: What is unusual is that I am going to have twice the sense of waking up. Why not have it twice? Why only once? And if I am tired in the afternoon—and obviously I am going to be tired by this—why not rest? Don't you take naps in the afternoon?

INT: It's a luxury I don't have.

JK: I can afford it. I'm a writer.

INT: What I'm getting at is this: don't you see yourself as having lived—I may be pressing—this simply incredible life, starting in Eastern Europe. You come to America, and every one of these experiences is a whole lifetime almost. All the things that you have done. What happens to your head stepping into those extremes?

JK: The head was formed, I think, by the time I was twelve or thirteen. What I am saying is that, to a large degree, when I arrived in this country, I brought with me a certain philosophy. To a large degree, one is responsible for one's own being. Maybe it's not that these things happened. Maybe I went after them in some way. Maybe I wanted to, maybe I felt that I ought to, because this is the only life I have. I honestly think that death—and this clearly I have seen, as most of us have—witnessed at very close range and confronted is something very intimate. I think about this very often. I have always thought about it. I thought about it on the way here. What if this car doesn't make it? What if the U-turn doesn't work? I wouldn't be here. Maybe that's why I like to think that every moment of life, including the time you and I are spending right now, is an independent unit of drama. You have to take it for what it is. You are at the mercy of this moment but, to a degree, you can be both at the mercy of the moment and in control of it as a dramatic unit. You have to create a fiction out of this moment. That is what I am trying to do with you.

On the American Dream

My life in the United States has gone through all the shades of the American ethos, from a truck driver in the beginning, a chauffeur, a student, a writer of nonfiction books. Graduate and postgraduate studies in the United States. My marriage which allowed me for ten years to scrutinize the American society in all its powerful components. Heavy industry, finance. Republican politics. After my marriage, teaching the sons and daughters of the American middle class for seven years. And also writing novels about all that.

The great thing about this country is that the Protestant ethic demands that you not remain passive. If you do, you are at the mercy of your vital existence and you are no longer a spiritual being. Now, to have that kind of a climate and the political freedom that accompanies it—my God, what else do you want?

PORT OF ENTRY

The International House, at 500 Riverside Drive in New York City, was conceived by the late YMCA official Harry Edmonds and funded through the philanthropy of John D. Rockefeller Jr. and the Cleveland H. Dodge family. Its distinguished alumni include Flora Lewis, Leontyne Price, and Jerzy Kosinski, all of whom were honored at an awards ceremony in 1990. At that ceremony Kosinski made a few brief remarks.

In America—a country the sociology of which I studied for years before I arrived here—I was greeted by my uncle Paul Lewinkopf, the brother of my father whom my father had not seen since Paul, at the age of thirteen, escaped from Russia to the United States to become a seaman. When I arrived in 1957, Paul was already over sixty years old. Born in 1895, he had served for thirty years on various American ships—the USS *America*, the *Leviathan*, the *Manhattan*, the *California*—and retired at fifty-six, after he was stricken by blindness. Yet until his death at the age of seventy, he remained, despite his blindness, a visionary.

He told me that as a seaman he knew the meaning of "port of entry": I was the future of the Lewinkopfs [the original name of the Kosinski family], and after my parents' death I was the last ship of the family "ship line." No other members of the clans that were once so numerous—the Weinrichs and Lewinkopfs—survived the Holocaust.

Immediately after my arrival in the United States, he told me he wanted me to stay at a place called the International House. He said that it overlooked the Hudson River on one side and faced the New York skyline on the other. This International House was a metaphor, metaphysically speaking, for a lighthouse—for people from seventy countries. I was to be one of them.

To me, the International House seemed a metaphor for the metaphysical. Now in Polish, *meta* means "winning, goal": *na dalszą metę*—long-term policy; *pierwszy na mecie*—to come in first.

Uncle Paul said that he had researched this particular lighthouse and found it better than any other lighthouse he had ever seen looking out from any of the ships on which he had served. The International House, he said, was founded by Harry Edmonds, who was born in 1883 and nicknamed "The Skipper," and made possible by the generosity of John D. Rockefeller Jr., who helped to open it in 1924.

Then Uncle Paul asked me to ensure that, after he died, he would be buried at sea. And, in fact, after his death on December 23, 1964, he was buried at sea, from on board the USS *United States*, on March 14, 1965.

Keep in mind that he was a seaman. When I first heard him speak of a "lighthouse" overlooking the Hudson River and a "port of entry" leading to New York, I thought that the International House was a ship, that Uncle Paul wanted me to live on a boathouse! Now I realize that the International House really was a boat of sorts, one that delivered me to the port that would become my new home, and a lighthouse that led me to a future—and to goals—that I could never have imagined when my visionary uncle first welcomed me to America.

THE LONE WOLF

Kosinski recognized Ernest T. Weir (the late husband of Mary Hayward Weir, Kosinski's first wife) as a titan of industry and as a man who—like Kosinski himself—had achieved the American Dream. He spoke often of Weir's accomplishments and even wrote about them, as in this essay, originally published in the *American Scholar* in 1972.

> *Well, well, I see the issue of these arms:*
> *I cannot mend it, I must needs confess,*
> *Because my power is weak and all ill left;*
> *But if I could, by him that gave me life,*
> *I would attach you all and make you stoop*
> *Unto the sovereign mercy of the king;*
> *But since I cannot, be it known to you*
> *I do remain as neuter. So, fare you well;*
> *Unless you please to enter in the castle*
> *And there repose you for this night.*

—the Duke of York in *Richard II*

On May 24, 1956, the American Iron and Steel Institute gave a dinner at the Waldorf-Astoria Hotel in New York City, and among those invited was Ernest T. Weir, a past president, director, and member of the executive committee of the institute, founder and chairman of the National Steel Corporation, this nation's fifth largest producer of steel. The institute's credo is "Right Makes Might," so it was indeed appropriate that the institute's president B. F. Fairless introduced as the evening's main speaker General Alfred M. Gruenther, USA, Supreme Allied Commander, Europe, and U.S. Commander in Chief, Europe. If Ernest T. Weir listened closely to General Gruenther's address, he must have listened with some detachment, for only a few weeks before, Weir himself had addressed the Poor Richard Club on Locust Street in Philadelphia. In his speech, Weir had introduced himself as "a propagandist for a point of view." His view was that since World War Two, America had embarked upon a course of hostility toward Communist nations and had become a country inclined toward the idea of war. This, he asserted, was the wrong policy for America because, for all its bluster, this policy was passive and static, another Maginot Line. If this does not sound like a traditional businessman's point of view in the mid-fifties, it is because Weir was not a traditionalist; while American businessmen seldom spoke on political matters Weir spoke often.

It was said in his native Pittsburgh that Ernest T. Weir was a man who would give in only to time. In a lifetime of nearly eighty-two years, Weir turned a rolling mill into a billion-dollar steel empire, founded Weirton, a town bearing his name, and took on the most powerful adversaries—the federal government, presidents, organized labor, and the steel industry itself. Born August 1, 1875, on Pittsburgh's North Side, when he was fifteen he was employed at three dollars a week in the Braddock Wire Company, doing work, as Weir recalled, that nobody else wanted to do. In 1901 he became chief clerk of the Monongahela Tin Plate Mills and a few years later, at the age of twenty-eight, was named the general manager of Monessen Mills, both subsidiaries of the American Sheet and Tin Plate Company. Rising higher in positions of bureaucratic responsibility to superiors was not his aim. No matter where he turned in Pittsburgh, he saw the chimneys rising as monuments to that sturdy breed of men of achievement: Carnegie, H. Clay Frick, Schwab, Henry Phipps Jr., and B. F. Jones. In 1905 Weir joined with J. R. Phillips in the reorganization of a decrepit tin plate company in Clarksburg, West Virginia. A few months later, after Phillips died in an accident, Weir took over as the company's president.

The business grew. In 1909 he bought land for a steel plant on the Ohio River, twenty miles above Wheeling, at what is now Weirton, West Virginia. By the end of the year the plant was working, and by 1915 the company, so recently a shoestring operation, had three plants and was the world's largest independent producer of tin plate.

Weir was an avid reader of nineteenth-century English novels. Perhaps it was from them that he acquired a sense of destiny. On his birthday in 1918, he changed the name of his company to Weirton Steel Company. Weirton remained for a long time America's largest unincorporated town.

At that time, the steel industry enforced a gentleman's agreement not to build mills in the Detroit area. This agreement supported the "Pittsburgh plus" plan, under which steel buyers had to pay freight from Pittsburgh regardless of where the product was produced. The Detroit automobile industry was then moving up from the third largest consumer of steel to first place, and Detroit was Weir's target. He broke the "Pittsburgh plus" agreement by allying Weirton Steel with the Michigan Steel and Great Lakes Steel corporations. And, as a result of these mergers, in 1929 Weirton Steel became the National Steel Corporation, the only large concern to show a profit from 1930 through 1934.

Weir was equally independent in his political allegiances. Under his direction, Weirton Steel was one of the few major companies to resist the CIO's organization attempts. To this day the National Steel Corporation has an independent company union. This caused many to brand Weir "a lone wolf" of American industry, an image he reinforced by publicly opposing United States Steel's capitulation to CIO pressure. When the National Recovery Act charged that Weirton Steel violated the collective bargaining provisions of the NRA by remaining a company union, Weir denied the charge, and in a widely publicized court case he upheld his position that the NRA provisions did not apply in the case of Weirton Steel.

Elsewhere a bitter feud developed between Franklin Delano Roosevelt and the New Dealers on one side and Weir on the other. It was said that FDR once called Weir "that feudal lord of Weirton" and that later in his life Weir would not visit any foreign capital that erected a monument to FDR or named one of its streets after him. To oppose Roosevelt, Weir became a member of the National Republican Finance Committee, which sought funds to combat the president's reelection. In 1940 Weir chaired that committee and saw his candidate, Wendell Willkie, run against, and lose to, FDR.

Before my arrival in the USA in 1957, I had always assumed American businessmen to be the chief exponents of political as well as business credos. Perhaps my view resulted from the traditional belief among European liberals that the American political establishment was a mere extension of the business community. In addition, here I learned that "the business of America is business"—just as the business of, let's say, the Kremlin is the total state. Instead, I found the phrase "big business" derogatory, and that even the most ardent Republicans, including Republican presidents, did not like to ally themselves openly with big business. One may well ask: are there any prominent businessmen in the present cabinet? University professors seem to have achieved a proximity to the presidency that big businessmen can only dream of. The Democrats, afraid of the taint of big business, openly long for contributions from big unions, which seem to me at least as formidably conservative as big business. Those traditional opponents, unions and big business, no longer seem politically so far apart.

It may be a tragic fact of the American power structure that, at the highest levels, it is the military that represents the products of big business. The generals mediate between the businessmen and the government; hence it is only natural that a general would retire into a business that has always surrendered its interests to him. Today the retired general advises the chairman of the board, but that board is not asked to advise the Pentagon.

I take Ernest T. Weir as an example because it might be of interest to listen to his advice now, even though in his own time few people in power listened: neither his Republican friends nor his Democratic enemies. In 1947, speaking to the joint meeting of the Engineering Society of Detroit and the American Society of Mechanical Engineers, Weir stated what was the guiding principle of his life.

The greatest need in the world today is the practical thinking and the practical action of practical men on its problems great and small. . . . For too many years . . . the direction of affairs has been in the hands of the other type of men—the unpractical thinkers. The unfortunate results of their handiwork are repeated in the dismal pattern around the world, and the pattern includes our own United States.

It is the engineer who, like the businessman, represented to Weir the rational mind at its most pragmatic. Accepting the profit-and-loss principle as Weir did and as indeed any business must do, Weir contrasted the man of industry, rational of necessity and predictable in his drive, with the American political leader who is bound by four to eight years' cadence of political power. Not content with the performance of his industry in the present, Weir looked with a practical eye far into the future of steel. What politician could or would speculate reasonably about his party in the year 2000?

Appearing in 1948 before the House Foreign Relations Committee, Weir stated: "To those who are alarmed with the prospect of an expansion of Russian Communism, I say that a serious depression in the United States is the greatest thing to fear." Opposing General Marshall and his "do-either-what-we-tell-you-or-nothing" attitude of Congress toward Europe, Weir argued:

If the nations of Western Europe were actually in danger of going communistic, then I believe that condition would be its own most powerful argument against giving any aid at all. Stated as "aid to stop Communism," the whole proposition reduces itself to a form of bribery. And we just can't make the bribe big enough—if, in fact, the political thinking of an entire people can be bought at any price. The aid that we could give to the extent of our practical ability, or even beyond it, would not be sufficient to produce a quick improvement in the lives of rank-and-file European peoples. If these peoples are to resist Communism it will not be because of billions from America but because of their own inner conviction that there is a better way of life and their own inner determination to have that better way of life.

And again, speaking twenty-one years before America's recognition of Red China and Nixon's trip to Peking, Weir said in his "Statement on Our Foreign Situation," released on January 5, 1951:

> The present Chinese Government is the result of the revolutionary fight which has been waged in China for many years and from which the Communist faction has emerged with total victory. As a result, they believe that Chiang Kai-shek is completely finished as a leader—that he has no influence in the affairs of China now and will not have in the future. In the opinion of our friends abroad, who know much more about China than we do, the overlord system which Chiang Kai-shek represented is completely ended.

From the factual standpoint, therefore, the present government of China represents the more than four hundred million Chinese—at least twenty percent of the world's population—and there is no apparent good reason why the United States should not have recognized this government as the representative of the Chinese people. If this had been done, it is felt, the present disastrous situation in Korea would not have developed. Our European friends believe that continued recognition of Chiang Kai-shek is unjustified by the facts of the situation and that persistence in this position simply stirs up additional resentment against the United States.

Even at that time Weir foresaw the necessity of distinguishing between Chinese and Soviet objectives.

> There is no natural bond between the Russians and the Chinese. From the Chinese standpoint, Russia is an occidental foreign power the same as the United States and other Western nations, and even now, observers with long experience in China report a growing resentment among the Chinese over the presence of Russians in China. It would be a gross error if the United States, through avoidable action, should provide the unifying bond that is now lacking between Russia and China by making our country their common enemy.

Weir brought to the debate on China a practical vision and a clearheaded sense of reality. Speaking on December 3, 1953, before the governing body of the National Industrial Conference Board in New York City, he said:

> China is a touchy subject. It is my opinion that whether or not we admit Communist China to the UN or sit down with her in five-power negotiations in the near future, eventually we are going to recognize her and deal with her in some way. Whatever mistakes may have been made in the past, we have to live in the world as it is now.

Without hysteria or passion, Weir predicted that American aggressive tendencies toward China would necessarily involve a larger conflict.

> Eventually, we must deal with a Chinese regime that we may not like unless we propose to replace that regime with one we do like. To do that, of course, would mean war, and bear in mind that it would not be war with China alone but war with all of Asia. My only comment on that will be to repeat a remark made to me by President Eisenhower during a conversation in Paris two years ago. He said: "War with Asia would be endless and hopeless."

In June 1953, in the climate of McCarthyism, Weir privately published a pamphlet, *Notes on the Foreign Situation Based on a Trip Abroad*. A large section of the pamphlet was devoted to a domestic problem: military spending. It is obvious that Weir wanted his point to be made as strongly as possible. His statement not only had been reprinted in many American newspapers and magazines, and even quoted by the Soviet *Pravda,* but in response to requests he distributed, at his own expense, over three hundred thousand copies. With a businessman's sense, Weir argued:

> When nations continue to enlarge their military machines, there is ever-present danger that the machines will be used. Of this I am sure. If such thinking should become the basis for our national course of action, the United States will become a leader without followers. . . . We would run the serious risk of really having to "go it alone." Some of our extremists indicate they are willing to do just that. I would hate to have on my conscience the burden of deciding

to take that action. . . . We have become so accustomed to a war economy that some people think we must have it to sustain employment and production. The plain fact is that war production is economic waste. Progress is not built on waste. All the great advances in human history have come in times of peace. If peace can be established, the prospects for development of the world economy are so great that there is not an individual anywhere who will not benefit.

I am often surprised at how many of us who oppose governmental policies, whether foreign or domestic, direct our efforts only against the politicians on Capitol Hill, in City Hall, at the courthouse, and the governor's mansion by either boycotting them or trying to seduce them into sharing our point of view, rather than by exploiting the polarization already existing within the business community. Especially today, the political man is a television image, a product of his own public relations men. The businessman, however, remains grounded in the almost tangible reality of his market, his profits, and his customers, whether actual or potential. Weir recognized these differences. At the annual convention of the National Association of Purchasing Agents on June 5, 1951, he criticized the businessman for being "a political neuter."

Why should businessmen withhold their talents from politics? What is it that makes these men, who are so conscious of their responsibility in their own jobs, think that they can shrug off their political obligations? Many of them do not even vote. And as for any more active participation, the response of the great majority is "that's not my game; that's for the politician." The truth is, in my opinion, that the average businessman is a political neuter because politics is a strange field to him; because he begrudges the time and effort he would have to give to it, and because he has the idea that the public is "anti-business" and thinks the safest thing to do is stay in his shell. And, in my opinion, none of these reasons is valid.

Yet Weir felt that the American businessman was by his very success a potentially powerful figure.

The average businessman has gotten where he is because he has *more* than average ability. He has the mental capacity for factual analysis that leads to sound conclusions and right actions. Obviously, his batting average has to be pretty good to keep him moving up—or at least keep him where he is. These talents are exactly the ones that must be applied to political activity if the tremendous power now contained in it is not to become an actual danger to the welfare of the people of this country.

According to Weir, two things kept the businessman from being a stronger force. First, while he applied the latest methods to his business to ensure profits and progress, the businessman chose to stand back from the political arena and merely complain about what government did. Second, the businessman faced the politicians' old tendency to keep him at arm's length. By contrast, Weir strongly believed that political activity of the American businessman was vital to a healthy national life. Weir mistrusted political leaders with equal strength and saw, perhaps more clearly than they, the instability of a nuclear balance of terror.

Wars have never been started by people but by leaders. And in many cases leaders have started wars for reasons of their own rather than for any true national purposes. But no leader has ever started a war unless he felt sure he would win, that he would benefit, and that the victory would be worth far more than its cost. No leader could ever feel less sure of any of those things than he can today.

Weir felt that political leaders themselves were bound by "horse-and-buggy" thinking in an age that demanded "jet plane" thinking. In a situation as delicate as that of the postwar nuclear world, Weir knew that the stakes were high: coexistence or annihilation.

In the meantime, the leaders of government must continue to deal with each other in a world in which war has become outmoded. The trouble is that the dealing is still by methods and conventions which include war as the final instrument of decision. And these old-fashioned methods may cause somebody to blunder into the new-fashioned war that nobody wants and everybody dreads. That is the danger we live under today.

These misgivings, articulated in a commencement address at Bethany College in June 1955, are even more appropriate today.

Both in his views and in his peripheral political role, Weir typifies the painful predicament of the American businessman. The American ethos credits him with the creation of the American way of life while denying him a direct share in this life as expressed by the political process. Unlike a politician's responsibility to an amorphous electorate, the businessman's responsibility is concrete. If and when his business fails, he must hold himself primarily responsible. I recall that when I visited the cemetery at Broadway and Wall Street, which is only one of many branches of the Trinity Church Corporation, the guide cheerfully reassured me that the majority of those buried there were businessmen, bankers, and other Wall Streeters who committed suicide in 1929. They killed themselves, I realized, when the Depression took from them the ultimate credibility of their existence. When I asked the guide, "Are there any politicians here?" she seemed surprised. "Politicians?" she asked. "Why would *they* kill themselves?"

I am convinced that American political life would benefit not only from our engaging the business community directly in our political process but also from our studying its views and pronouncements in the historical contexts from which they stem. And here I do not mean just a businessman's view on business theory or on philanthropy. As long as this country is founded on private enterprise, and regardless of our personal likes or dislikes of that system, an American businessman remains a central figure in the trinity of politician, businessman, and union leader.

EXPERIENCING AMERICA

Kosinski concluded an interview in 1989 with some thoughts on the uniqueness of the American experience.

The American experience is entirely different from any other. America was never occupied. The American psyche is therefore freer in many ways—but also more restricted. It simply doesn't know many things, and has experienced less. It knows less pain, less triumph. And it's therefore less able to withstand minor shocks. It screams at the sight of blood. It kills some sixty-five thousand people every year on the highways but doesn't talk about it. Instead, it gets preoccupied with thirty-eight hundred heroin addicts who die every year. Meanwhile, are safer highways being built? Are safer cars being built?

America is, at the same time, a country of free expression, and in many ways a country of massive philanthropy—yet it is also a country which will not help those who can no longer help themselves. The moral contradictions implicit in the American character are enormous. To a novelist, this is a fascinating culture precisely because of that. A new challenge: how do you become a storyteller in an environment which cannot understand many things that you could tell but which might not want to hear them in any case?

ACKNOWLEDGMENTS

The biggest debt is, of course, to Kiki Kosinski, without whom *Oral Pleasure* would never have been possible. Not only did she conceive of the volume; she also typed and prepared versions of many of the materials that appear here, often transcribing them from talks and lectures that she personally recorded on a small tape recorder. Moreover, through her recollections as well as from her diaries, she provided invaluable information about dates, places, and persons. Kiki was, in every respect, a force of nature, and she is greatly missed.

Dita von Fraunhofer-Brodin and Dr. Tony von Fraunhofer have long supported and encouraged this project. And after Kiki's death they served as executors of her estate and were instrumental in bringing this book to its conclusion. Just as Kiki sought to preserve her husband's legacy, Dita and Tony have been zealous in preserving hers.

At Grove/Atlantic, Morgan Entrekin and Amy Hundley encouraged and promoted the project and offered excellent suggestions for revision. Their interest in Kosinski and his work has been unflagging. I am also grateful to Michael Hornburg, managing editor, Zachary Pace, editorial assistant, and Don Kennison for his copyediting.

Kiki had many devoted friends—among them Ted Field, Warren Beatty, Ami Shinitzky, the late Henry Dasko, and the late Tomek Mirkowicz—and would surely have wanted to acknowledge their support.

The Polish Institute of Arts and Sciences of America, New York, played an important role in Jerzy Kosinski's life, particularly in the years immediately following his emigration from Poland in late 1957. The institute's quarterly journal the *Polish Review* and its past editors—Dr. Joseph Wieczerzak, Dr. Charles Kraszewski, and the late Dr. Ludwik Krzyzanowski—have fostered and promoted Kosinski scholarship over the years.

For information concerning Kosinski's address to the Century Association, I am grateful to Dr. Russell A. Flinchum, the Century Association Archives Foundation historian, and to Sidney Offitt, who served as Kosinski's proposer.

NOTES

On Autobiography as Fiction/Fiction as Autobiography

1 "My novels are always confrontational . . . ," Jerzy Kosinski, quoted by J. Sebastian Sinisi, "Polo? Or is It Life? A Dangerous Game," *Denver Post*, September 23, 1979.

1 "How can any novelist . . . ," Jerzy Kosinski, interview with Charlie Rose, *Nightwatch*, 1988.

2 Photo Credit: Kiki Kosinski.

3 Radio Interview with Barry Gray, *The Barry Gray Show*, April 25, 1982.

37 Radio Interview, BBC (British Broadcasting Corporation), December 1985.

44 Letter from Jerzy Kosinski to William Jovanovich, 1973.

48 Lecture sponsored by the *Toronto Star*, Toronto, May 3, 1987.

59 Interview on "Lifetime" television, Toronto, January 4, 1989.

On Writing

65 "Writing is the essence of my life . . . ," Jerzy Kosinski, quoted by Daniel J. Cahill, "Life at a Gallop," *Washington Post Book World*, September 16, 1979.

On Storytelling

On Censorship

119 "To reply [to the *Village Voice* controversy] . . . ," Jerzy Kosinski, quoted by Richard E. Nicholls, *Philadelphia Inquirer,* April 14, 1984.

119 "Whenever I learn of yet another journalist . . . ," Jerzy Kosinski, quoted by Daniel J. Cahill, "Life at a Gallop," the *Washington Post Book World,* September 16, 1979.

120 Photo Credit: Kiki Kosinski.

121 Interview with Lorrin P. Rosenbaum, "The Writer's Focus," *Index on Censorship* 5.1 (Spring 1976).

129 Address to American Civil Liberties Union, Crete, Nebraska, November 3, 1989.

139 New York Film Critics Awards ceremony, New York, New York, January 31, 1982.

141 Address to the Century Association, New York, New York, October 1, 1990.

On Autofiction

149 "I expose only what I want to expose . . . ," Jerzy Kosinski, quoted by Cheryl Lavin, *Chicago Tribune,* September 4, 1988.

149 "It's about a state of mind . . . ," Jerzy Kosinski, interview with Larry King, *The Larry King Show,* July 29, 1988.

149 "Why do I still have to write . . . ," Jerzy Kosinski, interview with David Firestone, "He Looks Kindly on the Poland He Fled," *Newsday,* August 1, 1988.

150 Photo Credit: Kiki Kosinski.

151 Lecture, Smithsonian Institution, Washington, D.C., 1988.

161 Interview with Joan Lunden, *Good Morning America,* ABC-TV, July 26, 1988.

164 Interview with Don Swaim, "Book Beat," WCBS-Radio, October 8, 1988.

166 Interview, originally published in *Manhattan* (February 1989).

On Poland

171 "It is the totalitarian system . . . ," Jerzy Kosinski, quoted by Art Silverman, "The Renegade Novelist Whose Life Is Stranger Than Fiction," *Berkeley Barb* (November 25–December 1, 1977).

171 "Poland may be a poor country . . . ," Jerzy Kosinski, quoted by David Firestone, "He Looks Kindly on the Poland He Fled," *Newsday*, August 1, 1988.

171 "The issue is not . . . ," Jerzy Kosinski, quoted by Lisa DeNike, "Jerzy Kosinski: Outcast Writer Migrates to New Reality in U.S.," [Baltimore] *Evening Sun*, November 10, 1981.

172 Photo Credit: Kiki Kosinski.

173 Interview with Bert Quint, CBS News, April 28, 1988.

175 Interview with Charles Osgood, *This Morning*, CBS-TV, June 6, 1989.

178 Interview with Faith Daniels, *This Morning*, CBS-TV, July 10, 1989.

181 Address on the occasion of Jerzy Kosinski's receipt of an honorary Doctorate of Humane Letters from Albion College, Albion, Michigan, April 20, 1988.

On the Holocaust

187 "No one can make me a Jew . . . ," Jerzy Kosinski, quoted by Harry James Cargas, "Jerzy Kosinski Electrifies Holocaust Survivors' Conference," *St. Louis Jewish Light* (March 31, 1982).

187 "How can I make them understand . . . ," Jerzy Kosinski, quoted by Richard E. Nicholls, interview on Holocaust remembrance, *Philadelphia Inquirer*, April 14, 1984.

187 "Remembering the Holocaust . . . ," Jerzy Kosinski, "The Second Holocaust," *Boston Sunday Globe*, November 4, 1990.

188 Photo Credit: Kiki Kosinski.

189 Excerpt from an address to Congregation Emanu-El, New York, New York, October 2, 1990.

195 Undated essay (ca. 1990).

201 Excerpt from a "Meet the Author" session hosted by the *Jerusalem Post*, Jerusalem, Israel, January 31, 1988.

204 Excerpt from a question-and-answer session following an address at Albion College, Albion, Michigan, on the occasion of the receipt of an honorary Doctorate of Humane Letters, April 20, 1988.

On Jewish Identity

On World Affairs

252 Address originally entitled "The Odyssey of One Man's Return to Eastern Europe," symposium on "Eastern Europe Policy in the Making: Free Market Seed in Socialist Soil," the Philadelphia Stock Exchange 200th Anniversary Symposium, Philadelphia, Pennsylvania, October 9, 1990.

258 Address, originally entitled "Totalitarian Polemics: The Theatre of the Absurd," Royal Theatre, Stockholm, Sweden, April 19, 1983.

On Sex

267 "Sex is the key force . . . ," Jerzy Kosinski, quoted by Maureen Kenney, "Beyond the Book: A Talk with Author Jerzy Kosinski," *Media People* (February 1980).

267 "The only thing . . . ," Jerzy Kosinski, interview on *Late Night with David Letterman,* undated (ca. 1982).

268 Photo Credit: Kiki Kosinski.

269 Excerpt from Czesław Czaplinski, "Kosinski's Passions: Interviews with Jerzy Kosinski" (translated by Peter Obst), *BIGnews* 5.41 (April 2004).

272 "Packaged Passion," originally appeared in the *American Scholar* (Spring 1973).

288 Excerpt from an address delivered at Franklin and Marshall College, Lancaster, Pennsylvania, March 9, 1988.

291 Excerpt from a radio interview with Barry Gray, *The Barry Gray Show,* April 25, 1982.

On Television

293 "In the little world of television, . . . ," Jerzy Kosinski, "TV as Baby-Sitter," comment, NBC-TV, September 3, 1972.

293 "By its nature, visual art . . . ," Jerzy Kosinski, quoted by Steve Davis, "Kosinski: The Literary Wanderer," *Daily Texan,* October 1, 1979.

293 "When you are watching television, . . . ," Jerzy Kosinski, quoted by Jeanie Blake, "Old Man River Lures Literary Giant to City," [New Orleans] *Times-Picayune,* October 21, 1979.

294 Photo Credit: Kiki Kosinski.

295 Comment, WNBC-TV, New York, New York, February 28, 1971.

298 Address to the National Council of the Teachers of English, Louisville, Kentucky, March 26, 1987.

301 Interview with Michael Spring, originally published in *Literary Cavalcade*, December 20, 1977.

306 Comment, later published in the *Los Angeles Times*, August 15, 1971.

On Acting

309 "Acting is something very opposite . . . ," Jerzy Kosinski, interview with Charlie Rose, *Nightwatch*, May 27, 1987.

309 "I was greatly surprised . . . ," Jerzy Kosinski, quoted by Blake Green, "Unforgettable and Obsessed with Sex," *San Francisco Chronicle*, March 3, 1982.

309 "I realized that I should be braver . . . ," Jerzy Kosinski, quoted by Carl Maves, "A 'Threatened' Celebrity Discovers There Is Another Side of Fame," *Peninsula Times Tribune Weekly*, March 1, 1982.

310 Photo Credit: Kiki Kosinski.

311 Presenter's remarks, Academy of Motion Picture Arts and Sciences, Los Angeles, California, March 29, 1982.

312 Interview with Mike Cerre, *Live on Four*, KRON-TV (an NBC affiliate), San Francisco, California, February 25, 1982.

315 Excerpt from an interview with Gene Shalit, *Today*, February 19, 1982.

317 Conversation with Barry Gray, *The Barry Gray Show*, April 25, 1982.

On Popular Culture

319 "I'm a wundkerkind . . . ," Jerzy Kosinski, quoted by Blake Green, "Unforgettable and Obsessed with Sex," *San Francisco Chronicle*, March 3, 1982.

319 "The creative self withers . . . ," Jerzy Kosinski, quoted by Richard E. Nicholls, interview on Holocaust remembrance, *Philadelphia Inquirer*, April 14, 1984.

320 Photo Credit: Kiki Kosinski.

321 Excerpt from a *Live at Five* interview with Sue Simmons and Liz Smith, NBC-TV, February 23, 1982.

On *Being There*

On Violence

On the American Dream

383 "My life in the United States . . . ," Jerzy Kosinski, quoted by George Christian, "A Passion for Polo," *Houston Chronicle,* October 7, 1979.

383 "The great thing . . . ," Jerzy Kosinski, interview with Merv Griffin, *The Merv Griffin Show,* 1982.

384 Photo Credit: Kiki Kosinski.

385 Awards presentation, International House, New York, New York, May 2, 1990.

387 Essay originally published in the *American Scholar* (Autumn 1972).

397 Excerpt from interview, originally published in *Manhattan,* February 1989.